TEACHER DEVELOPMENT SERIES
Series Editor: Andy Hargreaves

TEACHERS AND THE NATIONAL CURRICULUM

2006

8

TEACHERS AND THE NATIONAL CURRICULUM

edited by
Gill Helsby and Gary McCulloch

CASSELL

Cassell
Wellington House   PO Box 605
125 Strand   Herndon
London WC2R 0BB   VA 20172

First published 1997

British Library Cataloguing-in-Publication Data
A catalogue record for this book is available from the British Library.

ISBN 0-304-33654-8 (hardback)
     0-304-33648-3 (paperback)

Typeset by York House Typographic Ltd, London
Printed and bound in Great Britain by Redwood Books, Trowbridge, Wiltshire

Contents

Contents

Notes on Contributors

Sandra Acker is a Professor in the Department of Sociology in Education at the Ontario Institute for Studies in Education of the University of Toronto (OISE/UT). Her research interests are in gender and education, the sociology of the teaching profession and higher education. She has written a number of articles and chapters on these topics. She is editor of *Teachers, Gender and Careers* (Falmer Press, 1989) and author of *Gendered Education: Sociological Reflections on Women, Teaching and Feminism* (Open University Press, 1994). Currently she is directing a qualitative study of academic work in the fields of social work, education, pharmacy and dentistry and also participating in a research network on women and professional education, both funded by the Social Science and Humanities Research Council of Canada.

Susan Harris is a Lecturer in Education at the University of Sheffield. Between 1991 and 1994 she was a Research Fellow on an ESRC-funded project, 'Making Your Way Through Secondary School'. Her current research is on relationships between education policy and non-traditional curriculum areas (careers education and drugs education) and careers teachers' work in compulsory and post-compulsory education institutions. She is Director of a Home Office-funded qualitative study of a drugs education programme delivered through a 'family of schools' structure. She has published widely on students' experiences of secondary schooling and the role of careers teachers and careers education.

Gill Helsby is a Senior Researcher in the Centre for the Study of Education and Training at Lancaster University. Her research interests include the impact of recent curriculum initiatives on teachers' work practices and teachers' professional development. She is a member of an international research network on Professional Actions and Cultures of Teaching and has recently co-directed a two-and-a-half-year, ESRC-funded study exploring the relationship between teachers' professional cultures and the school curriculum.

Bob Jeffrey is a Research Fellow at the Open University in the Centre for Sociology and Social Studies department of the Faculty of Education. Prior to this he taught in London primary schools for over twenty years. He has an MA in Education Management and is currently working on a PhD focusing on the intensification of primary teachers' work. He was instrumental in gathering the data for a creative teaching project, which resulted in the publication of a book in February 1996, together with Professor Peter Woods of the Open University, entitled *Teachable Moments: The Art of Teaching in Primary Schools*. He is currently halfway through a three-year project funded by the ESRC on the effects of OFSTED inspections on primary teachers' work using similar ethnographic methods to the ones he used in the creative teaching project.

Edgar Jenkins taught chemistry in secondary schools in Leeds and the former West Riding of Yorkshire before joining the University of Leeds, where he is currently Professor of Science Education Policy within the School of Education. His published work is concerned with the social history and politics of school science education and with the role of science teachers in policy-making at school level. He is the editor of *Studies in Science Education* and is currently co-directing an ESRC-funded study of the factors governing change and continuity in the professional practice of teachers of science and of history.

Peter Knight works in the Department of Educational Research at Lancaster University. His research interests span schools and higher education. Recent publications include: *Transforming Higher Education* (1996, with Lee Harvey); *Active History in Key Stages 3 and 4* (1995, with Alan Farmer); and *Records of Achievement in Higher and Further Education* (1995).

Gary McCulloch is Professor of Education at the University of Sheffield. His research has focused on historical and policy issues relating to the school curriculum especially in Britain and New Zealand. His recent published work includes *The Secondary Technical School: A Usable Past?* (1989); *Philosophers and Kings: Education for Leadership in Modern England* (1991); *The School Curriculum in New Zealand: History, Theory, Policy and Practice* (ed., 1992); and *Educational Reconstruction: The 1944 Education Act and the 21st Century* (1994). He is currently working on a social history of mass secondary education in England and Wales and on the changing position of teachers in relation to the school curriculum since the 1940s.

Marilyn Osborn is Research Fellow and Deputy Director of the Centre for Curriculum and Assessment Studies, School of Education, University of Bristol. She researches and publishes in the field of teachers' work and professional perspectives, comparative education, and the education of adults. Currently she is directing an ESRC project on pupil perspectives of primary schooling in England and France and researching on the PACE project, a study of the impact of change in English primary schools. Her recent publications include *Liberating the Learner* (Routledge, 1996, with G. Claxton *et al.*); *Changing English Primary Schools* (Cassell, 1994, with A. Pollard *et al.*); *Perceptions of Teaching* (Cassell, 1993, with P. Broadfoot); and *The Changing Nature of Teachers' Work: Developing the National Curriculum at Key Stage 2* (NASUWT, 1994, with E. Black).

Margaret Roberts is a Lecturer in Education and a member of the Curriculum and Pedagogy Research Centre at Sheffield University Division of Education. Her research has focused on issues relating to geography teachers and the implementation of the Geography National Curriculum at Key Stage 3 in secondary schools.

Murray Saunders is a Reader in Education and Training, and Director of the Centre for the Study of Education and Training in the Educational Research Department at Lancaster University. He has interests in social change and education, curriculum change and educational innovation. In particular his research work has focused on the implementation and policy issues associated with vocational education, training and learning in the workplace. He is involved in collaborative research and evaluation activity in developing countries and participates in the promotion of evaluation and those engaged in it through the UK Evaluation Society.

Terry Warburton was a Research Associate in the Centre for the Study of Education and Training at Lancaster University. He has been working on an ESRC project entitled The Professional Culture of Teachers and the Secondary Curriculum. In addition he has been undertaking research into how teachers and teaching are represented in the press, particularly through cartoons. He is now Lecturer in Research Methods in the School of Education and Health Studies at Bolton Institute.

Peter Woods is Professor of Education at the School of Education, the Open University, Milton Keynes. He spent eleven years teaching before joining the Open University in 1972, where for a number of years he was Director of the Centre for Sociology and Social Research. His main research interest is school ethnography. He is the author of numerous articles and books, including *The Divided School, Sociology and the School, Inside Schools, The Happiest Days?* and *Teacher Skills and Strategies*. He has recently been researching 'creative teaching in primary schools'. His latest books, *Critical Events in Teaching and Learning* (Falmer Press), *Creative Teachers in Primary Schools*, and (with Bob Jeffrey) *Teachable Moments* (both Open University Press) are products of this research. A book on qualitative methodology, *Researching the Art of Teaching*, was published by Routledge in 1996. He is currently researching the effects of school inspections on primary teachers and their work.

Series Editor's Foreword

In Britain and Australia, they call it teaching. In the United States and Canada, they call it instruction. Whatever terms we use, we have come to realize in recent years that the teacher is the ultimate key to educational change and school improvement. The restructuring of schools, the composition of national and provincial curricula, the development of benchmark assessments – all these things are of little value if they do not take the teacher into account. Teachers don't merely deliver the curriculum. They develop, define and reinterpret it too. It is what teachers think, what teachers believe and what teachers do at the level of the classroom that ultimately shapes the kind of learning that young people get. Growing appreciation of this fact is placing working with teachers and understanding teaching at the top of our research and improvement agendas.

For some reformers, improving teaching is mainly a matter of developing better teaching methods, of improving instruction. Training teachers in new classroom management skills, in active learning, co-operative learning, one-to-one counselling and the like is the main priority. These things are important, but we are also increasingly coming to understand that developing teachers and improving their teaching involves more than giving them new tricks. We are beginning to recognize that, for teachers, what goes on inside the classroom is closely related to what goes on outside it. The quality, range and flexibility of teachers' classroom work are closely tied up with their professional growth – with the way in which they develop as people and as professionals.

Teachers teach in the way they do not just because of the skills they have or have not learned. The ways in which they teach are also rooted in their backgrounds, their biographies, and so in the kinds of teachers they have become. Their careers – their hopes and dreams, their opportunities and aspirations, or the frustration of these things – are also important for teachers' commitment, enthusiasm and morale. So too are relationships with their colleagues – either as supportive communities who work together in pursuit of common goals and continuous improvement, or as individuals working in isolation, with the insecurities that sometimes brings.

As we are coming to understand these wider aspects of teaching and teacher development, we are also beginning to recognize that much more than pedagogy, instruction or teaching method is at stake. Teacher development, teachers' careers, teachers' relations with their colleagues, the conditions of status, reward and leadership under which they work – all these affect the quality of what they do in the classroom.

This international series, *Teacher Development*, brings together some of the very best current research and writing on these aspects of teachers' lives and work. The books in the series seek to understand the wider dimensions of teachers' work, the depth of teachers' knowledge and the resources of biography and experience on which it draws, the ways that teachers' work roles and responsibilities are changing as we restructure our schools, and so forth. In this sense, the books in the series are written for those who are involved in research on teaching, those who work in initial and in-service teacher education, those who lead and administer teachers, those who work with teachers and, not least, teachers themselves.

This collection of work, solicited and edited by Gill Helsby and Gary McCulloch, brings together research findings on the impact of one of the most significant educational reforms in the world within the past decade: the construction and imposition of a detailed National Curriculum for England and Wales. Few reforms have ever been as unwanted by the teaching profession as this. The reforms were invented and undertaken with little or no input from the teaching profession, or from that other part of what was mockingly labelled 'the Educational Establishment' – the educational research community. The National Curriculum was based more on ideology than on expertise, prescribing a collection of academic subjects that was uncannily similar to those decreed by Robert Morant in 1904 as constituting the legitimate secondary school curriculum. With detailed imposition of curriculum content, an associated armoury of educational testing, and the erection of competitive league tables of performance through which pupil success in the National Curriculum would be judged, the implications for teachers and the work of teaching after this far-reaching reform have been monumental.

In a climate of scarce funding, the educational research community has responded in different ways. Some of the more hack writers and opportunist academics scurried off to write books or edit series of books on subject teaching in the National Curriculum. Some tried to introduce sense into Babel, by working on the inside, to develop technically defensible systems of National Curriculum assessment, for example. Many engaged in rhetorical battles against the very idea of a National Curriculum such as this, or against the excessive speed of its implementation. And too many, far too many, remained tight-lipped or modestly murmured that thoughtful teachers would simply find some way to make good of it – as if the discovery of small scale resistance was somehow a subsitute for criticizing the waging of war in the first place.

In time, though, as social science research recovered from the early onslaught of the Thatcherite Government, a knowledge base began to be built of what effects the National Curriculum was actually exerting, and of how teachers and pupils were responding to it. Some of this research has taken the form of small scale (but illuminating) case studies and some of it has been based on much larger samples, investigated by large research teams. The result is a body of knowledge, insight and understanding about the consequences of the National Curriculum, that is now quite formidable.

Helsby and McCulloch are the first researchers to bring together much of this body of work on the effects of the National Curriculum into one place. The research represented here looks at the National Curriculum's impact on teachers of different subjects and in different age ranges. It shows not only how what teachers taught in some of the higher status subjects such as mathematics came to be reproduced or redefined, but also how some subjects and their teachers were almost squeezed out completely by the reform efforts. Some teachers, especially at the secondary level, are depicted as feeling totally demoralized and deprofessionalized as a result of the National Curriculum. But in pockets, especially at the primary level, other teachers are shown as engaged in increased collegial effort to make sense of what has been imposed upon them.

Collectively, the evidence seems to indicate that the substance and scope of the National Curriculum have begun to bring about foundational shifts in what it means to be a teacher in England and Wales – many of these for the worse. It also shows that some groups of teachers have nonetheless been able to subvert or circumvent the changes to some extent.

At the time of going to press, National Curriculum requirements and the speed of their implementation have been eased somewhat, but all political parties remain committed to the concept. Nevertheless, the kind of evidence represented in this excellent collection provides sobering data for anyone in England and Wales and elsewhere who is intent on making further reforms, about how educational reform should or should not be managed, particularly in terms of its effects on those who are indispensable to making it work – the teaching profession. *Teachers and the National Curriculum* is solid, sensible reading, rich in research evidence and thoughtful in commentary. It is, in my view, an essential resource, which all proponents and recipients of fundamental efforts in educational change should study seriously.

Andy Hargreaves
Toronto, September 1996

Preface

The National Curriculum, which was introduced in England and Wales under the provisions of the Education Reform Act of 1988, represents a major departure in educational policy. Its implications for the different groups and interests involved in education, as for society as a whole, have only begun to be worked through and recognized. This book brings together a collection of original articles by leading researchers in the field to explore the complex and changing relationship between the National Curriculum and the teachers charged with putting it into practice in our schools.

On the one hand the following chapters examine the ways in which the National Curriculum affects the role of teachers in schools and classrooms. Has it produced systematic innovation in the way that teachers teach the curriculum, or in reality has it meant little difference from the practices and approaches adopted by teachers in the past? Does it constitute a loose framework within which teachers can exercise a due amount of autonomy, as its supporters would insist? Or, on the contrary, is it effectively a straitjacket that reduces teachers from autonomous professionals to the function of technicians, merely implementing orders that have been determined elsewhere?

On the other hand, however, teachers are not neutral agents, still less empty ciphers in their adoption of the National Curriculum, but tend to mediate it in many different and often unexpected ways. Accordingly the other key issue which is at the heart of this work is the question of how teachers affect the role and character of the National Curriculum. How far do they implement it as the designers intended? Or do they change or even transform it through the process of teaching, perhaps improving or perhaps subverting its underlying aims? Are there contextual factors which affect their responses?

This book seeks to understand the connections between teachers and the National Curriculum in terms of an interrelationship in which the dynamics operate in both directions, affecting both of the parties involved. The rapid development of this interrelationship inevitably raises fundamental questions about the role of teachers and about the aims of education, questions which are still being worked out in practice as the National Curriculum becomes more firmly established in our schools. The following chapters illustrate the ways in which this is happening in a variety of different contexts.

Gill Helsby and Gary McCulloch

Abbreviations

ASE	Association for Science Education
AT	Attainment Target
BAAS	British Association for the Advancement of Science
CDT	craft, design and technology
CEG	careers education and guidance
CPD	continuing professional development
DES	Department of Education and Science
DFE	Department for Education
DFEE	Department for Education and Employment
ERA	Education Reform Act
ESRC	Economic and Social Research Council
GCSE	General Certificate of Secondary Education
GNC	Geography National Curriculum
HE	home economics
HoD	Head of Department
INSET	in-service training
IT	information technology
ITE	initial teacher education
KS	Key Stage
LEA	local education authority
LMS	local management of schools
MPG	main professional grade
NACGT	National Association of Careers and Guidance Teachers
NATE	National Association of Teachers of English
NCC	National Curriculum Council
NEAB	Northern Examinations and Assessment Board
NHSS	New History and Sociology of Science
NICEC	National Institute for Careers Education and Counselling
OFSTED	Office for Standards in Education
PACE	Primary Assessment, Curriculum and Experience
PCT	Professional Culture of Teachers
PE	physical education
PSD	personal and social development

PSE	personal and social education
SAT	Standard Assessment Task
SCAA	School Curriculum and Assessment Authority
Sc1	scientific investigation
SEAC	School Examinations and Assessment Council
SMP	Schools Mathematics Project
TES	*Times Educational Supplement*
TGAT	Task Group on Assessment and Testing
TVEI	Technical and Vocational Education Initiative
WO	Welsh Office

Chapter 1

Introduction: Teachers and the National Curriculum

Gill Helsby and Gary McCulloch

BACKGROUND AND CONTEXT OF THE NATIONAL CURRICULUM

Gaining agreement on a desirable curriculum for state schools, and on the appropriate role for teachers within that curriculum, are familiar educational concerns. However, such concerns are thrown into sharp relief by the wave of educational reforms which have been sweeping across westernized democracies in recent years. Faced with the restructuring of world economies, the growth of global markets and the accompanying political uncertainties, many of the advanced industrialized nations have looked anew at the role of their educational systems in producing both the compliant citizenry and the skilled and flexible workforce deemed necessary to ensure social stability and economic success in the twenty-first century. This process of review, coupled with the widespread dismantling of the Keynesian welfare state in favour of monetarist and managerialist approaches (Clarke *et al.*, 1994; Ozga, 1995; Robertson, 1996) and with the general marketization of public services, has resulted in a remarkable degree of educational 'policy convergence' in western societies (Dale, 1992). The major restructuring of education which has ensued has had profound implications both for the nature of schooling and for the work of schoolteachers.

Key features of this restructuring which recur in different geographical and cultural locations are: administrative decentralization in the form of local school management; the introduction of stronger accountability mechanisms, including the use of teacher appraisal; and, significantly, a growing tendency to prescribe the curriculum of schools, often through the development of a national curriculum. Whilst clearly it is this latter reform, and its implications for teachers in the particular context of England and Wales, which is the focus of this book, it is important to remember that it has not been introduced in isolation but rather as part of a wide-ranging programme of fundamental changes.

Goodson (1994) has linked the recent emergence of national curricula in a number of countries with current economic and political considerations. On the one hand, a national curriculum may be presented as a blueprint for the development of the knowledge, skills and attitudes necessary for economic regeneration in a changed and increasingly competitive world, whilst on the other it can be seen as a reassertion of the power and ideology of the nation state at a time when this is perceived as being under threat from the forces of globalization. Thus the idea of a national curriculum has emerged in countries as diverse as Japan and Australia, Scotland and the USA, Sweden and England and Wales. However, whilst the overall aims and motivations may be similar, inspired by common concerns, the details of the various national curricula, and in particular the ways in which they are promoted, approached or introduced, vary significantly according to the historical, cultural and political context. Thus, for example, the governments of countries such as Sweden and the USA have chosen a gradual and progressive approach, conferring widely, emphasizing the role of teachers in helping to develop an agreed curriculum and appealing to their 'professionalism'. Others, however, have adopted a much more aggressive stance, involving minimal consultation, strong central prescription and draconian systems of assessment and accountability.

In England and Wales it has been the latter approach that has predominated, particularly in the early years of the National Curriculum, leading many commentators to suggest that teachers were being deskilled and proletarianized (e.g. Kelly, 1990; Kogan, 1989; Norton, 1994). At first sight, the use of such a strategy in this particular context is surprising, given the supposedly strong postwar tradition of teacher autonomy in the curriculum which preceded it, referred to by Grace (1987) as 'a distinctive feature of British democracy and schooling' (p. 212). However, in practice such autonomy was always relative (Hoyle, 1974) and, as McCulloch argues in Chapter 2 of this volume, may be seen as something of a myth, introduced for social and political purposes and subject to reinterpretation over time.

Whatever the degree of curriculum autonomy actually exercised by schoolteachers in England and Wales during the 'Golden Age of teacher control' (Lawton, 1980, p. 22), it seems clear that the tradition has been increasingly strongly contested since the mid-1970s. Initially, this contestation largely took the form of rhetoric, public debate and the publication of consultative documents: in this context the traditional failure of the centre–periphery model of educational change continued to hold sway. However, the launch of the Technical and Vocational Education Initiative (TVEI) in 1983 marked a watershed in active state involvement in the curriculum. This initiative, which was virulently attacked at the time as unwarranted state interference in 'professional' matters, aimed to promote a curriculum for 14- to 18-year-olds that would combine general and vocational education and which would equip students with the necessary skills for adult and working life. Despite the aggressive tone of its announcement, participation was voluntary (albeit virtually ensured by the lure of additional educational funding in economically difficult times) and the degree of central prescription within this early 'national' curriculum amounted to little more than a broad framework, within which teachers were able to develop appropriate programmes and courses for their students. In practice, the initiative was largely seized by educationalists who 'hijacked' the associated curriculum development (Harland, 1987; Helsby, 1989).

By 1987, however, buoyed up by a third successive electoral victory, the Conservative government was ready to adopt much more stringent measures in its introduction of the promised National Curriculum. Abandoning the overtly vocational imperative that had characterized TVEI, the July Consultation Document (DES, 1987) laid out an intensive programme of ten traditional school subjects (plus Welsh language in Wales) which, it was initially suggested, would occupy at least 90 per cent of curriculum time for all 5- to 16-year-olds. Programmes of Study were to be developed which would specify what children should know, understand and be able to do at each of four 'Key Stages' during their period of compulsory schooling, and there would be a system of national assessment at ages seven, eleven, fourteen and sixteen. Significantly, the period of 'consultation' over this fundamental and wide-ranging reform was exceptionally brief (from July to September) and coincided with the school holidays.

As Goodson (1994) points out, the list of compulsory subjects detailed in the Consultative Document was almost identical to that embodied in the Secondary Regulations of 1904, thereby reflecting a preference for the traditional and elitist grammar school curriculum. In many ways this appeared to be at odds with many aspects of existing practice: primary school teachers had, since the 1960s, increasingly adopted progressive and topic-centred teaching approaches and TVEI had encouraged the development of integrated, student-centred and skill-based courses in secondary schools. The proposed National Curriculum, however, appeared to mark an abrupt volte-face, with its emphasis upon the teaching and learning of discrete bodies of knowledge within a more directive framework. This change can be seen as marking a significant disturbance in the 'classification' and 'framing' of educational knowledge (Bernstein, 1971). 'Classification' refers to 'the degree of boundary maintenance between contents', whilst 'framing' refers to 'the degree of control teacher and pupil possess over the selection, organization and pacing of the knowledge transmitted and received in the pedagogical relationship' (*ibid.*, pp. 49–50). According to Bernstein, changes in the strength of classification and framing are associated with disturbances in existing patterns of authority and control.

Such disturbances are also reflected in other initiatives introduced at around the same time, for example the removal of teachers' pay bargaining rights, proposals for compulsory teacher appraisal, increased powers for school governors, the specification of minimum contractual hours for teachers, the addition of five compulsory school-based training days each year and a sharp increase in central authority over both pre-service and in-service teacher education. All of these developments point towards a fundamental shift in control of the education system away from teachers and other educationalists and towards the state. Moreover, teacher morale was under threat both because of the after-effects of the bitter but unsuccessful Teacher Action of the mid-1980s and also as a result of the government's continuing 'discourses of derision' (Ball, 1990). Within these discourses, it was consistently asserted that there was a serious problem with education, that standards were too low, that the fault for this lay within the educational establishment, and particularly with 'trendy teachers', and that it was only action at national level that could rescue the situation.

In these circumstances of apparently increased control of teachers' working lives and potentially low morale in schools, it might be expected that the imposition of an extensive and tightly prescribed National Curriculum, with a rigorous system of inspection and national testing, would mark the final disintegration of the tradition of professional autonomy in the school curriculum. In this scenario, the teacher's role would be reduced to that of mere technician, carrying out the plans of others and held accountable for certain quantifiable and pre-specified outcomes. Indeed, there was a strong line of research in the early years of National Curriculum implementation which tended to emphasize changes in structure because of this imposition. It was suggested that proletarianization or deprofessionalization were resulting both from this assumed loss of autonomy (e.g. Kelly, 1990) and from the general 'intensification' of working life (Apple, 1986; Hargreaves, 1994).

STRUCTURE, AGENCY AND CULTURE

Such structural approaches can offer only partial explanations of reality, since they tend to ignore the importance of agency – the active part played by teachers in developing and defining the National Curriculum – as well as the strong influence of different work cultures upon the responses of individual teachers. Ozga and Lawn, for example, who had earlier drawn upon the work of Braverman to suggest that schoolteachers were undergoing a process of proletarianization even before the introduction of the National Curriculum, later rejected his critique as having 'lost much of its explanatory value because of its reduction of the active role of workers in contesting or resisting or adapting this process' (Ozga and Lawn, 1988, p. 329). Certainly, any research into the implementation of a centrally developed and prescriptive National Curriculum in a context such as England and Wales, with its strong tradition of local curriculum autonomy, inevitably puts into sharp focus questions about the role of teachers and about the ways in which they accept, accommodate, modify or contest the new requirements. To what extent should classroom teachers be viewed as passive victims, disempowered by some monolithic structure which prescribes their actions and removes their autonomy? Alternatively, how far can they be seen as active agents, using their professional judgement in their day-to-day work and making key decisions which fundamentally shape the development and form of the new curriculum?

Inevitably, the overall reality is more complex than is suggested by either of these two extreme scenarios and is a composite of varying responses in different contexts. Drawing upon the ideas of Roland Barthes, Bowe and Ball (1992) suggested that teachers confronted with National Curriculum policy texts retained a degree of choice as to whether they adopted a 'readerly' or 'writerly' approach to such texts. Whilst the former approach implies an unquestioning acceptance of the texts as prescriptions for action, the latter involves critical scrutiny, interpretation and selectivity. Neither approach is inevitable, and neither is universal: in some cases, the 'structure' of National Curriculum prescription will predominate, at other times the 'agency' of teachers will be highly significant. To understand the whole picture, therefore, account must be taken of the duality of structure (Giddens, 1984) and of its interdependent relationship with human action. The notion of 'strategy' is also useful here, since it both accepts the existence of constraints and opportunities within which people must operate and emphasizes the active role of participants in adapting, adjusting and managing those constraints and opportunities (see Crow, 1989 and Evetts, 1994, for helpful discussions of this concept).

As already indicated, the ways in which individual teachers respond to the National Curriculum is heavily influenced by the professional and work cultures within which they operate. Although the notion of 'culture' is complex, two aspects are significant in this respect, namely the 'content' and 'form' of such cultures (Hargreaves, 1992). 'Content' refers to the collection of values, beliefs, norms and myths shared by a particular group: where there are strong commitments to fundamental principles within a group, for example to a particular way of teaching or to the importance of individual professional judgement, then teachers are less amenable to external direction. The term 'form' of culture denotes the varying patterns of association between teachers. Since colleagues are potentially important sources of norms and sanctions for teachers (Talbert and McLaughlin, 1996), the degree to which teachers work in isolation or in collaboration can be highly significant. Where there is a high degree of collegiality, as in the case of Hillview school in Chapter 3 of this book for example, evidence suggests that teachers are more likely to have the confidence to assert their own interpretations upon situations and to take an active and constructive part in curriculum development.

THE NATIONAL CURRICULUM

Before considering how the particular interrelationship between structure, agency and culture has developed in practice, it is important to take on board the specific characteristics of the National Curriculum as it has developed since its inception, and also of teachers as individuals, in different groupings, and as a group.

The so-called 'National Curriculum' must be understood in relation to the boundaries of its statutory authority. Like so much in educational legislation, it has force in England and Wales, but not in Scotland, nor in Northern Ireland. Three 'core' subjects (English, maths and science) were the central focus of the National Curriculum, together with seven 'foundation' subjects: art, geography, history, music, physical education, technology, and (in secondary schools) modern languages. Religious education remained a statutory requirement as it had been created under the Education Act of 1944. There were in addition five 'cross-curricular themes': careers education and guidance, education for citizenship, economic and industrial awareness, environmental education, and health education. All subjects and topics for inclusion in the school curriculum had either to be incorporated within this framework, or seek provision in a crowded timetable as an 'optional' subject outside the compulsory framework.

The relevance of this curriculum to schools in Wales has been a matter of some contention (e.g. Jones, 1994), but the 'Cwricwlwm Cymreig', or Welsh Curriculum, formed within the framework of the National Curriculum, supposedly gave children in Wales 'an understanding of the influence which the uniqueness of their country has on their lives' (DFE, 1992, para. 14.4). Separate curriculum orders in geography, history, art and music, together with a special one for the Welsh language, reflected the 'distinctive features of Wales' (*ibid.*). Much of the debate over the National Curriculum and its constituent parts, however, has revolved around its implications for the character of national 'culture' and 'identity' at the end of the twentieth century.

The National Curriculum was also specifically intended only for state schools rather than for independent schools. This was a major limitation in a context where the maintenance of an independent sector often seemed to perpetuate the existence of 'two nations' in education. Nor did it apply to nursery schools, or to children after the compulsory leaving age of 16, but only to primary schools (generally for children aged from 5 to 11) and, within secondary schools, for those aged from 11 up to 16. It was organized through four 'key stages': Key Stage 1 for infants in Years 1 and 2; Key Stage 2 for juniors in Years 3, 4, 5 and 6; Key Stage 3 for the early years in the secondary school in Years 7, 8, and 9; and Key Stage 4 in the final years of compulsory education in Years 10 and 11. Progress was to be assessed at the end of each Key Stage through 'Standard Assessment Tasks' (SATs) at 7, 11, 14 and 16. This related machinery for assessment helped to tie the National Curriculum in with wider issues such as the accountability of schools for the progress of their pupils. At a time of major policy emphasis on the need for 'choice' and 'diversity' in schools, it represented a countervailing tendency to establish national benchmarks for 'quality' and 'standards'.

A further preliminary point about the specific characteristics of the National Curriculum is that it has changed significantly since it was first introduced in the late 1980s. Over this time its role and character have been continually contested among the groups and interests involved to such an extent that any reference to the 'National Curriculum' needs to take account of its phase of development no less than of its different subjects and Key Stages. The nature of its phased introduction itself raised important issues in the way that it tended to reinforce divisions between school subjects and undermine integration. In broad terms, three main phases of development may perhaps be identified in terms of innovation, control and settlement, although these have not been by any means clearly demarcated and distinct, and the nature of the 'settlement' continues to be marked by vigorous contestation of principles and practices.

First was the stage of *innovation*, in which the outlines of syllabuses for the National Curriculum were drawn up by working parties in each subject, and then introduced into the schools. This involved high politics among the 'movers and shakers' in and around the Conservative government of the late 1980s at a time when right-wing pressure groups were exerting increasing pressure on the direction of educational reform. A major teachers' dispute over pay between 1984 and 1986 had ended in public confrontation and low morale among teachers, and reflected scant sympathy for teachers' claims on the part of the government (Pietrasik, 1987). The work of Kenneth Baker as Secretary of State for Education in introducing the National Curriculum was affected by these influences (see, e.g., Taylor, 1995; Barber, 1996), as well as by the public 'discourses of derision' that have already been noted (Ball, 1990; Wallace, 1993). These also constituted major constraints and influences for the National Curriculum Council under first Duncan Graham and then David Pascall (Graham, 1993), and the individual working parties (e.g. Evans and Penney, 1995).

Second was the phase of *bureaucratic control* over the curriculum, as the National Curriculum asserted its new position in the schools. This phase was implicit in the original design for the National Curriculum under Kenneth Baker as Secretary of State for Education. It reached a spectacular and unsustainable climax during 1993 as John Patten (Baker's third successor as Education Secretary after John MacGregor and Kenneth Clarke) attempted to enforce testing for 7- and 14-year-olds in the face of a widespread boycott by teachers. Over the longer term, control was maintained especially through the effects of the national assessment system that was introduced (Radnor *et al.*, 1995) and through the Office for Standards in Education (OFSTED) under the controversial Chief Inspector, Chris Woodhead (e.g. Hodges, 1996).

The polarized debates of 1993 were hastily succeeded by what might be described as a *settlement* phase. This was symbolized in the review of the National Curriculum undertaken by Sir Ron Dearing, the chairman of the School Curriculum and Assessment Authority (SCAA), whose *Final Report* was published at the start of 1994. In this report, Dearing recommended that the requirements of the National Curriculum should be 'slimmed down' in order to allow teachers what he called 'scope for professional judgement' (Dearing, 1994, p. 20). This 'professional judgement' appeared to relate in particular to non-compulsory areas of the curriculum, since Dearing proposed a division of the curriculum orders into, on the one hand, 'the essential matters, skills and processes which any school must by law teach' and, on the other, 'the optional material which can be taught according to the professional judgement of teachers' (*ibid.*, pp. 20–1). For children between 5 and 14 (Key Stages 1, 2 and 3) the existing National Curriculum would be streamlined to release one day per week for schools to use at their own discretion. The Dearing Review aspired towards 'increased trust for teachers', beyond what had often been shown in the early years of the National Curriculum, but it also insisted that this trust should be matched on the part of teachers by 'accountability to parents and society, including that from simple tests in the core subjects' (*ibid.*, p. 25). At the same time, it sought a reduction in the workload of teachers, which had grown as a result of the National Curriculum, and reduced demands for testing and recording. It also suggested that 'alternative pathways' should be constructed for Key Stage 4 from the age of 14. These pathways would be academic, vocational and occupational respectively, and they should be 'of equal quality, leading to parity of esteem' (*ibid.*, p. 20).

All of these aspirations – for professional judgement, trust, accountability, reduced workloads and 'parity of esteem' – were open to debate as to how and whether they were likely to be achieved, and each had high potential to produce further controversy despite the soothing balm applied by the Dearing Review. Even so, after the conflict and alienation manifest under Patten, this general shift in the balance of the National Curriculum seemed to offer the opportunity of a lasting accommodation with teachers and the wider educational community, an opportunity that was further enhanced when Patten was replaced as Education Secretary in 1994 by a more conciliatory figure in Gillian Shephard. It was Dearing's hope that the 'new', more flexible National Curriculum would be phased in and then given five years before any further substantial changes were made. However, it would be misleading either to associate the process of 'settlement' simply with the Dearing Report, or to suggest that major points of contention did not remain even after its publication. The White Paper *Choice and Diversity*, published in July 1992, could assert in relation to the National Curriculum that 'What was hotly contested in the mid-1980s is now widely accepted. Debate is no longer about the principle of a national curriculum but about the detail' (DFE, 1992, para. 1.12). As so often, the devil was in the detail, and this has continued to be the case in subsequent years. Even more to the point, disputes over the detail should not be seen simply as teething problems, as the sponsors of the National Curriculum would no doubt have preferred to think, but as continuing contestation over the principles and practices involved.

TEACHERS' RESPONSES

The responses of teachers are central to understanding the development and the general significance of the National Curriculum, and also in highlighting the importance of the school and classroom context as distinct from the national scene. These involve responses by individual teachers on an everyday level as well as collective judgements arrived at by groups of teachers and their representatives in a range of associations, formal and informal. It is important also to gauge the ways in which teachers have been able not only to draw on their own earlier experiences in responding to the National Curriculum, but also to adapt and accommodate their practices, often growing in confidence as they have begun to find spaces for manoeuvre within its framework.

The problems faced by teachers in responding to the National Curriculum as an innovation are well exemplified by Eleanor Rawling in her presidential address to the Geographical Association in April 1992. She was involved in the Geography Working Group appointed by the government to determine the framework for geography in the 5–16 curriculum, and was acutely aware of a 'mismatch between the intentions of the Working Group and the reality of how these intentions were translated into the Order'. The outcome, as she described it, was that 'geography teachers have been launched on a major curriculum development journey without the benefit of an adequate map', and it was this lack of 'curriculum sense' that explained the difficulties that the teachers subsequently suffered (Rawling, 1992, p. 294). In many different areas, the translation of the National Curriculum from the initial conception to Working Group design to Curriculum Order and thence to school and classroom led teachers into uncharted waters in adapting not simply to change, but to experiment.

Rawling's comments are highly pertinent in so far as they reflect both the opportunities for curriculum development that appeared to be offered in the form of the National Curriculum, and the nature of the major hazards and contradictions involved. Other critics have perceived the hazards as far outweighing, indeed undermining, any possible opportunities in relation to teachers, as they warned that the incursion of the state into the classroom had the potential of destroying the relative autonomy of teachers in the curriculum domain. It was this prospect that was emphasized, for example, by Professor Helen Simons (Simons, 1988, p. 80):

> the national curriculum will take the place of local professional judgement of common provision, testing and schemes of work will confine pedagogy to what is conducive to publicly comparable performance, and the responsibility for curriculum experimentation, development, growth and change – the hallmark of educational professionalism – will no longer be the concern of teachers, schools or localities. They are destined to become the implementers of curricula, judged nevertheless by the success of treatments they no longer devise.

Viewed from the perspective of the National Curriculum as bureaucratic and centralized management, the key issue is how far teachers have fallen victim to restrictions and how far they have been able to overcome or transcend them.

The National Curriculum as a form of educational settlement also places teachers at the centre of the equation, for it is they who must negotiate a meaningful role in relation to the state. Michael Barber, former education officer of the National Union of Teachers, emphasizes this perspective when he suggests that teachers are 'learning to love' the National Curriculum. Barber points out that although their influence at national level is 'strictly circumscribed at least in the short term', teachers still 'retain influence in the schools' in their task as 'pragmatists making sense out of nonsense and providing as coherent a bill of fare for their pupils as is possible in a world where politicians have become as fickle and interfering as the Red Queen in *Alice in Wonderland*' (Barber, 1993, p. 22). When viewed in this light, the key focus is on the scope or freedom that teachers may have, in the rapidly changing educational and political situation of the 1990s, to determine the curriculum in the classroom. Following on from this major issue, too, are the questions of where are the limitations of teachers' freedom, and what they choose to do with it when they have it.

Embedded in teachers' relationships with the National Curriculum, too, is a key distinction between *what* is to be taught and *how* to teach it. This separation of 'content' and 'method' has been explicitly recognized in the National Curriculum as a policy since its origins in the consultation document of July 1987 through to the Dearing Review. It was clearly acknowledged that in translating the National Curriculum from policy into practice, the 'organization of teaching and learning' should remain 'a professional matter for the head teacher and his or her staff' (DES, 1989, para. 4.3). Moreover,

> What is specified will allow teachers considerable freedom in the
> way in which they teach, examples and materials used, selection of
> content and context, use of textbooks, etc. The legislation does not
> allow particular textbooks or teaching methods to be prescribed as
> part of a programme of study. (Ibid., para. 4.15)

A key issue here is how teachers have worked out the implications of this key distinction in terms of their own teaching practice, or whether indeed the notion of such a separation of powers is itself a contradiction in practical terms.

It needs to be emphasized, though, that teaching methods were also increasingly under attack during this same period, particularly in the primary schools for their supposedly 'trendy' and 'progressive' approaches. The report on curriculum organization and classroom practice conducted for the government by the 'Three Wise Men' in 1992 was a major contribution to this debate (Woods and Wenham, 1995), which was further sustained in critical reports produced by OFSTED and in increasingly strong statements in favour of going 'back to basics' by the Labour Party spokesperson on education, David Blunkett (*The Independent*, 1996a, 1996b). These public debates were bound to be influential in the further development of the National Curriculum itself.

Each of these issues needs to be addressed in relation to teachers in their individual and everyday classroom duties, no less than for teachers in association. For teachers as individuals, confronted with the task of interpreting a prescribed curriculum, there are many dependent variables that must be considered. The personal biography of the teacher is one such specificity, taking into account the stage of career, and the nature of the teacher's training and ongoing professional development. The 'professional lives' of teachers (Hargreaves and Goodson, 1996) go through many different stages, and the responses of particular teachers to the National Curriculum may well depend in part on their location in what Huberman (1993) describes as their 'life-cycle'. Moreover, as Hargreaves (1991, p. 251) puts it, 'Teachers are people too. They have interests; they have lives; they have selves.' This suggests that teachers' individual responses may be based in a range of often conflicting emotions as much as in rational calculation (see also Hargreaves, 1994), and that further research into the relationship between teachers' thinking and practice would be appropriate (see also Carlgren *et al.*, 1994).

The position of individual teachers in relation to the curriculum and management hierarchies of schools is another variable that is highly significant for an appraisal of their relationship to the National Curriculum. In terms of teachers' roles in groups, it seems important to assess their relationships within subject groupings, for example within school departments and also more broadly in subject teaching associations, as well as in representative associations such as the National Union of Teachers. The forms of subject organization within which teachers operate, especially in secondary schools (see especially Goodson, 1992; Siskin, 1994; Siskin and Little, 1995), are key frameworks for understanding teachers' responses to the National Curriculum. As Paechter (1995, p. 85) observes in relation to the design and technology curriculum, for example, 'while presenting enormous possibilities for student-centred learning', the National Curriculum has at the same time 'allowed teachers to insist that certain items of content (such as their entire previous syllabuses) are crucial and must be covered'. Issues of power involving gender differences are also a major potential source of differing kinds of response (e.g. Paechter and Head, 1996).

Responses to the National Curriculum also provide a useful gauge by which to appraise the nature of the 'professional community' of teachers, and indeed may well come to have a central role in its development. As has been noted in the USA, collegial groups of teachers vary markedly in terms of their intensity, their inclusivity and their orientation, as well as in the nature of their networks within and between schools (Little, 1992; Little and McLaughlin, 1993). Much of this dimension of teachers' responses revolves around their value judgements and their shared, often tacit understandings of their 'professional responsibility' (Broadfoot and Osborn, 1988; Pollard *et al.*, 1994) and of what makes a good colleague.

TEACHERS AND THE NATIONAL CURRICULUM IN PRACTICE

As the introduction of the English and Welsh National Curriculum progressed, it became clear that teachers' responses varied from school to school and even, in the secondary sector, from department to department (Bowe and Ball, 1992). Whilst very many teachers undoubtedly experienced a profound sense of disempowerment and stress, others adopted a more proactive role in seeking to impose their own interpretations upon the requirements (see, for example,

Campbell and Neill, 1994; Croll *et al.*, 1994; Woods, 1994). Given the degree of detail embodied in the early Curriculum Orders and in the system of national assessment, this was not always an easy thing to do, and certainly required a degree of 'professional confidence' amongst teachers (Helsby, 1995). Evidence from Bowe and Ball (1992) suggests that such confidence, and a sense of autonomy, are more likely to be present in schools and departments with high *'capacity'* (teacher experience in responding to change), *'commitment'* (firmly held subject or pedagogical paradigms) and *'history'* (of curriculum innovation and development).

Certainly, with growing experience of the National Curriculum, evidence is beginning to emerge of gradual increases in teachers' confidence and in their ability to identify and exploit the 'spaces for manoeuvre' within the legislative framework (Bowe and Ball, 1992; Helsby, 1996). These spaces are sometimes used to accommodate what teachers themselves regard as educationally valuable experiences for their students but which are not a part of the National Curriculum. Equally, as demonstrated in the early chapters of this book, they are used to reconcile conflicting demands and approaches. It is apparent in the literature surrounding the National Curriculum that the notion of 'spaces' and of the active role of teachers in 'creating policy in practice' (Croll *et al.*, 1994) have become increasingly important themes for research and development over time.

As the evidence of this book shows, teachers in both primary and secondary schools are not necessarily passive victims of some monolithic piece of state machinery but, in many cases, are key actors in the realization of the National Curriculum in practice. Whilst all are constrained to a greater or lesser extent by the enforced requirements, the National Curriculum itself is far from being fixed and immutable, but instead is subject to interpretation and reinterpretation over time. In other words, the relationship between teachers and the National Curriculum is at once mutually dependent and dynamic, with each side both shaping and being shaped by the other.

This changing relationship is put into its historic context by McCulloch in Chapter 2, which examines the long-standing tradition in England and Wales that links the notion of 'teacher professionalism' with teachers' supposed control over the school curriculum. Whilst this tradition was always problematic, it has not been eclipsed by the National Curriculum, but rather subjected to continuing contestation. On the one hand, it has continued to exert a strong influence upon the way in which the reforms developed; on the other, it has itself been constantly reinterpreted to meet the new challenges. The issue is, as yet, unresolved.

Chapters 3–5 focus upon the changes which have taken place in English primary schools, which were the first to feel the effects of the National Curriculum and which, arguably, have experienced the greatest degree of disturbance to the status quo. Since the gradual withdrawal and the effective demise of the eleven-plus examination as a national system of pupil assessment at the end of the primary phase of compulsory education, primary school teachers have enjoyed an unusually high level of curriculum autonomy. Encouraged by the

Plowden report of the 1960s, a strong primary tradition has developed v
rhetoric emphasizes progressive pedagogy, with integrated topic work and c
centred learning favoured over more didactic and subject-based approac
Accordingly, the strongly classified, bureaucratic and technical/rational view of
teaching embodied in the new National Curriculum appeared to be at odds with
the professional commitments and practices of many primary teachers.

Acker, in her detailed and evocative study of a primary school in the early
years of National Curriculum implementation (see Chapter 3), explores the
developing relationship between the reforms and existing school and teacher
cultures. Whilst vividly describing how increased central control created a new
context for teachers' work, making it more systematic and less spontaneous, she
also shows how the teachers' common commitment to a caring and child-centred
approach enabled them to mould the new curriculum to accommodate this.
Looking at the wider lessons that can be drawn from these data, she concludes
that there is no simple correspondence between changes in policy and changes in
teachers' work, and that hegemony is not total:

> We learn that school cultures cannot survive untouched by
> imposed change, but that material realities and school cultures
> influence the form taken by innovation. We have, in effect, a case
> study of the intricate and changing relationships of agency,
> culture and structure. (Chapter 3, p. 47)

Osborn, in Chapter 4, also eschews simplistic conclusions and rejects claims
of either widescale passivity and deskilling of teachers or strong contestation and
concerted resistance to the reforms. Drawing upon extensive data from a
national study of change in primary schools in the wake of the 1988 Education
Reform Act, she argues that the conflicts which arose between the National
Curriculum and teachers' existing values and beliefs were most frequently
resolved through a process of 'creative mediation'. Working within the framework of the new requirements, many teachers nevertheless interpreted the
policies in the light of their own values before translating them into practice. In
this way, the notions of both structure and agency are again preserved as
important influences upon practice: indeed, Osborn argues that, insofar as
different teachers adopt similar responses and their resultant actions have
system-wide effects, they are in practice transformed into policy-makers in their
own right.

The contradictions and paradoxes arising from the introduction of the
National Curriculum into primary schools are again apparent in Chapter 5, by
Woods and Jeffrey, which focuses specifically upon 'creative teachers'. Whilst all
of the indications point towards a lessening of the opportunities for teachers to be
creative, nonetheless they are able to identify ways in which some 'creative
teachers' are able to maintain innovation, ownership, control and relevance in
their teaching. Despite the inevitable tensions between the rational, bureaucratic and ends–means philosophy of recent government policy and the

emotional, child-centred and process-oriented approaches of creative teachers, examples are given of the successful adoption of strategies of resistance, appropriation and even enrichment in the face of the new requirements. Although some of the teachers in their study are unable to adapt, resulting in stress, burnout and even exit from teaching, Woods and Jeffrey conclude that 'some of the more intangible, but highly significant, constituents of the art of teaching [are] still alive and well in some areas, despite the National Curriculum' (p. 76).

The situation in English and Welsh secondary schools differs in many ways from that in the primary sector. Not only are secondary schools larger and more complex organizations, mostly subdivided according to subject areas, but their curriculum has traditionally been overshadowed by the university-led public examinations system. Secondary teachers as a group are less female-dominated than their primary counterparts, traditionally less compliant and often more highly qualified, with an emphasis upon subject rather than pedagogical expertise. In these circumstances, it might be expected that the impact of the subject-dominated National Curriculum and its associated assessment system might be less severe than in primary schools. Once again, however, the reality is varied and complex, as evidenced by the data in chapters 6–9.

Teachers' subject backgrounds and cultures are important variables in determining their responses to National Curriculum requirements, as demonstrated in Saunders and Warburton's comparison of maths and technology teachers (Chapter 6). For maths teachers, wide and long-standing agreement on the content of the secondary maths syllabus, coupled with the subject's established position in the curriculum hierarchy, meant that they had to contend with only minimal change as a result of the new requirements. Indeed, there were suggestions that the National Curriculum served largely to confirm both the pre-eminence of maths as a subject and the status quo. For technology teachers, however, things were very different, as the National Curriculum brought in sweeping changes both in curriculum content and in the organization of teaching in this area. Teachers with long years of experience in teaching craft skills in such disparate areas as woodwork and home economics were suddenly thrust into integrated teams and expected to work together to develop design skills in their students. To make matters worse, ongoing policy changes meant a total lack of stability within the area as the National Curriculum developed, leading to a good deal of wasted effort and confusion.

Subject differences were not, however, the sole determinant of reactions to the National Curriculum, as is illustrated graphically in Roberts's study of geography teachers (Chapter 7). Here, prior experience and beliefs about the subject are the crucial factor in shaping not only teachers' attitudes to the reforms but also their practical responses. Thus, for example, the head of department who had previously chosen a highly prescriptive examination syllabus and based his courses on a series of textbooks found relatively little difficulty in adjusting to the National Curriculum: he simply substituted one form of external prescription for another. By contrast those who been committed to developing a unique curriculum within their department based on strongly held subject and pedagogical beliefs encountered much more difficulty in reconciling the dilemmas presented by the new central requirements: the extent to which they were able to do so determined the degree of resistance which they felt towards the National Curriculum.

Jenkins's study of the development of one of the Attainment Targets for science (Chapter 8) provides a timely reminder both of the limits of central prescription and of the ultimate reliance upon teachers to turn educational policy into practice. Whilst there was widespread agreement amongst both teachers and policy-makers on the desirability of developing skills of 'scientific investigation' in students, the lack of clarity about what the Attainment Target might involve and how it might be taught led to considerable difficulties and frustration in schools. In the absence of clear and authoritative guidance, despite many attempts to provide it from the centre, it was left to teachers and their representatives to develop the policy into practice by 'continuously drawing upon their professional experience and "teacherly knowledge"' (p. 126).

In the final example of the effects of the National Curriculum in secondary schools, Chapter 9 explores its impact upon one of the five designated cross-curricular themes. Harris's research on careers teachers underlines the way in which the National Curriculum reinforced the importance attached to traditional bodies of academic knowledge at the expense of activities which crossed existing subject boundaries. Thus careers teachers, whose work had been emphasized at the time of TVEI and associated developments, found that both their activities and their budgets were being squeezed by the escalating timetable and other demands of traditional subjects. At the same time the increasingly competitive ethos promoted by other government initiatives threatened the student-centred approaches developed both in careers education and in the wider area of personal and social education. Despite a rhetoric of improvement, the position of careers teachers has certainly not been enhanced by the National Curriculum, and in many cases they been made more vulnerable.

The introduction of a new National Curriculum inevitably had important implications for the professional development of all teachers, whether in primary or secondary schools. The final chapter, by Helsby and Knight, examines evidence of recent changes in formal in-service training (INSET) provision and of teachers' views of their own professional development in the context of National Curriculum implementation. It concludes that, whilst formal provision has been predominantly instrumental and limited for some teachers, engagement with colleagues in developing the new curriculum has often led to much informal professional development. However, the increased workload and pressures have left many feeling beleaguered and unsupported, and the *ad hoc* and 'do-it-yourself' model of professional development may be judged inappropriate for such a wide-ranging national initiative.

15

REFERENCES

Apple, M. W. (1986) *Teachers and Texts: A Political Economy of Class and Gender Relations in Education*. New York: Routledge.

Ball, S. J. (1990) *Politics and Policy Making in Education: Explorations in Policy Sociology*. London: Routledge.

Barber, M. (1993) Teachers and the National Curriculum: learning to love it? In M. Barber and D. Graham (eds), *Sense, Nonsense and the National Curriculum*. London: Falmer Press, pp. 10–25.

Barber, M. (1996) Why are you still smiling Kenneth? *Times Educational Supplement*, 31 May.

Bernstein, B. (1971) On the classification and framing of educational knowledge. In M. F. D. Young (ed.), *Knowledge and Control: New Directions for the Sociology of Education*. London: Collier-Macmillan, pp. 47–69.

Bowe, R. and Ball, S. J. with Gold, A. (1992) *Reforming Education and Changing Schools*. London: Routledge.

Broadfoot, P. and Osborn, M. with Gilly, M. and Paillet, A. (1988) What professional responsibility means to teachers: national contexts and classroom constraints. *British Journal of Sociology of Education*, 9(3): 265–87.

Campbell, R. J. and Neill, S. R. St J. (1994) *Secondary Teachers at Work*. London: Routledge.

Carlgren, I., Handal, G. and Vaage, S. (eds) (1994) *Teachers' Minds and Actions: Research on Teachers' Thinking and Practice*. London: Falmer Press.

Clarke, J., Cochrane, A. and McLaughlin, E. (eds) (1994) *Managing Social Policy*. London: Sage.

Croll, P., Abbott, D., Broadfoot, P., Osborn, M. and Pollard, A. (1994) Teachers and educational policy: roles and models. *British Journal of Educational Studies*, 42(2): 333–47.

Crow, G. (1989) The use of the concept of strategy in recent sociological literature. *Sociology*, 23(1): 1–24.

Dale, R. (1992, April) National reform, economic crisis and 'New Right' theory: a New Zealand perspective. Paper presented to the annual conference of the American Educational Research Association, San Francisco.

Dearing, R. (1994) *The National Curriculum and its Assessment: Final Report*. London: HMSO.

DES (Department of Education and Science) (1987) *The National Curriculum 5–16: A Consultation Document*. London: HMSO.

DES (1989) *The National Curriculum: From Policy to Practice*. London: HMSO.

DFE (Department for Education) (1992) *Choice and Diversity: A New Framework for Schools*. London: HMSO.

Evans, J. and Penney, D. (1995) The politics of pedagogy: making a National Curriculum Physical Education. *Journal of Education Policy*, 10(1): 27–44.

Evetts, J. (1994) *Becoming a Secondary Head Teacher*. London: Cassell.

Giddens, A. (1984) *The Constitution of Society*. Cambridge: Polity Press.

Goodson, I. (1992) *School Subjects and Curriculum Change*, 3rd edn. London: Falmer Press.

Goodson, I. (1994) *Studying Curriculum: Cases and Methods*. Buckingham: Open University Press.

Goodson, I. F. and Hargreaves, A. (eds) (1996) *Teachers' Professional Lives*. London: Falmer Press.

Grace, G. (1987) Teachers and the state in Britain: a changing relationship. In M. Lawn and G. Grace (eds), *Teachers: The Culture and Politics of Work*. Lewes: Falmer Press, pp. 193–228.

Graham, D. (1993) *A Lesson for Us All: The Making of the National Curriculum*. London: Routledge.

Hargreaves, A. (1991) Curriculum reform and the teacher. *Curriculum Journal*, **2**(3): 250–8.

Hargreaves, A. (1992) Cultures of teaching: a focus for change. In A. Hargreaves and M. G. Fullan (eds), *Understanding Teacher Development*. London: Cassell, pp. 216–40.

Hargreaves, A. (1994) *Changing Teachers, Changing Times: Teachers' Work and Culture in the Post-Modern Age*. London: Cassell.

Hargreaves, A. and Goodson, I. (1996) Teachers' professional lives: aspirations and actualities. In I. Goodson and A. Hargreaves (eds), *Teachers' Professional Lives*. London: Falmer Press, pp. 1–27.

Harland, J. (1987) The TVEI experience: issues of control, response and the professional role of teachers. In D. Gleeson (ed.), *TVEI and Secondary Education: A Critical Appraisal*. Milton Keynes: Open University Press, pp. 38–54.

Helsby, G. (1989) Central control and grassroots creativity: the paradox at the heart of TVEI. In A. Harrison and S. Gretton (eds), *Education and Training UK 1989: An Economic, Social and Policy Audit*. Newbury: Policy Journals, pp. 78–83.

Helsby, G. (1995) Teachers' construction of professionalism in England in the 1990s. *Journal of Education for Teaching*, **21**(3): 317–32.

Helsby, G. (1996) Defining and developing professionalism in English secondary schools. *Journal of Education for Teaching*, **22**(2): 135–48.

Hodges, L. (1996) On the rocks with Machiavelli. *Times Educational Supplement*, 9 February.

Hoyle, E. (1974) Professionality, professionalism and control in teaching. *London Educational Review*, **3**(2): 13–19.

Huberman, M. (1993) *The Lives of Teachers*. London: Cassell.

Jones, G. E. (1994) Which nation's curriculum? The case of Wales. *Curriculum Journal*, **5**(1): 5–16.

Kelly, A. V. (1990) *The National Curriculum: A Critical Review*. London: Paul Chapman Publishing.

Kogan, M. (1989) Accountability and teacher professionalism. In W. Carr (ed.), *Quality in Teaching*. London: Falmer Press, pp. 135–44.

Lawton, D. (1980) *The Politics of the School Curriculum*. London: Routledge & Kegan Paul.

Little, J. W. (1992) Opening the black box of professional community. In A. Lieberman (ed.), *The Changing Context of Teaching*. Chicago: University of Chicago Press, pp. 157–78.

Little, J. W. and McLaughlin, M. W. (eds) (1993) *Teachers' Work: Individuals, Colleagues and Contexts*. New York: Teachers' College Press.

Norton, J. (1994) Primary teachers experiencing change. In H. Constable, S. Farrow and J. Norton (eds), *Change in Classroom Practice*. London: Falmer Press, pp. 127–36.

Ozga, J. (1995, January) Teacher professionalism: an overview rooted in current concerns. Paper presented at the Inaugural Conference of the Professional Studies Forum, Queens Hotel, Leeds.

Ozga, J. and Lawn, M. (1988) Interpreting the labour process of teaching. *British Journal of Sociology of Education*, **9**: 323–36.

Paechter, C. (1995) Subcultural retreat: negotiating the design and technology curriculum. *British Educational Research Journal*, **21**(1): 75–87.

Paechter, C. and Head, J. (1996) Power and gender in the classroom. *British Educational Research Journal*, **22**(1): 57–69.

17

Pietrasik, R. (1987) The teachers' action, 1984–1986. In M. Lawn and G. Grace (eds), *Teachers: The Culture and Politics of Work*. Lewes: Falmer Press, pp. 168–89.

Pollard, A., Broadfoot, P., Croll, P., Osborn, M. and Abbott, D. (1994) *Changing English Primary Schools? The Impact of the Education Reform Act at Key Stage One*. London: Cassell.

Radnor, H., Poulson, L., Turner-Bisset, R. (1995) Assessment and teacher professionalism. *Curriculum Journal*, **6**(3): 325–42.

Rawling, E. (1992) The making of a national geography curriculum. *Geography*, **77**(4): 292–309.

Robertson, S. (1996) Teachers' work, restructuring and postfordism: constructing the new 'professionalism'. In I. F. Goodson and A. Hargreaves (eds), *Teachers' Professional Lives*. London: Falmer Press, pp. 28–55.

Simons, H. (1988) Teacher professionalism and the National Curriculum. In D. Lawton and C. Chitty (eds), *The National Curriculum*. Bedford Way Papers 33, London: Institute of Education, University of London, pp. 78–90.

Siskin, L. S. (1994) *Realms of Knowledge: Academic Departments in Secondary Schools*. London: Falmer Press.

Siskin, L. S. and Little, J. W. (eds) (1995) *The Subjects in Question: Departmental Organization and the High School*. New York: Teachers' College Press.

Talbert, J. E. and McLaughlin, M. W. (1996) Teacher professionalism in local school contexts. In I. F. Goodson and A. Hargreaves (eds), *Teachers' Professional Lives*. London: Falmer Press, pp. 127–53.

Taylor, T. (1995) Movers and shakers: high politics and the origins of the National Curriculum. *Curriculum Journal*, **6**(2): 161–84.

The Independent (1996a) Report blames poor reading on teacher training. 8 May.

The Independent (1996b) Labour goes back to basics on teaching. 30 May.

Wallace, M. (1993) Discourse of derision: the role of the mass media within the education policy process. *Journal of Education Policy*, **8**(4): 321–37.

Woods, P. (1994) Adaptation and self-determination in English primary schools. *Oxford Review of Education*, **20**(4): 387–410.

Woods, P. and Wenham, P. (1995) Politics and pedagogy: a case study in appropriation. *Journal of Education Policy*, **10**(2): 119–41.

Chapter 2

Teachers and the National Curriculum in England and Wales: Socio-historical Frameworks

Gary McCulloch

Among the many problematic aspects of the current cycle of educational reforms in England and Wales, the relationship between teachers and the new National Curriculum has been one of the most powerfully evocative in terms of broader social, political and cultural issues. Well publicized conflicts over the character and implications of the National Curriculum could be depicted in terms of 'a battle over who controls the nation's classrooms, the way children are tested and how far the government should prescribe what pupils are taught' (*Sunday Times*, 1993). In order to fully understand the relationship between teachers and the National Curriculum, however, it is necessary to locate it in a longer-term socio-historical framework. Developing such a framework helps to explain the ways in which the National Curriculum impinges on 'teacher professionalism' in England and Wales. It also begins to shed light on the kinds of responses made by teachers themselves in a changing context.

TEACHER PROFESSIONALISM AND THE SCHOOL CURRICULUM

The notion of teacher professionalism is notoriously beset with conceptual difficulties and ambiguities (see, e.g., Burrage and Torstendahl, 1990; Eraut, 1994; Hoyle and John, 1995). At least in the case of England and Wales, however, it has been strongly associated with teachers' involvement in the school curriculum. It is necessary first to make a distinction between the ideas of 'professionalization' and 'professionalism' in relation to teachers, and to understand them both in terms of distinct socio-historical 'traditions'. In the USA, Linda Eisenmann has suggested that whereas professionalization denotes issues of status, professionalism concerns the rights and obligations of teachers to determine their own tasks in the classroom, that is, how teachers use their own knowledge (Eisenmann, 1991). This distinction seems particularly apt in the English context, where it holds strong historical resonance, although this more specific notion of professionalism has also been expressed as 'professionality' (e.g. Foreman, 1995; Hoyle and John, 1995).

The idea of professionalization is highly familiar in the historical literature on English education as the quest on the part of teachers to be publicly acknowledged as 'professionals', and of teachers' unions and associations to establish teaching as a recognized 'profession' on the same level as, for example, medicine or law. The classic works on teachers' history emphasized what they perceived as the 'evolution of a profession'. Asher Tropp, for example, sought to document the 'growth of the teaching profession' by investigating the historical role of the National Union of Teachers in facilitating a gradual rise in 'professional status'. The major achievements that are viewed as relevant to this process include the enlarging of qualifications, the exclusion of uncertificated teachers, the improvement of conditions of work, the obtaining of security of tenure, promotion to the highest ranks, salary and pension schemes, increased influence and importance as a professional group, the growing trust of parents, increasing unity among teachers' groups, and the creation of a more favourable image or stereotype for teachers and their unions. Tropp's work also exemplifies a liberal model of teachers' development towards public esteem, as it concludes:

> The position of the school teachers could well be regarded by other
> professions and would-be professions. Without any of the
> advantages of the older professions, they have fought successfully
> for the welfare of the schools and for an increase in their status.
> (Tropp, 1957, p. 270)

The role of teachers in the classroom, or of their relationship to the school curriculum, finds very little place in this discussion. Similarly Peter Gosden's account of the 'contribution of teachers' associations to the development of school teaching as a professional occupation' emphasized the importance of attaining 'a reasonable level of salaries, pensions, security of tenure, sound training and qualifications and some recognition by the community of the profession's right to influence the way in which the service it offers is administered' (Gosden, 1972, foreword).

More recent works have developed this general line of analysis without necessarily sharing in the liberal assumptions about gradual progress that had been so strong. The struggle of women teachers and their associations for increased security and status has been well documented (e.g. Widdowson, 1983). The means by which teachers' groups enhanced their public status through channels such as the media have also recently attracted greater attention (e.g. Cunningham, 1992). There has also developed a powerful counter-argument that has contradicted the notion of professional aspirations and instead emphasized the idea of teachers as workers, highlighting the importance of class solidarity and industrial action in relation to teachers (e.g. Lawn, 1985). Issues to do with how teachers have been 'deskilled' or 'proletarianized' in recent educational changes also have a great deal of bearing on this notion of 'professionalization' in terms of their effects on teachers' status in society as an occupational group. At the same time, they link up with ideas about professionalism, especially through their general inference that teachers' effective autonomy in the classroom domain has been reduced to the role of a functionary or technician in 'implementing' orders produced elsewhere. The view that teachers' work has undergone a process commonly described as 'intensification' also contrasts with received ideals of professionalism, no less than of professionalization.

The concept of 'teacher professionalism' strikes a different historical chord to that of 'professionalization', and relates in particular to teachers' supposed control and autonomy in the curriculum domain. Here, the familiar storyline is about teachers acquiring a striking degree of freedom in this area by the 1940s, but coming under pressure from other interested parties and then from a massive incursion on the part of the state after the self-styled 'Great Debate' of the late 1970s. Denis Lawton has described the period between the 1940s and the 1960s as 'the Golden Age of teacher control (or non-control) of the curriculum' in England and Wales, evoking both the opportunities that existed in that period and a common tendency on the part of teachers and their representatives to fail to make use of these (Lawton, 1980, p. 22). The curriculum was widely recognized both as the chief domain of teachers' autonomy and as the major source of their professionalism. Indeed, the link is often made in explicit terms in accounts such as that of J. F. Kerr in the late 1960s: 'The teachers worked hard to achieve some degree of professional autonomy and by the 1950s it was generally accepted they were free to decide what and how they should teach' (Kerr, 1968, p. 13).

Gerald Grace's notion of 'legitimated professionalism' provides a socio-historical model that strongly evokes this phase of relative curricular freedom and a notion of its subsequent decline. Grace suggests that in the 1950s and 1960s, an educational settlement between teachers and the state gave rise to considerable professional autonomy in relation to the curriculum despite set-backs in teachers' terms and conditions of service, to the extent that

> In contrast to highly centralised and controlled systems of state
> schooling in other socio-political contexts, the de-centralised
> autonomy of British teachers with respect to curriculum selection
> and pedagogic methods was taken to be a distinctive feature of
> British democracy and schooling. (Grace, 1987, p. 212)

By the mid-1980s, however, in Grace's terms, successive state initiatives appeared to have eroded this kind of professionalism no less than they had weakened the position of teachers in other areas, such as their terms and conditions of service. This view can lead to a straightforward notion of the undermining and eventual collapse of teacher control and autonomy in the curriculum domain in the face of state involvement, with the National Curriculum representing the logical final stage in this long-term process (see, e.g., Chitty, 1988). Indeed, Lawn goes so far as to argue that 'In retrospect, teacher autonomy as an exploratory idea in curriculum control in England and Wales may now be seen as historically specific to the period 1925–80' (Lawn, 1987, p. 227). Whereas in this period 'it appears to provide an explanation for events in which teachers are seen as "professionals" engaged in "partnership" with local and central government', Lawn maintains, 'In recent years a shift in educational policy and a return to overt, centralised administrative controls in education have muted or replaced this once common explanation in the curriculum field of autonomy, professionalism and partnership' (*ibid.*; see also, e.g., Chitty and Lawn, 1995).

On this straightforward historical model, therefore, the significance of the National Curriculum is that it completed the process of eclipsing teachers' 'professionalism'. It is possible to interpret the relationship between teachers and the National Curriculum in more problematic terms, however, again in relation to its long-term historical context. In particular, a greater emphasis on the role of contestation between different interests and ideologies tends to suggest not a simple model of the decline of teachers' influence, but a framework that involves continuing debate among teachers and other interested groups, including the agencies of the state. Such contestation implies at its most severe an open confrontation between opposing parties. It also allows for more complex mediation and interactions among the groups and individuals involved, including those interactions that have taken place among teachers themselves. Fundamentally, too, it provides scope for understanding the continuing efforts of teachers and others to reinterpret received notions of their role in a rapidly changing educational and political context.

Awareness of these more complex relationships is central to developing a fuller understanding of teachers and the school curriculum. An important example of this is the career of the Technical and Vocational Education Initiative (TVEI) in the 1980s. This scheme was originally introduced under the auspices of the Manpower Services Commission to foster greater economic productivity, emphasizing a strongly instrumental rationale. It gave rise to well-founded suspicions that it was intended to undermine ideals of liberal education and also teachers' 'professional prerogative to think and to plan' (Proud, 1984). In the event, however, the TVEI did not simply follow the lines originally anticipated, but developed in unexpected ways that often appeared to enhance the roles of the teachers involved in the scheme. Janet Harland notes in relation to the TVEI what she calls the 'central paradox' of

> the simultaneous emergence of two apparently or potentially
> conflicting features: on one hand, strong central control of a kind
> which has permitted the detailed intervention of a central
> government agency right down to the level of the classroom; and
> on the other a teacher response which is, in many of the pilot
> schemes, creative and innovative, and often indeed experimental
> and downright risky. (Harland, 1987, p. 39)

Harland describes the teachers 'leading the TVEI crusade' as 'released prisoners'. These, however, are a 'very particular set of teachers', many of them drawn from the practical/technical/applied areas of the curriculum, who have 'in many schools led rather isolated and low-status professional lives' (*ibid.*, p. 47). On this view, teachers interpret state policy in different ways, often leading it in directions unanticipated by its initiators (see also, e.g., Gleeson, 1987; Helsby and McCulloch, 1996).

Another way of problematizing the relationship between teachers and the school curriculum in a rapidly shifting educational and political context is to understand it in terms of the reinterpretation of an established 'tradition'. As Goodson argues, the National Curriculum may be read as a major initiative to rebuild the nation state and to re-establish national identity and ideology, in response to fears of economic decline, cultural dissolution, and a loss of national power (Goodson, 1994, ch. 7). And yet the National Curriculum itself posed a series of challenges to another socially constructed national tradition, the idea of teacher professionalism defined in terms of autonomy and effective control in the curriculum domain, which had become established earlier in the century.

Eric Hobsbawm has suggested that traditions are 'invented' for social and political purposes, often to establish or reinforce the status of particular institutions and to define the ways they are allowed to develop (Hobsbawm, 1983). In Scottish education, for example, as R. D. Anderson has persuasively argued, the notion of a distinctively democratic and egalitarian 'Scottish tradition' has developed to become a potent factor that itself influences the nature of reform. Anderson describes this Scottish tradition as a 'powerful historical myth', not in order to signify that it is untrue or false, but to suggest its character as 'an idealisation and distillation of a complex reality'. It takes on ideological and political force as it informs change, 'interacting with other forces and pressures, ruling out some developments as inconsistent with the national tradition, and shaping the form in which the institutions inherited from the past are allowed to change' (Anderson, 1983, p. 1). The idea of teacher control over the curriculum may be taken as another example of a 'tradition', invented for social and political reasons in the mid-twentieth century, which has undergone a strenuous process of reinterpretation, especially since the 1970s. On this view, the tradition of teacher control in this domain has not gone into a total eclipse but has continued to exert an influence on the character of reforms, and has itself mutated to emphasize particular and perhaps surprising characteristics.

It is possible to exaggerate the strength of this 'tradition' even in the so-called 'Golden Age' of the 1940s and 1950s, especially when seeking to contrast it with the more recent developments of the 1980s and 1990s. Teachers' autonomy and control in the curriculum field was always limited and in many ways contradictory in nature. Lawn suggests that the role assumed by teachers still allowed the state to maintain a form of 'indirect rule' in this area (Lawn, 1987). The Education Act of 1944 provided for the school day to begin with 'collective worship' and for religious instruction to be given – the first time that these had been made statutory obligations for schools. The so-called 'tripartite' system of grammar, technical and modern schools that was promoted in the 1940s and 1950s clearly also constituted a major influence upon the character of the school curriculum (see McCulloch, 1989, ch. 4). The hierarchical nature of school subjects, and the close relationship between this hierarchy and the position of teachers in schools, created a further set of limitations (Goodson, 1992). Teacher professionalism could look very different from the vantage point of a male physics teacher in a grammar school, or a male craft teacher in a technical school, or a female English teacher in a modern school, or to teachers in different areas of primary schools. The strength of university-based examining boards also generated powerful challenges to teachers' supposed autonomy and control in respect to assessment of the curriculum, and it appears that teachers tended to be loath to assert themselves strongly in this area despite the fact that it clearly influenced and limited their own role in the curriculum domain (McCulloch, 1993). Constraints affecting teachers in primary schools often differed from those in secondary schools, and they varied in different schools depending on factors such as the role of the headteacher and the importance attached to the eleven-plus examination and other selection devices.

It seems clear, then, that the school curriculum was never quite the 'secret garden' for teachers that it was imagined to be from the vantage point of the Ministry of Education. Even so, in spite of such important variations between the espoused 'myth' and the lived 'reality', the idea of teacher professionalism in this particular sense became well established during this period. Appraising the relationship between teachers and the National Curriculum may therefore be seen as a way to investigate the changing nature of 'teacher professionalism' itself in England and Wales in the 1990s. To what extent has this idea of teacher autonomy been undermined, how far may it be said to have been contested, and in what ways if any has it been reinterpreted through the introduction of the National Curriculum?

REINTERPRETING TEACHER PROFESSIONALISM

The discourse developed by the British government in its education reforms of the 1980s and 1990s has placed an emphasis not on undermining or abandoning the tradition of teacher professionalism, but of reinterpreting it to meet new challenges. The strategic aim has been to ensure broad acceptability for the National Curriculum among teachers and the public, and in general this has been achieved by recasting received and inherited ideals. Where the development of the National Curriculum has met with concerted public opposition, as it did in the early 1990s, the eventual response has been to reiterate the entrenched role of teachers' 'professional judgement' in the curriculum domain. The overall effect has been to obscure the extent to which the National Curriculum has limited and reduced the former role of teachers in this domain, but at the same time to limit the intrusive nature of the National Curriculum itself.

The notion of teacher professionalism developed by the government in this period, while often vague and highly elastic in nature, has generally, although not always, related to teachers' involvement in the curriculum domain. In 1983, the major policy document *Teaching Quality* could still articulate an idealized, not to say inaccurate vision of 'the national tradition of an undivided school teaching profession, united by a common purpose and with parity of esteem for all its members' (DES, 1983, p. 1). It suggested somewhat vaguely that

> Teachers' professionalism should be encouraged by improved
> policies for career development within schools and local
> authorities, and a clearer definition of individual teachers' tasks
> within the school and of their responsibilities to parents and to
> those to whom the school is ultimately accountable. (*ibid.*, p. 27).

Over the following decade, the government's growing commitment to a National Curriculum and the conflicts to which this gave rise encouraged more specific discussion of the notion of teacher professionalism in a changed educational context. This was especially the case as the government's educational reforms also strongly emphasized the rights of parents as consumers, as against what were seen as the entrenched privileges of teachers, local education authorities, and the so-called 'educational Establishment'.

The Secretary of State for Education in the early 1980s, Sir Keith Joseph, was concerned to raise standards of pupil attainment, and in order to do so devised objectives for each main area of the curriculum. On the other hand, Joseph denied any intention of 'seeking to impose a centrally controlled curriculum, and to suppress the freedom to define the details of what is taught which had traditionally resided at local level' (Joseph, 1984, p. 147). This reflected a continuing awareness of the strength of this tradition. Joseph attempted to articulate a changing relationship between local and national responsibilities, while still paying homage to teachers' established role in this area. Thus he stressed that 'the detail of how subjects are taught will continue to be decided in each school, in the context of the local education authority's curricular policy', while at a national level there would be objectives for the range and balance of the curriculum, with defined levels of attainment to be reached at the ages of 11 and 16 (*ibid.*). This was the general line that was maintained in the White Paper *Better Schools*, published in 1985, although the idea of teacher professionalism in more general terms continued to be somewhat ill-defined and amorphous, as in the following declaration:

> Like other professionals, teachers are expected to carry out their
> professional tasks in accordance with their judgment, without
> bias, precisely because they are professionals. This
> professionalism requires not only appropriate training and
> experience but also the professional attitude which gives priority
> to the interests of those served and is constantly concerned to
> increase effectiveness through professional development.
> (DES, 1985, p. 44)

During the development of the National Curriculum in 1987–8, the need to raise standards and improve accountability was stressed even more strongly, but government statements continued to support a strong role for teachers. For

25

example, the consultation document on the National Curriculum, published in July 1987, noted that 'legislation should leave full scope for professional judgment and for schools to organise how the curriculum is delivered in the way best suited to the ages, circumstances, needs and abilities of the children in each classroom' (DES, 1987, p. 11). Similarly, it was emphasized two years later that in translating the National Curriculum from policy into practice, the 'organisation of teaching and learning' should remain 'a professional matter for the head teacher and his or her staff' (DES, 1989, para. 4.3). Moreover, the DES pointed out,

> What is specified will allow teachers considerable freedom in the way in which they teach, examples and materials used, selection of content and context, use of textbooks, etc. The legislation does not allow particular textbooks or teaching methods to be prescribed as part of a programme of study. (*Ibid.*, 1989, para. 4.15)

In retrospect, such policy statements were drawing a distinction between the content of the school curriculum, which teachers would not be able to control, and the methods by which the curriculum would be delivered, which would remain within the domain of teachers. They were also concerned to maintain a role for teachers in curriculum development. The relationship between the delivery and the assessment of the curriculum, meanwhile, was unclear. Despite these important adjustments, however, a notion of teacher professionalism as being related in a distinctive way to the curriculum domain was preserved.

Kenneth Baker, who as Secretary of State for Education was chiefly responsible for the introduction of the National Curriculum as part of the Education Reform Act of 1988, also attempted to allay the concerns of 'some teachers' that the National Curriculum would 'prescribe how they go about their professional duties'. He insisted that 'We want to build upon the professionalism of the teacher in the classroom – the professionalism of the many fine and dedicated teachers throughout our education system' (House of Commons Debates, 1987). It was not intended, he continued, 'to lay down how lessons should be taught, how timetables should be organised, or which textbooks should be used'. Indeed, according to Baker, the National Curriculum would provide ample 'scope for imaginative approaches developed by our teachers', such as the teaching of science in primary schools and in the TVEI (*ibid.*). On this account, the National Curriculum would provide a loose framework for teachers' work, to maintain and even enhance their autonomy in curriculum development.

Autobiographical accounts also help to explain differences in the attitudes of the key policy-makers of the late 1980s in forging a relationship between teachers and the National Curriculum. In particular, they highlight the different ways in which the established tradition of teacher professionalism could be reinterpreted to suit changing educational, social and political purposes. In his highly revealing political memoirs, Kenneth Baker emphasizes the need for a curriculum plan that would 'match the needs of twenty-first-century Britain' (Baker, 1993, p. 169). It should therefore comprise not simply a core curriculum of 'basic' subjects redolent of nineteenth-century needs, but should include a full range of ten subjects together with the requisite cross-curricular themes. By contrast, the then Prime Minister, Margaret Thatcher, preferred to concentrate on the core subjects, alongside

> a nationally recognised and reliably monitored system of testing at various stages of a child's school career which would allow parents, teachers, local authorities and central government to know what was going wrong and right and take remedial action if necessary. (Thatcher, 1993, p. 590)

She envisaged the establishment of a basic syllabus for English, mathematics and science with simple tests for each: 'There ought then to be plenty of scope for the individual teacher to concentrate with children on the particular aspects of the subject in which he or she felt a special enthusiasm or interest' (*ibid.*, p. 593).

Thatcher also relates this priority to a more general attempt to reinterpret the established tradition of teachers' autonomy in a changing context. She acknowledges the existence of a strong tradition of teacher control in the curriculum area: 'The fact that since 1944 the only compulsory subject in the curriculum in Britain had been religious education reflected a healthy distrust of the state using central control of the syllabus as a means of propaganda' (*ibid.*, p. 590). At the same time, Thatcher maintains the view that the state should not try to 'regiment every detail of what happened in schools', and argues that the French 'centralised system' would 'not be acceptable in Britain' (*ibid.*, p. 591). It is in this context that she seeks the retention of 'plenty of scope' for individual teachers. Indeed, she emphasizes with the benefit of hindsight, 'I had no wish to put good teachers in a straitjacket' (*ibid.*, p. 593). The established 'tradition' of the teacher in the curriculum domain is acknowledged and treated as a starting point, to be encouraged and incorporated in current reforms as far as possible, and providing a sanction for the kinds of reform that were seen as acceptable.

CONTESTING A TRADITION?

In spite of the official discourse which continued to avow an important place for teacher professionalism in the new order, many critics of the government's reforms feared that they signalled the abandonment of this tradition. The more general emphasis in the new education policies upon parental choice and the greater accountability of schools suggested a hidden agenda in which the National Curriculum would effectively undermine the position of schoolteachers even in their most established domain. As Kenneth Baker's memoirs indicate, there were strong grounds for such fears. Despite his public affirmations of 'the professionalism of the teacher in the classroom', Baker later recalled that his preference for a 'full prescribed curriculum' had been partly in order to avoid schools being left 'adrift in a sea of fashionable opinions about what students should not, rather than should, be taught and at what age' (Baker, 1993, p. 198). Moreover, he adds, 'Vagueness and lack of detail will allow an inadequate and lazy teacher to skip important parts' (*ibid.*). Here, a much more negative notion of the role of the teacher is reflected, as the National Curriculum is rationalized in terms of the need to limit teachers' influence in the classroom and to provide greater control over teachers themselves. These connotations of the National Curriculum were closely associated with the hostile stance adopted by the government towards teacher unions, and a dominant negative media discourse that was antagonistic towards the supposed abuses of teachers' rights.

Critics of the National Curriculum, alert to this polarized debate, therefore tended to assert the tradition of teacher professionalism in order to challenge the validity of the new reforms. Helen Simons, for example, emphasized 'the professional role of the teacher and the loss to our education system of the pedagogical and curriculum developments that have taken place over the past twenty-five years' (Simons, 1988, p. 78). She opposed the National Curriculum on the grounds that teachers would lose this professional role and become instead merely 'the implementers of curricula, judged nevertheless by the success of treatments they no longer devise' (*ibid.*, p. 80). Similarly, Peter Gilroy warned that 'the professional autonomy of the teacher cannot long survive a situation where they have little or no control over the content of a curriculum which they are obliged by law to implement and test' (Gilroy, 1991, p. 3). These fears were heightened in the early 1990s as the implementation of the National Curriculum proved to be highly bureaucratic and intrusive in its effects. It was noted that teachers' 'professional knowledge' was 'at risk of becoming undermined by a heavily prescriptive, bureaucratic and managerial view of the curriculum, with an over emphasis on predetermined attainment targets and rigid forms of testing and assessment' (Ackland, 1992, p. 88).

There was evidence, moreover, that teachers themselves were conscious of losing their former role in this area. It was observed in 1993 that 'The two points on which the overwhelming majority of teachers agree are that the introduction of the curriculum has placed a heavy burden on their time, and that their professional concerns have been casually disdained' (*The Independent*, 1993). According to one history teacher, interviewed by Robert Phillips,

> My main objection to the concept of a National Curriculum is that
> it negates my professionalism and integrity as a teacher and a
> historian. The history course I have devised in my school works for
> me, my department and my pupils. It is one I can justify in

breadth, scope, detail and balance. I am being asked to dismantle
a syllabus I have faith and experience in, for one that is artificial,
contrived and lacks integrity. Whereas I have always welcomed
debate, suggestions and guidelines, I resent bitterly now having to
teach someone else's package ... I am a qualified history teacher
with ten years' teaching experience and as such feel more than
capable of making my own decisions regarding the curriculum.
(Phillips, 1991, p. 22)

Phillips concludes: 'The State's new regulatory requirements have forced the
history teacher to re-examine his/her role as autonomous curricular decision-
maker' (*ibid.*).

At the same time, critics were also able to draw on the tradition of teacher
professionalism either to suggest alternatives to the National Curriculum as it
had been developed, or to argue for ways in which it might be maintained even in
these unpromising circumstances. Philip O'Hear, for example, set out a case for
'a broader but less prescriptive curriculum based on overall aims, rather than the
differently conceived content of 10 subjects, themselves chosen arbitrarily'. In
such a model, he proposed, 'recognition of teachers' professionalism and knowledge of the learning needs and potential of their pupils would be given by
allowing them a good deal of control of the content, order and delivery of the
curriculum' (O'Hear, 1994, p. 56; see also O'Hear and White, 1991). Other critics
recognized the deeply rooted 'professional ideology' of teachers, and suggested
that this would continue to influence their notion of their role. According to one
group of researchers,

> The passionately held commitment of most primary teachers in
> England and Wales to professional autonomy in both curriculum
> and pedagogy, the freedom of the individual school to decide how
> to educate its children, and the child-centred ideology which
> supports a pedagogy that aspires to be individualist, are all ideals
> that are held at the cost of a not inconsiderable sacrifice among
> English teachers. (Broadfoot and Osborn, 1988, p. 283)

On this view, teachers' own conception of their professionalism played a fundamental role in what teachers do at an everyday level, with the further implication
that 'If policy changes ride roughshod over such ideologies, and fail to take them
into account, the result is likely to be widespread resentment, a lowering of
morale, and with it, a reduced effectiveness' (*ibid.*). On the other hand, as Ball
and Bowe suggest, the 'whole notion of teacher professionalism' may still survive
'to provide a powerful critical vocabulary of aspects of the National Curriculum'
(Ball and Bowe, 1992, p. 108).

BACK WITH THE TEACHERS?

The continuing scope for contesting and reinterpreting the tradition of teacher professionalism in the domain of the curriculum is highlighted in the Dearing Review of the National Curriculum and its assessment. This followed a phase in which the demands of the National Curriculum were producing protests among teachers, reaching a climax in 1993 when there was a widespread teachers' action to boycott tests for 7- and 14-year-olds. Much of this agitation again revolved around notions of teacher professionalism, and the Dearing Review may be read as an initiative designed to reinterpret this tradition in a new way that would be more acceptable for teachers. The then Education Secretary, John Patten, was obliged to concede a distinctive professional role for teachers in the development of their teaching methods. The Dearing Review then restated an explicit link between teacher professionalism and the school curriculum by recognizing that reducing the amount of prescriptive material in the National Curriculum would 'give more scope for professional judgement' (Dearing, 1994, p. 17). In doing so, it made an important distinction between 'the essential matters, skills and processes which every school must by law teach' and 'the optional material which can be taught according to the professional judgement of teachers' (Dearing, 1994, pp. 21–2). It remained to be seen whether this formula would provide the basis for lasting accommodation, but at least initially it could be argued that the National Curriculum was 'back with the teachers' (*Times Educational Supplement*, 1994b).

There remained many unresolved issues to be worked out following the publication of the Dearing Review and the new curriculum orders. Some continued to argue for greater scope for teacher autonomy, for example through 'greater day-to-day control of their classroom and curriculum organisation' (Siraj-Blatchford, 1994). Others questioned the major role assigned to external marking of examinations:

> To take the marking out of the hands of teachers may be a smart
> tactical move, and many may welcome the removal of the
> workload, but it also takes away a large measure of their
> professionalism and any hope that the tests might be put to
> constructive use. (TES, 1994a)

On the other hand, the Dearing Review provided those involved in developing the National Curriculum with a new opportunity to promote its role. For instance, Chris Woodhead, Chief Executive of the School Curriculum and Assessment Authority, could acknowledge that

> To have any effect, the words on the page of a National
> Curriculum Order need to be brought to life by teachers who have
> a confident grasp of the knowledge, understanding and skills
> encapsulated in each order, who are skilled classroom

practitioners, and whose daily work brings real professional satisfaction. (Woodhead, 1994)

If the 'overload' of the curriculum had 'undermined that satisfaction', he continued, the Dearing Review had now defined 'a significantly slimmer curriculum which will allow scope for the exercise of professional judgment' (Woodhead, 1994; see also Tate, 1994).

CONCLUSIONS

It is clear that the relationship between teachers and the National Curriculum will continue to be fiercely debated among the parties involved, and the eventual outcome of this long-term process still cannot be predicted. This chapter has argued, however, that the parameters of this debate are rooted in the socio-historical tradition of teacher autonomy in the curriculum domain that in the context of England and Wales is closely associated with the idea of 'teacher professionalism' itself. This tradition has not gone into a sudden eclipse with the introduction of the National Curriculum. The issue of whether it has lapsed into a longer-term decline is also problematic, and there is a continuing need for research into changes in the roles and attitudes of teachers in different kinds of schools, in different areas of the curriculum, and in different phases of the policy-making process. In general terms, it has continued to exert a strong influence on the kinds of reform that are permitted, while itself being restructured in the same process. The tensions that have arisen and which continue to arise may therefore be read in terms of the contestation of this tradition, reflecting differences about how to affirm, challenge, and reinterpret teacher professionalism in a radically changing educational and political context.

ACKNOWLEDGEMENTS

I should like to acknowledge the Economic and Social Research Council for its support for the research project 'The professional culture of teachers and the secondary school curriculum' (no. R000234738); also my colleagues in this project, Gill Helsby, Peter Knight, Murray Saunders and Terry Warburton. Thanks also to members of the Professional Actions and Cultures of Teaching (PACT) conference, London, 2–4 April 1995, for their helpful comments on an earlier version of this chapter.

REFERENCES

Ackland, J. (1992) The National Curriculum and teachers' professional knowledge. In *The National Curriculum in Practice*, Perspectives 46. Exeter: School of Education, University of Exeter, pp. 88–93.

Anderson, R. D. (1983) *Education and Opportunity in Victorian Scotland: Schools and Universities*. Edinburgh: Edinburgh University Press.

Baker, K. (1993) *The Turbulent Years: My Life in Politics*. London: Faber and Faber.

Ball, S. and Bowe, R. (1992) Subject departments and the 'implementation' of National Curriculum policy: an overview of the issues. *Journal of Curriculum Studies*, **24**(2): 97–115.

Broadfoot, P. and Osborn, M. with Gilly, M. and Paillet, A. (1988) What professional responsibility means to teachers: national contexts and classroom constraints. *British Journal of Sociology of Education*, **9**(3): 265–87.

Burrage, M. and Torstendahl, R. (eds) (1990) *Professions in Theory and History: Rethinking the Study of the Professions*. London: Sage.

Chitty, C. (1988) Central control of the school curriculum 1944–87. *History of Education*, **17**(4): 321–34.

Chitty, C. and Lawn, M. (1995) Introduction: redefining the teacher and the curriculum. *Educational Review*, **27**(2): 1–4.

Cunningham, P. (1992) Teachers' professional image and the Press 1950–1990. *History of Education*, **21**(1): 37–56.

Dearing, R. (1994) *The National Curriculum and its Assessment: Final Report*. London: HMSO.

DES (Department of Education and Science) (1983) *Teaching Quality*, Cmnd 8836. London: HMSO.

DES (1985) *Better Schools*, Cmnd. 9469. London: HMSO.

DES (1987) *The National Curriculum 5–16: A Consultation Document*. London: HMSO.

DES (1989) *The National Curriculum: From Policy to Practice*. London: HMSO.

Eisenmann, L. (1991) Teacher professionalism: a new analytical tool for the history of teachers. *Harvard Educational Review*, **61**(2): 215–24.

Eraut, M. (1994) *Developing Professional Knowledge and Competence*. London: Falmer Press.

Foreman, K. (1995) Teacher professionality and the National Curriculum: management implications. In H. Busher and R. Saran (eds), *Managing Teachers as Professionals in Schools*. London: Kogan Page, pp. 89–106.

Gilroy, P. (1991) The loss of professional autonomy. *Journal of Education for Teaching*, **17**(1): 1–5.

Gleeson, D. (ed.) (1987) *TVEI and Secondary Education: A Critical Appraisal*. Milton Keynes: Open University Press.

Goodson, I. (1992) *School Subjects and Curriculum Change*, 3rd edn. London: Falmer Press.

Goodson, I. (1994) *Studying Curriculum: Cases and Methods*. Buckingham: Open University Press.

Gosden, P. (1972) *The Evolution of a Profession: A Study of the Contribution of Teachers' Associations to the Development of School Teaching as a Professional Occupation*. Oxford: Basil Blackwell.

Grace, G. (1987) Teachers and the state in Britain: a changing relationship. In M. Lawn and G. Grace (eds), *Teachers: The Culture and Politics of Work*, London: Falmer Press, pp. 193–228.

Harland, J. (1987) The TVEI experience: issues of control, response and the professional role of teachers. In D. Gleeson (ed.), *TVEI and Secondary Education: A Critical Appraisal*, Milton Keynes: Open University Press, pp. 38–54.

Helsby, G. and McCulloch, G. (1996) Teacher professionalism and curriculum control. In I. Goodson and A. Hargreaves (eds), *Teachers' Professional Lives*. London: Falmer Press, pp. 56–74.

Hobsbawm, E. (1983) Introduction: inventing traditions. In E. Hobsbawm and T. Ranger (eds), *The Invention of Tradition*. Cambridge: Cambridge University Press, pp. 1–14.

House of Commons Debates (1987, 1 December) *Parliamentary Debates*, vol. 123, 1987–8, col. 774.

Hoyle, E. and John, P. (1995) *Professional Knowledge and Professional Practice*. London: Cassell.

Joseph, Sir K. (1984) Postscript. *Oxford Review of Education* **10**(2): 147–8.

Kerr, J. F. (1968) The problem of curriculum reform. In J. F. Kerr, *Changing the Curriculum*, London: University of London Press, pp. 13–38.

Lawn, M. (1985) Teachers in dispute: the Portsmouth and West Ham strikes. *History of Education*, **14**(1): 35–47.

Lawn, M. (1987) The spur and the bridle: changing the mode of curriculum control. *Journal of Curriculum Studies*, **19**(3): 227–36.

Lawton, D. (1980) *The Politics of the School Curriculum*. London: Routledge and Kegan Paul.

McCulloch, G. (1989) *The Secondary Technical School: A Usable Past?* London: Falmer Press.

McCulloch, G. (1993) Judgement of the teacher: the Norwood Report and internal examinations. *International Studies in Sociology of Education*, **3**(1): 129–43.

O'Hear, P. (1994) An alternative National Curriculum. In S. Tomlinson (ed.), *Educational Reform and its Consequences*. London: Institute for Public Policy Research/Rivers Oram Press, pp. 55–72.

O'Hear, P. and White, J. (1991) *A National Curriculum for All*, Education and Training Paper 6. London: IPPR.

Phillips, R. (1991) National Curriculum history and teacher autonomy: the major challenge. *Teaching History*. **65**: 21–4.

Proud, D. (1984) Nothing but vinegar sponges. *Times Educational Supplement*, 14 December.

Simons, H. (1988) Teacher professionalism and the National Curriculum. In D. Lawton and C. Chitty (eds), *The National Curriculum*. Bedford Way Papers 33, London: Institute of Education, University of London. pp. 78–90.

Siraj-Blatchford, I. (1994) Back to the future? *Times Educational Supplement*, 24 June.

Sunday Times (1993) Patten's big test. 11 April, p. 11.

Tate, N. (1994) Target vision. *Times Educational Supplement*, 2 December.

Thatcher, M. (1993) *The Downing Street Years*. London: HarperCollins.

The Independent (1993) Boycotts and other distractions (editorial). 24 April, p. 16.

TES (Times Educational Supplement) (1994a) Deskilling teachers (editorial). 8 July, p. 14.

TES (1994b) Back with the teachers (editorial). 11 November, p. 14.

Tropp, A. (1957) *The School Teachers: The Growth of the Teaching Profession in England and Wales from 1800 to the Present Day*. London: Heinemann.

Widdowson, F. (1983) *Going up into the Next Class: Women and Elementary Teacher Training, 1840–1916*. London: Heinemann.

Woodhead, C. (1994) Letter. *Times Educational Supplement*, 15 July.

Chapter 3

Primary School Teachers' Work: The Response to Educational Reform

Sandra Acker

INTRODUCTION

Government interventions in the late 1980s and early 1990s created a new context for teachers' work in England and Wales. The interventions could be seen to have various purposes: educational, political and ideological. Supporters claimed that the reforms would accomplish educational purposes such as improved standards, better measures of achievement, greater comparability of performance across the nation, heightened accountability, more choice and a stronger voice for parents. Critics argued that what were being served were political and ideological purposes disguised as educational ones. The political agenda aimed to weaken potential centres of opposition in local government, unions and professional associations. The ideological agenda was the promotion of supposedly traditional values such as the sanctity of the family, the rewards of hard work and individual effort, the importance of competition, the virtues of capitalism over socialism, and the centrality of British history, literature and culture. Social justice concerns were conspicuously absent in the new educational order (Arnot, 1992; Burton and Weiner, 1990; Skeggs, 1994).

The extent of the educational interventions left commentators struggling to find sufficiently dramatic terms of description. Particularly remarked upon were the political means to the educational ends: the 'huge extensions of the control of the centralized state' (Burgess, 1989) or the 'massive extension of state power over schools' (Brehony, 1990). Efforts were made to increase central control over curriculum, assessment, teachers' work conditions, teacher education, finance, governance, and other aspects of educational activity, reaching a high point, if not a stopping point, in the Educational Reform Act of 1988 (Hellawell, 1992).

Despite the draconian nature of the intended changes, there is many a slip between intent and outcome. And in this case, in between intent and outcome were the teachers. In this chapter, I shall describe the efforts to use legislation and other forms of persuasion to alter the ways in which teachers, especially primary school teachers, approached their work. I concentrate on the events between 1988 and 1991. Despite the enormity of the changes imposed in this period, there were always signs of contradiction, struggle and contestation, culminating in the boycott of Standard Assessment Tasks (SATs) in 1993 and

1994, the review of the National Curriculum and its assessment by Sir Ron Dearing and consequent new 'slimmed down' curriculum Orders in 1994, and various other concessions over the curriculum and assessment procedures. These more recent events will be described elsewhere in this book. Here I shall concentrate on the early effects of the legislation on the work of primary school teachers, drawing on my ethnographic research in an English primary school which I call by the pseudonym 'Hillview'.[1] I argue that while the reforms had definite impacts on the culture of Hillview and other schools, the occupational and workplace cultures of teachers significantly influenced the fate of the changes that central government hoped for.

THE CONTEXT: CONTROLLING TEACHERS

It is well known in the literature on educational innovation that top-down efforts to bring about change frequently fail. One reason for their failure is the class-room focus of teachers; as it is impossible to have total surveillance of every teacher in every classroom, there is plenty of scope to sidestep unreasonable prescriptions. Teachers are thought to accept innovations when they can see sufficient potential and practicality to make the effort worthwhile (Doyle and Ponder, 1977).[2] The British government might have proceeded by trying to bring the teachers on board and convince them of their important role in the innovations, using the rhetoric of empowerment common in North American reform efforts but conspicuously missing in British ones (Chard, 1994; Lawn, 1995). Instead, it went the prescriptive route, buttressed by other efforts to control and contain teacher opposition.

Over time, teachers in Britain had strengthened their claims to profession-alism, despite the well-known divisions among them, given concrete form in the multiple and competing teacher unions. By the 1970s, however, relationships among central government, local government and teachers' unions had begun to show signs of strain (Grace, 1987). In the 1980s, teachers demonstrated their disaffection by a prolonged and bitter period of 'industrial action' from 1984 to 1986 (Pietrasik, 1987).

The central government's response was to weaken further the occupational autonomy of the teachers. The 1987 Teachers' Pay and Conditions Act abolished the old negotiating body that had included representation from local education authorities and teachers' unions; power to establish pay and conditions went to the Secretary of State, aided by an advisory committee to which he would appoint members. This body became the School Teachers' Review Body, which reports annually, making recommendations for pay awards and other conditions of service. Teacher autonomy was typically more evident in the classroom than in the ability of the occupation to control entry or work conditions. In 1987, the government also specified teachers' hours and responsibilities. Details of new contracts and conditions were announced, setting a fixed number of days for teaching and in-service work and dividing teachers' time into three categories, including 1265 hours per year that would be 'directed' by the headteacher. Headteachers and deputy headteachers also had specified responsibilities. The salary scale for teachers was revised from its previous version into a Main Professional Grade (later called the Standard Scale) that could be topped up with one of five levels of 'incentive allowances', with a limited number available for each school. Since that time, teachers have also been subject to new requirements for appraisal, and the pay scale has been revised yet again with incentive allowances deleted but points given on the scale for various qualifications and responsibilities. Also suggested have been performance-related pay and local pay scales. Teachers' work is, of course, not only affected by legislation that directly targets pay and conditions but by changes in curriculum, assessment, finance, management, and other features of the education system. For example, decentralized management and financing of schools has serious effects on teachers' work and career opportunities. Schools are tempted to hire 'cheaper' teachers, including those on short-term contracts, to save money (Hellawell, 1992); school governors have been given greater powers over hiring, salaries and rewards for teachers, enabling them to act 'as if they were the school owners and the teachers were their workforce' (Lawn, 1995, p. 354). Having moved to implement direct controls over teacher work and reward systems, the government turned its attention to altering the context and content of schooling itself, most notoriously through the 1988 Education Reform Act.

INTRODUCING THE NATIONAL CURRICULUM AND ASSESSMENT

The 1988 Education Act gave a broad outline of the curricular framework to be used in all state schools in England and Wales. Working Groups in each subject area were appointed and given directions by the Secretary of State; results of the working group deliberations, when converted into statutory orders, were sent to schools. The National Curriculum Council (NCC) coordinated the curriculum changes and provided advice to schools. The Act specified that children should be assessed on their knowledge of the new curriculum at the end of 'Key Stages', that is, at the ages of approximately 7, 11, 14 and 16 years. The School Examinations and Assessment Council (SEAC), a companion body to the NCC,[3] was charged with overseeing the development of assessment instruments, working within a framework set by a committee known as TGAT: the Task Group on Assessment and Testing (DES, 1988). The TGAT framework specified a ten-level grading system, across all ages, with 'average' attainment defined at each of the Key Stages, for example as Level 2 at age 7. Teachers were to conduct and report both their own assessments and others selected from a bank of Standard Assessment Tasks, known as SATs.

PUTTING PRIMARY SCHOOLS IN THE LIMELIGHT

A decision to begin the introduction of the assessment procedures with 7-year-olds shone an unaccustomed spotlight on infant teachers (those who taught 5-to-7 year-olds) and on primary schools. It was widely believed, by parents as well as teachers, that age 7 was too young for testing and might have traumatic effects on sensitive children, yet the scheme went ahead as planned with pilot SATs for mathematics, English language and science in 1990, and expectations for all schools to conduct and report teacher assessments and SAT results for 7-year-olds starting in 1991.

Results of individual schools were not made public in 1991, but some summary figures for local education authorities were reported, accompanied by widespread protests about both the lack of standard procedures from one classroom or school to another, and the difficulties of interpreting raw data without controls for factors such as socio-economic disadvantage. There were also many complaints about the extended time and energy required for the administration of the SATs. The 1992 versions cut the number of attainment targets covered from nine to six, and more of the assessment was designed to be done with the whole class.

Throughout the first years of the implementation of the National Curriculum and assessment, advice was liberally provided to schools instituting the changes. As well as receiving the 'Orders' that gave details of the curriculum, schools were showered with additional documents from various sources, including SEAC, NCC, the government itself, and local education authorities, clarifying or changing requirements or assisting in implementation. There was an air of patent unreality about some of the expectations placed upon teachers, especially evident in some of the 'nonstatutory advice' from SEAC and NCC. The underlying problem was that if taken literally, the new work required of teachers, especially in revising the curriculum and recording children's progress towards hundreds of attainment targets, would be impossible to accomplish within any semblance of a normal day. As I noted in 1990:

> Primary school teachers would [be expected to] review all aspects
> of a school's work, including the use of time and resources; produce
> school policy statements, schemes of work, forward plans and
> lesson plans for each subject; incorporate assessment into
> curriculum development plans, staff development plans and head's
> management plans. They are also, of course, expected to
> assimilate all the attainment targets, make up for gaps in their
> own subject knowledge and experiment with means of recording
> what is taught and how much of it is mastered by each child.
> (Acker, 1990b, p. 260)[4]

The credibility of both the advice and the arrangements for the curriculum and assessment were also undermined by the frequency with which alterations were made, itself due to the rush with which most of the reforms were being implemented and the under-representation of practitioners among those devising the policies. Moreover, the changes themselves were repeatedly 'altered, amended and reoriented' (Ball, 1992, p. 2). The documents and politicians' pronouncements showed little recognition of the variation among schools. In the real world of schools, children can be ill or disruptive, plans come unstuck, spare time is scarce, equipment breaks down (Acker, 1990a). Not all children have English as a first language; not all children turn 7 at the same moment of the year. Some schools have such high pupil turnover that the children entering at 5 are not the ones being tested at 7, let alone 11. In contrast, advice in the advice manuals appears to be most suitable for a relatively small, quiet, stable, middle-class classroom setting (Osborn, 1996a). An overloaded curriculum, oversize classes and inadequate resources were not taken seriously as constraints, reinforcing the impression that the individual teacher is the sole agent of bringing about or thwarting children's learning (Woods and Wenham, 1995, p. 123).

TARGETING PEDAGOGY

Through legislation, the central government had introduced major alterations in two of the 'message systems' (Bernstein, 1971) of the school – curriculum and evaluation. For the government and right-wing educational critics, the third of the message systems, pedagogy – the actual process of teaching – needed equal attention. The reforms envisioned by the New Right involved more than alterations to institutions: reformers wanted to create an appropriate character structure to go with the new institutions. Socialization of children into 'appropriate' values clearly starts from the first days of school and so it is not surprising that primary education was newly scrutinized.

In an effort to make the reforms more palatable, politicians and those writing circulars and curriculum documents had repeatedly denied intentions to tell teachers 'how to teach'. Initial government attempts at altering pedagogy had been indirect, for example via changes in teacher training criteria or through the structuring of the National Curriculum around discrete subjects when many primary schools preferred to integrate subjects into topics or themes. In the later months of 1991, perhaps stimulated by the imminence of a general election (Woods and Wenham, 1995), there were a number of attacks by government figures on 'standards' in primary schools, culminating in a statement (Clarke, 1991) sent from the Secretary of State for Education to all primary school headteachers, announcing the appointment of a body of 'Three Wise Men' to produce over the next few months a report on the current state of primary education.

Clarke's statement was very negative about the 'dogmatic orthodoxy' of discovery methods and child-centred teaching. It urged greater consideration of 'more effective' traditional methods of formal, didactic and whole class teaching;

specialist teachers; increased use of setting or other methods of ability grouping. The subsequent report (Alexander *et al.*, 1992) also criticized 'highly questionable dogmas' and advocated more subject-based and specialist teaching. It called for a better balance among modes of organizing teaching such as individual, small group and whole class teaching. The document noted difficulties that teachers experienced in implementing the new curriculum and assessment procedures, but tended to regard them as 'teething troubles' rather than indications of flaws in the procedures themselves.[5]

CREATING A SUPPORTING DISCOURSE

Attacks on primary pedagogy were supported by the appearance of a discourse that applauded moves towards tradition and away from progressive styles of teaching and school organization. A number of New Right groups, such as the Centre for Policy Studies, the Hillgate Group, the Adam Smith Institute, the Campaign for Real Education, etc., often with the same or similar membership, seemed to have had disproportionate influence on government educational policy in this period.

A large segment of the media is notorious for its obsequious support of Conservative policy and practices, and education became front page news. Even the educational press such as the *Times Educational Supplement* or the *Guardian*'s Education Section regularly reported on utterances, speeches and pamphlets of members of these groups, in sharp contrast to the fate of most educational scholarship, noted in passing or not at all.

The tone of much of the press coverage of educational matters around 1991 exemplifies what Ball (1990) calls the 'discourse of derision'. Scorned were the 'loony left' local education authorities; socialism; anti-racism and anti-sexism and other curricular initiatives such as 'peace education'; and trendy 'sixties' teachers and teacher trainers. Coursework was compared unfavourably to examinations, as was small group teaching to whole class instruction. Education professionals or 'producers' were dismissed as having vested interests and therefore unable to contribute to the debate; teachers in general came under suspicion for being insufficiently rigorous and politically suspect. The government reforms were presented as an inevitable result of the previous decades of too much teacher power and too little concern for conservative values.

The workings of this discourse of derision can be seen particularly clearly in the efforts to influence pedagogy in primary schools. Brehony (1990) describes the phenomenon as a manufactured problem, a sense that 'something is wrong' created by repeated statements in the press by government figures. Whatever the shortcomings of child-centred teaching, the form taken by the critique suggested an ideological rather than an educational impetus (Brehony, 1990). Exaggeration was commonplace. Speeches were reported with headlines such as: 'It ain't on, Baker tells the trendies' or 'Clarke frees pupils from grip of Sixties' (*Daily Express*, 3 December 1991). Even the more respectable *Sunday Times* gave us 'Scandal in our schools: one in three can't count' (27 October 1991, p. 1).

The educational press, despite its critique of the tabloid outlets, still supported the rhetoric by its choice of articles and headlines. A detailed review that I conducted of four months of articles in the *Times Educational Supplement* (*TES*), from October 1991 through January 1992, clearly showed the hammering home of the message that 'something is wrong' with primary education. It was reported that primary teachers are not confident in technology, history or geography (18 October 1991, p. 2); that 'Pupils do worst in maths SATs' (15 November 1991, p. 16); and that 'Heaven knows where earth is' (3 January 1992) – the latter an article about teachers' poor skills in astronomy.

Headlines in the *TES* tended to take alarmist form, such as 'Reading tests pick up poor standards' (1 November 1991); 'Primary system "fails to deliver" ' (1 November 1991, p. 3) or 'Standards seen to fall' (31 January 1992). In such cases, the content of the article or report would often permit a less negative headline. Even if the majority of 7-year-olds could read, a headline would highlight those who could not and label the standards 'poor'. Teachers who were not confident about technology were more confident in science, but that observation did not make it into the headline. And if pupils 'do worst' in maths SATs, they 'do best' in something else.

Along with this rash of reports came pronouncements by ministers, along the lines mentioned earlier. Some of these were especially quaint. Michael Fallon, then the Schools Minister, spoke to a conference of headteachers criticizing topic work. At worst, he said, this kind of practice would make primary schools like pre-school playgroups, with 'much happiness and painting but very little learning' (Hofkins, 1991, p. 15). Kenneth Clarke, the Secretary of State for Education at the time, made similar remarks about 'child-centred education': 'at its weakest there is a lot of the sticking together of egg boxes and playing in the sand' (Rafferty, 1991, p. 3). Conservative backbenchers even called for less 'project work' in nursery schools, one critic commenting 'We are worried about the level of education these schools provide. They shouldn't just be about play' (Hackett, 1991, p. 1).

Perhaps the primary school was simply seen as an easy target. It is, after all, the province of female teachers. The teachers of the 7-year-old 'failures' are overwhelmingly female. The politicians are overwhelmingly male; the cabinet in question – John Major's team after Mrs Thatcher's resignation and prior to the 1992 election – had no women members. Note also the imagery of 'Three Wise *Men*'. Almost all of the pronouncements on primary school pedagogy were made by men, few of whom were likely to be intimately familiar with child-centred, topic-based practices in nursery or primary schools. The campaign can also be seen as an attack on values traditionally associated with women, and perhaps even an attack on women themselves. Some of the most scathing sneers were directed at 'Plowden' – the Report that was said to put the seal of approval on progressive, child-centred education in the 1960s, or at Lady Plowden herself (Hofkins, 1992, p. 11). We see a familiar phenomenon of men controlling the work of women teachers, and as Grumet (1988, p. 23) puts it, 'blame is deflected from the men who establish [the] policies onto the women who teach the children who fail'.

IN THE SCHOOLS: RESPONDING TO REFORM

Thus primary schools and teachers had to respond not only to the details of the National Curriculum, assessment and other changes, but to widespread charges about their supposed dogmas, excesses and failings. Whether or not teachers were being deskilled, they were certainly not being empowered. Yet they were not without resources for resistance. I locate these in the culture and structure of primary school teaching as an occupation, and in the local workplace cultures where teachers discussed events of the day. I illustrate this argument with my research in an English primary school as well as with the research of others.

Culture, structure and gender

Although all teachers suffered from the pressure of new expectations and the problems associated with lack of clarity and frequent revisions of guidelines, primary school teachers faced several additional difficulties with the National Curriculum.[6] One stemmed from the typically generalist nature of their work. British primary schools are usually relatively small, with between 200 and 400 pupils, and work on a class teacher system. Each teacher is responsible for teaching all, or nearly all, subjects to a class. While schools in North America often feature specialists in areas such as music, art or physical education, as well as classroom aides, special needs and resource teachers, the typical British primary school has few such personnel. Deputy headteachers often have a full class assignment, and even headteachers do a certain amount of teaching, especially in small schools. Increasingly, teachers do take responsibility for specific curriculum areas, but they are rarely given more than a small amount of time away from their class to fulfil them. One consequence of this structure was that primary school teachers faced the expectation that they would become competent practitioners of every subject in the National Curriculum – a recipe for anxiety, especially about some elements of science teaching and about technology, areas that had not necessarily been part of the teacher's own training (Bennett *et al.*, 1992).

The other major problem for primary school teachers, especially infant teachers, was the ideological clash between their progressive, child-centred tradition and the subject model upon which the National Curriculum was based (Osborn, 1996b). While teachers did not always in practice adhere to a progressive model of teaching (Galton, 1989), neither did they typically divide the day rigidly into chunks designated 'geography', 'history' or 'science'. Project-oriented work often combined several subject areas. Perhaps more important than their actual practice was the widely shared ethos that revolved (at least rhetorically) around the needs of the child. It was a strong plank in the occupational culture, not easily dislodged, to which we could add the preservation of classroom autonomy, i.e. relatively unimpeded decision-making in the classroom by the individual teacher. Ever since the demise of the eleven-plus examination and the competition for entry to selective secondary schooling, primary school teachers in Britain had enjoyed a level of classroom autonomy far above their counterparts in many other countries.

Also significant, as suggested above, is the fact that almost all teachers who were to begin the assessment of the National Curriculum were women. In 1990, 81 per cent of teachers in nursery and primary schools in England and Wales were women. In separate infant schools (with children aged 5 to 7), the percentage rose to 98 per cent (DES, 1992; Acker, 1994). Elsewhere I have explored extensively the relationships between gender and teachers' work (Acker, 1992, 1994, 1995a, 1995/96). What is important is not so much that these teachers are women *per se*, but that they are influenced by social expectations about caring, nurturing roles for women.

At the same time, the older model of a teacher with a half-hearted commitment to the job because of her competing domestic commitments, if ever true, had been superseded by a new model of the professional (woman) teacher. Changing social conventions, easier divorce, maternity leave provisions, and an economic recession created a new context for teachers' careers. Older women teachers had left the profession for child-rearing and returned years later. But by the 1980s it was common for teachers who were mothers to continue working, either full-time with brief interruptions, or by means of part-time and short-term contracts.

The pattern could be seen clearly at Hillview, where the older teacher-mothers had returned after a career break, while the younger teachers had minimal time out of the system. One teacher came in for staff meetings during her maternity leave when expecting her third child. Most of the younger teachers were also pursuing master's degree courses in education and by 1995 had become heads or deputy heads at other primary schools (see Acker, 1992, 1994, 1995b). Statements about careers, however, both in interview and in everyday interaction, rarely expressed ambitions in the traditional sense. Instead, as with Nias's (1989) interviewees, commitment meant dedication to doing the best possible job rather than moving up a career ladder.

Working hard, doing good, feeling bad

If I extrapolate from my findings and those of others such as Osborn (1996b), the group of teachers who were to spearhead the National Curriculum and assessment were female, child-centred and highly conscientious. In some respects they suited the government's purposes perfectly, as they could be relied on to try hard to do what was expected of them, even against the odds. The cultural script for women caring for young children leads to an ethos of putting others first, even to the point of exploitation (Acker, 1995a, 1995/96; Griffith and Smith, 1991; Grumet, 1988; Walkerdine, 1986). Over-conscientiousness on the part of such teachers, and the resulting fatigue and exhaustion, has been noted both in the context of the National Curriculum (e.g. Campbell and Neill, 1994a, Campbell *et al.*, 1991b) and outside it (e.g. Hargreaves, 1994; McPherson, 1972).

There is now considerable evidence that the curricular and assessment reforms increased teachers' workloads and heightened their stress and anxiety levels (Acker, 1990a, 1991; Ball and Bowe, 1992; Bowe and Ball, 1992; Broadfoot and Abbott, 1991; Campbell and Neill, 1994a, b; Campbell *et al.*, 1991a, b; Chard, 1994; Osborn 1996a, b; Osborn and Broadfoot, 1991; Osborn and Pollard, 1990; Pollard *et al.*, 1994). Infant teachers interviewed by Campbell *et al.* (1991b, p. 6) shared the view that workloads were 'unreasonable and unmanageable even for experienced teachers'. They were working approximately 55 hours per week, of which about 60 per cent was not in pupil contact but spent on preparation, administration, recording and in-service work. Moreover, in adjusting to the new requirements, teachers were not simply acquiring technical skills, but making a 'major reconstruction of their self-identity' (Stone, 1993, p. 188).

My study also found teachers becoming increasingly anxious over the period 1987–91 (see also Acker, 1990b). Although praising certain aspects of the draft specifications for technology in the curriculum, Dennis Bryan, Hillview's deputy headteacher, commented, 'It's ridiculous to expect ordinary mortals to do this'. Rosalind Phillips, a teacher at Hillview, provided an example of what Campbell *et al.* (1991b) call the 'running commentary syndrome'. She said:

> To do all that's expected is impossible ... you've got to come to
> terms with that. You're always looking at components ... you can't
> remember it all. I'm enjoying what I do, but if I look ahead I panic.
> I wander around with a book in my hand trying to work out what
> attainment target something is.

Hillview teachers found themselves spending large amounts of time record-ing children's progress. Betty Chapman, the teacher responsible for the class that took the first round of SATs in 1991, estimated that she was spending an extra hour and a half working on records every weekend. During the weeks when SATs were administered, each school had to find ways to find cover for the children not being 'SATed' at any given time. The class teacher might be listening to a child read, or working with a small group investigating which of a number of items would float or sink (a science SAT), but meanwhile the other children needed looking after. Broadfoot and Abbott (1991) noted that arrangements varied so much from classroom to classroom, school to school, that serious questions might be raised about the validity of the testing practices. For the main teacher involved, as Betty said, 'it was just my life for six weeks'.

By 1991, Betty Chapman and others in the school had come round to accepting much of the principle of a National Curriculum and more systematic teacher assessment as having some positive features. This outcome might be predictable as a means of reducing the cognitive dissonance produced by beliefs at odds with actions. The SATs were regarded as a good experience for the children who were doing them at any one time, because such children enjoyed getting so much of their teacher's attention, but as problematic for other children. Maintaining any kind of effective instruction during those weeks was difficult. Having a supply teacher take the class for long periods of time led to a restless class of children who lost several weeks of learning time and were difficult to settle down afterwards. The teachers believed they learned little from the results that they did not already know.

Hillview teachers' concerns went beyond extra work. They worried about the curriculum becoming unbalanced: 'Music's gone by the board completely', one teacher said. Mathematics, science and English were the core subjects in the curriculum and introduced first, with technology, history and geography following. Mathematics and English were familiar territory for infant teachers (Bennett *et al.*, 1992), but the science curriculum brought new challenges. Bennett *et al.* (1992) found that primary school teachers' confidence in science increased considerably between 1989 and 1991. Betty Chapman suggested that science (a subject that had been relatively de-emphasized in my 1987–88 observations) was now taking a major role in the curriculum. She explained how at one point, worried about neglecting the rest of the curriculum, she finally 'abandoned' science to do a history topic. The headteacher, Liz Clarke, feared that the arts and the 'affective curriculum' were being crowded out. The teachers were also concerned about how the school could afford to purchase the necessary materials for areas such as technology.

Other activities traditionally promoted by the school were being squeezed out. Comments I recorded in meetings in 1990 included: 'There's no way we're going to have a concert, we don't have the energy'; 'We'll have a deliberately low-key Christmas this year'; 'I can't face another Harvest Assembly'. And Mrs Clarke told me in 1991, 'For the second year, we've not had a big celebration in summer'. Osborn (1996b) reported similar findings, commenting that there was 'clear evidence that KS1 teachers felt compelled to narrow their priorities to concentrate on basic skills at the expense of broader academic and nonacademic activities'.

For the headteacher, there were multiple sources of strain during this period (see also Hellawell, 1992). Perhaps even more than the teachers, the head needed to develop a new style, one that departed in significant ways from her preferences. In British primary schools, headteachers often do some class teaching, perhaps one afternoon a week to relieve a teacher for another task, or to substitute for a teacher who is away. Liz Clarke enjoyed making some teaching input into the school, both for the closeness it gave her to the children and for the credibility it might give her with the staff. With the increased pressure brought by other aspects of the 1988 legislation, Liz found little time for teaching. She was out of school more often, as the local authority sent headteachers on short courses to help them with new responsibilities such as delegated budgets. Moreover, the introduction of open enrolment meant increased numbers of children in the same space, bringing additional control problems, especially for the dinnertime staff. Coming back to school after a meeting with other local primary school head-teachers, she commented that they were 'tired looking ladies, just like me'. Her main regret was greater distance from parents: 'I'm no longer Mrs Available Clarke who is there whenever you want to call in about anything.'

Doing it all

Teachers tried to square the circle: adapting to the new requirements while preserving their traditional ideologies. The effects could be seen in schools such as Hillview. In many ways, the workplace culture of Hillview was changing dramatically. In an earlier article (Acker, 1990b), I described the workplace culture of Hillview teachers as casual, humorous, warm and caring. Collabora-tion and participation were highly valued. Roles overlapped and responsibilities were shared. There was a strong concern about the social as well as the intellec-tual development of the children. The headteacher tended to respond to new developments with a 'wait and see' philosophy, which often proved wise due to the fluid and changing nature of events, both before and after the reforms.[7] The school ran on a model that was more like a family than a corporation.

A number of changes could be discerned over the period 1987–91 in the direction of structure rather than spontaneity. There was more delegation and less whole-staff discussion of matters such as setting up the timetable and making arrangements for taking children to local swimming pools. Individual responsibilities for aspects of curriculum were delineated more clearly. Staff meetings were more orderly; curriculum reviews more systematic; record-keeping procedures clarified and agreed upon by all. Ways of keeping track of materials and identifying those in need of replacement were suggested. Resources in the staffroom were reorganized. The secretary finally got a com-puter. Curriculum policies were written down and accessible. A helpful booklet for new or temporary teachers was produced. The requirements of the legislation were responsible for at least some of these changes, as schools were now being asked to produce systematic records, school development plans, reports to par-ents and so forth.

Finding a way to record progress in the many statements of attainment for all the subjects taxed teachers at Hillview, as it did teachers in primary schools across the country. Much discussion concerned the best ways of making such records and what procedures should be adopted across the school. Comments such as 'We've got to start being more disciplined' appear in my notes of meetings. In July 1991, the headteacher told me, 'The assessment process is very much more clearly defined in our minds' and in March 1992, 'We have been forced to plan more carefully.'

At the same time, staff tried hard to preserve the ethos of the school and the aspects of their workplace culture that they most valued. There was, for example, continuing emphasis on the child-centred, socially concerned agenda of the school. In a 1989 staff-meeting discussion of special needs, Liz Clarke said 'Everything we do should aim to give the children a positive self-image.' The school developed anti-racism and anti-sexism policies and an elaborate strategy to improve behaviour in the school.

Also still evident among the Hillview teachers and headteacher was a participatory, democratic, collegial and caring way of working together (Acker, 1995a). One of the positive side-effects teachers have applauded about the new requirements is greater collegiality (Osborn, 1996b), but at Hillview the traditions of isolation and independence so often remarked upon in the literature were not a feature of this particular teacher culture. Nevertheless, although later staff meetings retained the collaborative approach to planning major school activities, developing a school policy or solving a major problem such as children's bad behaviour at lunchtime, minor and administrative matters were less often tackled collectively.

The determination to preserve valued elements of the culture, combined with the newly systematic approach, was evident with the hiring of Amanda Prentice, who entered the school with the clearly delineated responsibility for developing science activities. During 1989–90 she conducted a number of staff meetings to introduce aspects of the science curriculum to colleagues and to work with them to shape the school science policy. She prepared carefully for the meetings and used flip charts and handouts. At the same time, she was at pains to encourage teachers not simply to accept what was on paper, but to voice their own priorities, so that policy would not simply come from 'on high'. Similarly, the school worked to develop records of children's achievements that not only met the criteria set down by government but allowed other accomplishments of the children to be displayed. Reports to parents did not simply follow the approved format but were modified to incorporate the kind of communication the teachers believed was important.

These examples show an intensification of teachers' work beyond the extra hours needed to study, teach and assess the National Curriculum, one that appears almost paradoxically self-induced (Campbell and Neill, 1994a). Yet it seems less freely chosen when one notes it is consistent with efforts to preserve the teacher 'self' (Nias, 1989; Pollard, 1985); with the culture of teaching in this school and more generally; and with the cultural script for women noted above. Moreover, the necessity to adapt policies to suit a school with a large ability and social class range, together with poor provision of material resources, was not internally generated.

CONCLUSION

In trying to get to grips with the effects of the reforms, it is hard not to over-generalize about 'teachers' and their response. Osborn (1996a, b) and McCallum *et al.* (1993) remind us that there are a range of possible responses, even among apparently similar teachers in the same school. Moreover, there are changes over time in such responses, paralleling changes in the politics and policies surrounding the reforms. Osborn's (1996b) work shows that anxiety and concern among Key Stage 1 teachers rose between 1990 and 1992, then declined again by 1994. As interactionist theories in the sociology of education would predict, teachers respond creatively with a certain amount of agency, rather than mechanically and as victims of forces beyond their control. On the other hand, it is unlikely that there is simply an infinite scatter of possible responses, or that individuals can wish away the real constraints and consequences caused by the policies and other features of the British educational system.

Ideally, researchers would go beyond simply charting changes in workload, classroom practices, or stress levels. What larger lessons can we learn from the stories of teachers' responses to the government interventions into the curriculum and other aspects of schooling in Britain in the late 1980s and early 1990s? We learn that changes in educational policy have their counterparts in changes in the nature of teachers' work, but that there is no simple correspondence. We learn, not for the first time, that hegemony is never total; that in the world of education, the outcomes are rarely quite what was what intended – itself not always obvious or agreed upon (Bowe and Ball, 1992; Woods and Wenham, 1995). There is no possibility of policing every classroom every minute of the day, and modifications of the original policies are bound to occur as they are shaped and stretched to fit realities of school and classroom life.

We learn, or should learn, that stereotypes about teachers' inevitable reluctance to collaborate, or women teachers' domestic responsibilities and lack of job commitment, or the ease of teaching young children are difficult to reconcile with what we see around us. We learn that there are different interpretations and different responses to what seems the same event, and that we need ways to conceptualize these individual and group differences. We learn that school cultures cannot survive untouched by imposed change, but that material realities and school cultures influence the form taken by innovation. We have, in effect, a case study of the intricate and changing relationships of agency, culture and structure.

The struggles of teachers such as those at Hillview did not go unnoticed. While the 'overconscientiousness' of the mostly women infant school teachers appeared in the first instance to work in favour of government reform – a more substantial revolt was to await the disaffection of secondary school English teachers (Waters, 1995) – it had paradoxical consequences. The caring script also stood in the way of simple acceptance of the reforms: child-centredness was hard to reconcile with testing, subject orientation and regimentation (Osborn,

1996a, b). Teachers in schools like Hillview insisted on holding onto the values they cherished, even at personal cost. Gradually the media, parents, heads and others came to respect and sympathize with these dedicated teachers who were clearly trying so hard to make sense of the challenge with its many impossible expectations and built-in flaws. Eventually the government, its popularity on the wane, would be forced to make some concessions. It is noticeable that in 1994 and 1995 issues of the *Times Educational Supplement*, the discourse of derision had diminished.

With the pervasiveness of school improvement and school effectiveness rhetoric, it is also tempting to evaluate schools like Hillview as more or less 'effective' before and after the 1988 Act. Certainly, Hillview became more structured and systematic in its ways of working. Already members of a collaborative culture, Hillview's teachers found working together presented no huge challenges. But there were costs, too, both to individual teachers who worked hard and struggled to make sense of the new curriculum and assessment requirements, and to the headteacher who lost much of her satisfaction in working with children and parents. For the children, there were likely gains and losses, too. Perhaps, in time, we will learn what these were.

ACKNOWLEDGEMENTS

I would like to thank the editors of this volume for their comments on draft versions of this chapter; Andy Hargreaves for an invitation to speak at a conference several years ago where the first thoughts about this text surfaced; Lisa Richards for invaluable help in tracing and photocopying recent and relevant references; and of course the headteacher and teachers of Hillview School.

NOTES

1 Hillview is an inner-city, Church of England primary school containing about 200 children from age 4 to 11. There is considerable diversity among the children in both social class and ethnic terms. There are seven classes. The exact number of teachers fluctuated slightly during my study but the usual complement was a headteacher, a deputy headteacher, and eight others, three of whom were part-time teachers. I spent about 880 hours at Hillview during 1987–89. My time in the school was limited after December 1990 as I had moved to Canada. I was interested in the nature of primary teachers' work and the extent to which their work was shaped by a teacher culture within the school. I did not enter Hillview in order to study the effect of the 1988 legislation as it had not even been proposed at my point of entry. For more details about the school and my methods, see Acker 1990a, 1990b, 1991, 1992.

2 Wideen (1994), however, argues that the practicality ethic may operate only for top-down innovations; in his study of an innovation devised by a school, practical problems were regarded as a challenge (pp. 96–7).

3   These two bodies were later combined into one, the School Curriculum and Assessment Authority.

4   For ease of readability, I have deleted references to particular SEAC and NCC publications in the original quotation. They can be found in the 1990 article.

5   Woods and Wenham (1995) provide a fascinating account of the 'career' of this document, from inception to implementation. Some of their material is based on interviews with the three authors, who are quite disparate in their own ideologies and agendas. The role of the media (to whom the document was released several weeks before it was made public) is highlighted in the article.

6   Waters (1995) gives a particularly vivid account of the adaptations required (and resisted) by English teachers and departments in secondary schools.

7   My notes are full of equipment breakdowns, coaches not turning up, visitors arriving unexpectedly, television programmes not as advertised, children with leading roles in a production being ill, new children arriving with little or no English, and numerous other events for which the most sensible response was to be very flexible and able to change plans at short notice (Acker, 1990a). Throughout the period covered by my research, teachers retained this ability to tolerate ambiguity and switch gears rapidly.

REFERENCES

Acker, S. (1990a) Managing the drama: the head teacher's work in an urban primary school. *Sociological Review*, **38**(2): 247–71.

Acker, S. (1990b) Teachers' culture in an English primary school: continuity and change. *British Journal of Sociology of Education*, **11**(3): 257–73.

Acker, S. (1991) Teacher relationships and educational reform in England and Wales. *Curriculum Journal*, **2**(3): 301–16.

Acker, S. (1992) Creating careers: women teachers at work. *Curriculum Inquiry*, **22**(2): 141–63.

Acker, S. (1994) *Gendered Education: Sociological Reflections on Women, Teaching and Feminism*. Buckingham: Open University Press.

Acker, S. (1995a) Carry on caring: the work of women teachers. *British Journal of Sociology of Education*, **16**(1): 21–36.

Acker, S. (1995b) The head teacher as career broker: Stories from an English primary school. In P. Schmuck and D. Dunlap (eds), *Women Leading in Education*. Albany, NY: State University of New York Press, pp. 49–70.

Acker, S. (1995/96) Gender and teachers' work. In M. Apple (ed.), *Review of Research in Education 21*. Washington, D.C.: American Educational Research Association, pp. 99–162.

Alexander, R., Rose, J. and Woodhead, C. (1992) *Curriculum Organisation and Classroom Practice in Primary Schools: A Discussion Paper*. London: DES.

Arnot, M. (1992) Feminism, education and the New Right. In M. Arnot and L. Barton (eds), *Voicing Concerns: Sociological Perspectives on Contemporary Education Reforms*. Oxford: Triangle, pp. 41–65.

Ball, S. J. (1990) *Politics and Policy Making in Education*. London: Routledge.

Ball, S. J. (1992, April) Changing management and the management of change: educational reform and school processes, an English perspective. Paper presented at the Annual Meeting of the American Educational Research Association, San Francisco.

Ball, S. J. and Bowe, R. (1992) Subject departments and the 'implementation' of National Curriculum policy: an overview of the issues. *Journal of Curriculum Studies*, **24**: 97–115.

Bennett, S. N., Wragg, E. C., Carré, C. G. and Carter, D. S. G. (1992) A longitudinal study of primary teachers' perceived competence in, and concerns about, National Curriculum implementation. *Research Papers in Education*, **7**(1): 53–78.

Bernstein, B. (1971) On the classification and framing of educational knowledge. In M. F. D. Young (ed.), *Knowledge and Control*. London: Collier-Macmillan, pp. 47–69.

Bowe, R. and Ball, S. J. with Gold, A. (1992) *Reforming Education and Changing Schools*. London: Routledge.

Brehony, K. J. (1990) Neither rhyme nor reason: primary schooling and the national curriculum. In M. Flude and M. Hammer (eds), *The Education Reform Act, 1988: Its Origins and Implications*. London: Falmer Press, pp. 107–31.

Broadfoot, P. and Abbott, D. with Croll, P., Osborn, M. and Pollard, A. (1991) Look back in anger? Findings from the PACE project concerning primary teachers' experiences of SATs. Unpublished paper, Bristol: School of Education, University of Bristol.

Burgess, T. (1989) The great pretenders. *Times Educational Supplement*, 17 March, A17.

Burton, L. and Weiner, G. (1990) Social justice and the National Curriculum. *Research Papers in Education*, **5**(3): 203–27.

Campbell, R. J. and Neill, S. R. St J. (1994a) *Primary Teachers at Work*. London: Routledge.

Campbell, R. J. and Neill, S. R. St J. (1994b) *Teacher Commitment and Policy Failure*. Harlow: Longman with the Association of Teachers and Lecturers.

Campbell, R. J., Evans, L., Neill, S. R. St J. and Packwood, S. (1991a) *Workloads, Achievement and Stress*. London: Assistant Masters and Mistresses Association.

Campbell, R. J., Evans, L., Neill, S. R. St J. and Packwood, S. (1991b) The use and management of infant teachers' time: some policy issues. Paper prepared for the Policy Analysis Unit Seminar, Coventry, Warwick University.

Chard, S. (1994) The National Curriculum in England and Wales. In P. Grimmett and J. Neufeld (eds), *Teacher Development and the Struggle for Authenticity*. New York: Teachers College Press, pp. 101–20.

Clarke, K. (1991) Primary education: a statement by the Secretary of State for Education and Science, 3 December 1991. London: DES.

DES (Department of Education and Science) (1988) *Task Group on Assessment and Testing – A Report*. London: HMSO.

DES (1992) *Statistics of Education: Teachers in Service, England and Wales, 1989 and 1990*. London: DES.

Doyle, W. and Ponder, G. A. (1977) The practicality ethic in teacher decision-making. *Interchange*, **8**: 1–12.

Galton, M. (1989) *Teaching in the Primary School*. London: David Fulton.

Grace, G. (1987) Teachers and the state in Britain: a changing relationship. In M. Lawn and G. Grace (eds), *Teachers: The Culture and Politics of Work*. Lewes: Falmer Press, pp. 193–228.

Griffith, A. and Smith, D. E. (1991) Constructing cultural knowledge: Mothering as discourse. In J. Gaskell and A. McLaren (eds), *Women and Education*. 2nd edn. Calgary: Detselig, pp. 81–97.

Grumet, M. (1988) *Bitter Milk: Women and Teaching*. Amherst: University of Massachusetts Press.

Hackett, G. (1991) Checks on nursery schools. *Times Educational Supplement*, 13 December, p. 1.

Hargreaves, A. (1994) *Changing Teachers, Changing Times: Teachers' Work and Culture in the Post-Modern Age*. London: Cassell.

Hellawell, D. (1992) Structural changes in education in England. *International Journal of Educational Reform*, 1(4): 356–65.

Hofkins, D. (1991) Streaming 'may begin at nine'. *Times Educational Supplement*, 8 November, p. 15.

Hofkins, D. (1992) Barking up the wrong dogma. *Times Educational Supplement*, 31 January, p. 11.

Lawn, M. (1995) Restructuring teaching in the USA and England: moving towards the differentiated, flexible teacher. *Journal of Education Policy*, 10(4): 347–60.

McCallum, B., McAlister, S., Brown, M. and Gipps, C. (1993) Teacher assessment at Key Stage One. *Research Papers in Education*, 8(3): 305–27.

McPherson, G. (1972) *Small Town Teacher*. Cambridge, MA: Harvard University Press.

Nias, J. (1989) *Primary Teachers Talking: A Study of Teaching as Work*. London: Routledge.

Osborn, M. (1996a) Identity, career and change: a tale of two teachers. In P. Croll (ed.), *Teachers, Pupils and Primary Schooling*. London: Cassell, pp. 53–68.

Osborn, M. (1996b) Teachers mediating change: Key Stage 1 revisited. In P. Croll (ed.), *Teachers, Pupils and Primary Schooling*. London: Cassell, pp. 35–52.

Osborn, M. and Broadfoot, P. with Abbott, D., Croll, P. and Pollard, A. (1991, April) The impact of current changes in English primary schools on teacher professionalism. Paper presented at the Annual Meeting of the American Educational Research Association, Chicago.

Osborn, M. and Pollard, A. with Abbott, D., Broadfoot, P. and Croll, P. (1990, August) Anxiety and paradox: teachers' initial responses to change under the National Curriculum. Paper presented at the Annual Meeting of the British Educational Research Association, Roehampton, London.

Pietrasik, R. (1987) The teachers' action, 1984–1986. In M. Lawn and G. Grace (eds), *Teachers: The Culture and Politics of Work*. Lewes: Falmer Press, pp. 168–89.

Pollard, A. (1985) *The Social World of the Primary School*. London: Holt, Rinehart and Winston.

Pollard, A., Broadfoot, P., Croll, P., Osborn, M. and Abbott, D. (1994) *Changing English Primary Schools? The Impact of the Education Reform Act at Key Stage One*. London: Cassell.

Rafferty, F. (1991) Primary system 'fails to deliver'. *Times Educational Supplement*, 1 November, p. 3.

Skeggs, B. (1994) The constraints of neutrality: The 1988 Education Reform Act and feminist research. In D. Halpin and B. Troyna (eds), *Researching Education Policy*. London: Falmer Press, pp. 75–93.

Stone, C. (1993) Questioning the new orthodoxies. *School Organization*, 11(3): 187–98.

Walkerdine, V. (1986) Progressive pedagogy and political struggle. *Screen*, 27(5): 54–60.

Waters, S. (1995) At the core: 'Oh, to be in England'. In J. Bell (ed.), *Teachers Talk about Teaching: Coping with Change in Turbulent Times*. Buckingham: Open University Press, pp. 110–22.

Wideen, M. with Pye, I. (1994). *The Struggle for Change: The Story of One School*. London: Falmer Press.

Woods, P. and Wenham, P. (1995) Politics and pedagogy: a case study in appropriation. *Journal of Education Policy*, 10(2): 119–41.

Chapter 4

Policy Into Practice and Practice Into Policy: Creative Mediation in the Primary Classroom

Marilyn Osborn with Paul Croll, Patricia Broadfoot, Andrew Pollard, Elizabeth McNess and Pat Triggs

INTRODUCTION

The requirement to implement a National Curriculum and to carry out national assessment imposed changes which were in fundamental conflict with the values and deeply held beliefs of many primary teachers in England and Wales. The Education Reform Act of 1988 and the processes of multiple change which followed it, including the introduction of new forms of management into schools, new forms of evaluation of teachers' work, and the infiltration of the values of the market-place into education, highlighted particularly strongly the debate over the professional role of teachers with regard to the formulation and implementation of educational policy. There were fears that the changes would deskill teachers and reduce them from being professionals exercising judgement to mere classroom technicians (Apple 1986; Densmore, 1987; Lawn and Ozga, 1981). The notion of teachers as passive 'victims' forced to implement educational policy in a largely uncritical way was placed in opposition to accounts of teachers' ability to resist or to contest policy change (Croll et al., 1994).

However the main argument of this chapter is that, on the whole, the majority of primary teachers in England have adopted neither of these extreme positions. Although there has been some resistance and contestation of policy, notably the 1993 action of the teachers' unions over national assessment, in general there has been neither strong resistance nor passive acceptance of government policy by teachers. The research evidence from PACE (Primary Assessment, Curriculum and Experience), a national study of educational change under the National Curriculum (Croll, 1996; Pollard et al., 1994), and from a number of other studies (Campbell et al., 1993; Cox and Sanders, 1994; Osborn and Black, 1994; Woods, 1995) consistently suggests that primary teachers have accepted and internalized the National Curriculum, but that they work with it in a way that suits their beliefs, enables them to preserve what they consider to be best about their practice, to protect children, and in some cases to be very creative, although working within a prescribed framework. I have suggested that such a response may be seen as 'creative mediation' (Osborn, 1996a).

In addition to this strategic response from some older and more experienced teachers who were in post before the 1988 Education Reform Act, there have been further developments as a new generation of teachers has entered schools since 1988. These teachers who were trained within the National Curriculum and who have accepted this as their 'taken-for-granted' way of working are developing their own forms of practice which have a National Curriculum framework as an initial starting point, but which go beyond this to produce innovative and creative ways of teaching.

In general the main concern expressed by primary teachers now in connection with the reforms is not so much with the National Curriculum as a principle, but with the extensive demands for knowledge and subject coverage it makes at the upper end of primary school, with the effect of standardized assessments on children and schools, and with recent developments such as OFSTED inspections of schools which impose further control and constraint on teachers. This chapter therefore draws upon an alternative model of teachers' work which presents them as creative mediators, who in some instances have the ability to transform themselves into 'policy-makers in practice' in the classroom (Croll *et al.*, 1994). In this view, teachers have the ability to mediate educational policy in the light of their own beliefs about teaching and the constraints which operate on them in the classroom.

This model of teaching suggests that as teachers attempt to reconcile external demands with their belief in professional autonomy and with the practicalities of the working situation, they must make choices about the way in which they carry out their work. Where numbers of individual teachers faced with a similar situation mediate change in similar ways and take communal, although not collective action, they effectively become makers of policy in their own classrooms as well as implementers of policy (Croll *et al.*, 1994).

This view of teachers acting communally to make parallel policy to that intended by government is one suggested particularly by the evidence from the PACE study. Other researchers have written of stronger or weaker versions of teachers' actions as subverting, resisting, transforming or appropriating government policy. However, all the accounts have in common a notion of the filtering of policy through teachers' values before it is translated into classroom practice. For example, Bowe *et al.* (1992) describe how secondary teachers successfully appropriated the TVEI initiative to 'very different purposes to those intended by the policy', while Vulliamy and Webb (1993) write of new policies having 'to be mediated through teachers'. Woods (1995) gives case study examples of 'creative teaching' within the National Curriculum. Troman (1995, p. 4) talks of 'new professionals', teachers who largely accommodated to the reforms but 'nevertheless, in some instances, contested and resisted them'.

Although teachers in England have traditionally believed more strongly in their professional autonomy than teachers in many other countries (Broadfoot and Osborn, 1993), the research evidence suggests that the ability to mediate is a feature of teaching as a profession which transcends national and cross-cultural differences. When confronted with change, and in particular with reform imposed from above, a proportion of teachers in many countries, even those working in highly prescriptive, centrally controlled systems, will respond by subverting, mediating, reinventing, or developing an innovative response. Darmanin (1990), for example, demonstrates how Maltese teachers subverted some aspects of educational change. There is evidence of some teachers in Greece ignoring a rigid, over-prescriptive curriculum in selective ways (Krespi, 1995), while Hargreaves's study of Canadian primary teachers and the introduction of 'preparation time' suggested that although there was evidence for the intensification of teachers' work, this could not account for the whole range and complexity of teachers' response (Hargreaves, 1992). In a recent study comparing the response of primary teachers in France and England when confronted with reform imposed from above, some French primary teachers talked of the need to 'internalize the changes, to be selective', and of the importance of 'taking the best from the reforms, but using their own judgement in the end' (Broadfoot *et al.*, 1994; Osborn, 1995).

Of course, not all teachers adopt this strategy when confronted with change. Teachers in the PACE sample adopted alternative responses of 'compliance', 'incorporation', and 'retreatism' as well as 'creative mediation' and 'resistance' (Osborn *et al.*, 1992; Pollard *et al.*, 1994). Troman (1995), in a case study of one primary school, writes of the 'old professionals' who stuck to what they felt works, regardless of policy directives. There were many such teachers in the French study cited above, carried out by Broadfoot *et al.* (1994); these teachers justified their refusal to change by arguing that the reforms were inappropriate and that they lacked the necessary training and resources to change.

However, the concern of this chapter is particularly with those teachers who have had the confidence, and also the support from within their school, to enable them to become creative mediators, to be selective in how they implement National Curriculum policy, to prioritize, and to develop new forms of practice in pedagogy and assessment. Four strategies of creative mediation, which I have termed 'protective', 'innovative', 'collaborative' and 'conspiratorial' will be identified, drawing mainly upon the PACE data. While some of these represent teachers acting solely at an individual level, it will be argued that most of the examples suggest that because of either similar structural and situational constraints or because of similar ideologies teachers have acted in similar ways, taking common actions in response to the realities of their working situations (Croll *et al.*, 1994). Insofar as this is the case, these actions can be seen to have systematic effects and may effectively redirect educational activities in a way that transforms teachers into policy-makers. First, however, I want to identify some key features in the development of primary teachers' response to change over the six years since the National Curriculum (and the PACE study) began.

DEVELOPMENTS IN TEACHERS' RESPONSE TO CHANGE

The PACE study provides a unique means of studying teachers' response to change over time from the initial implementation of a National Curriculum and assessment up to the Dearing Report and the introduction of the revised National Curriculum. Samples of teachers and children have been studied over six years and the same group of children have been followed from their time in Year 1 (aged 5) until the end of their time in Year 6 (aged 11). Successive samples of approximately 90 teachers have been interviewed at roughly yearly intervals. Some of the teachers interviewed in the study were different at each round of data collection as the children moved into new classes. However, teachers of the same Year Groups in the same schools were revisited on subsequent occasions both at Key Stage 1 (in 1994) and at Key Stage 2 in 1995. Full details of the research design are given in the two books published by the research team (Croll, 1996; Pollard *et al.*, 1994).

Initially, most Key Stage 1 teachers interviewed by the PACE team in 1990 welcomed at least some aspects of the National Curriculum, particularly the curriculum clarification and focus it provided. However, there were strong feelings about many aspects of the reforms, in particular the standardized assessment tasks (SATs), and the sheer pace and extent of change. While many argued that some of the National Curriculum equated with good practice and was what good teachers were doing already, it was striking that a majority of all teachers interviewed felt that they had to make substantial changes to their teaching approach, to their working day and to their role as a teacher as a result of the Education Reform Act (ERA). However, most teachers continued to hold strong personal value commitments and felt responsible and accountable in many, often conflicting directions. Overall teachers' work was perceived to have intensified following the reforms, but many Key Stage 1 teachers were unwilling to give up their expressive commitment to children and their 'extended' sense of professional responsibility.

Nevertheless, they experienced their work as far more stressful and regretted the decrease in their professional autonomy and the loss of spontaneity in their work with children as a result of the time constraints imposed by the need to cover an overloaded curriculum. In general, the level of stress, intensification, and sense of deskilling experienced and the corresponding loss of fulfilment and enjoyment in teaching increased and became more marked between 1990 and 1992. There were considerable differences in response between older and younger teachers and between teachers working in different socio-economic catchment areas. Older, more experienced teachers were more depressed about the changes than younger, newer teachers. Many felt close to burn-out and argued that the nature of teaching was now such that it could no longer be a job for life. Levels of drop-out through stress and early retirement increased dramatically. Teachers of special needs children and those working in inner-city schools felt the National Curriculum to be particularly inappropriate for their pupils' needs.

However, by 1994, when the Dearing Review was already under way, some Key Stage 1 teachers, in particular, began to feel a decline in pressure and an increased sense of optimism about the future. These teachers argued that they now experienced a greater sense of focus and clarity about their role. Perceptions of deskilling had diminished and a considerable proportion of those who had remained in teaching and had become 'survivors' (Woods, 1977) of the changes thus far, saw themselves as having acquired new professional skills and having developed creative ways of working and assessing within the National Curriculum. There was an increasing sense that it was possible to maintain their own beliefs and good practice and even to enrich their work within a prescribed curriculum.

Key Stage 2 teachers, who by 1995 were experiencing the pressure of national assessment at the upper end of the primary school, felt, on the whole, somewhat less reassured by the Dearing Review and subsequent report. Dearing had argued that content and prescription of the curriculum would be reduced and the professional judgement of teachers increased by the freeing of one day per week for discretionary, non-curricular activities (Dearing, 1994). However, after the first term of the revised National Curriculum, many Key Stage 2 teachers interviewed by the PACE team argued that they had experienced no perceptible difference in curriculum overload. When pressed, some did say that more time had been released for catching up, for activities which had previously been squeezed out such as art, music, a school or class production which might not otherwise have been possible, or for concentrating on children with particular needs. Some also argued that they now felt 'freed up' to do those things which they thought were important, or 'released from a feeling of guilt' at taking time out to digress from National Curriculum topics. For others, it had made them more 'relaxed about time' and put them 'in a more legally tenable position'.

Overall, the evidence suggested that teachers at both Key Stage 1 and Key Stage 2 had adopted coping strategies in response to change ranging from compliance (complete acceptance), through incorporation (fitting the changes into existing means of working), mediation, and retreatism (dropping out of teaching or submission to change without any fundamental change in values) to resistance (Osborn *et al.*, 1992; Pollard *et al.*, 1994). Many had managed, to varying degrees, to incorporate the changes into existing ways of working. Most of those who remained in teaching after an unprecedented level of drop-out had adopted strategies which enabled them to mediate the pressures of change imposed from above through the filter of their own particular values in relation to teaching. For many of the teachers studied, this produced a particular, personal response to change which was evident in their professional ideology and their classroom practice (Osborn, 1996b). As a result they had been able to work with the National Curriculum in a way that suited their beliefs, and enabled them to preserve what they considered to be most important about their practice. In some cases they felt that having guidelines and a framework to work within had left them free to develop creative ways of teaching.

I have argued that such teachers may be seen as 'creative mediators' filtering change through their own values, which are in turn influenced by gender, social class, previous experience in the classroom, professional training and other historical and biographical factors (Osborn, 1996b). However, the argument may be taken a stage further. In this mediating role, teachers may well act in similar ways, so that the effect on classrooms and schools is much greater, and more powerful, and in so doing they may effectively be seen to have become makers of policy in their own classrooms as well as implementers of policy (Croll *et al.*, 1994). This model of teachers as 'policy-makers in practice' implies a communal rather than a collective action by teachers.

The PACE research suggests several different strategies of creative mediation adopted by teachers which may contribute to policy-making in practice. These are 'protective mediation', 'innovative mediation', 'collaborative mediation' and 'conspiratorial mediation'. Although these strategies are often adopted at an individual level, and by particular groups of teachers at particular times, they have been used in common by many teachers to the extent that they form a particular pattern of response which may have far-reaching implications for primary practice.

PROTECTIVE MEDIATION

As protective mediators, teachers have been particularly concerned with the effect of external directives such as the SAT requirements, the time pressure to cover a vast curriculum, and the pressures of more rigorous assessment procedures on children, and have striven to protect the children from what they deem to be the worst effects of these.

For example, right from the outset of the implementation of the National Curriculum teachers were determined to protect the good relationship they had with children from the pressures on teachers' time resulting from the need to cover a broad and prescriptive curriculum. They emphasized the need to maintain spontaneity and the ability to respond to children's interests even where this did not involve the coverage of an attainment target. Many teachers made a deliberate and sustained attempt to maintain this freedom to respond in spite of the pressures.

Examples such as this became more prevalent by 1994 when more teachers gained the confidence to follow their own instincts and to feel, as one Year 2 teacher put it,

> far more in control now, feeling Yes, I can do this again. It is
> possible, and I'll be able to gradually get back to focusing on maths
> and English, and the other things being a very important
> enrichment.

By resisting the pressures to stick closely to a prescribed curriculum, such teachers were taking a common action which had consequences unintended by government policy, and were in effect making parallel National Curriculum policy in the classroom.

Examples of protective mediation were particularly striking in the area of assessment, where teachers of all year groups in primary schools mediated the impact of assessment on the children in a way which accorded with their beliefs and concerns about children's needs. The common action taken by many teachers was a response not to a collective decision but to the similarity of the situation in which teachers found themselves and the ideas which informed their actions.

Key Stage 1 teachers were deeply concerned about the stress and anxiety which the SATs might cause 7-year-olds and worked hard to counteract any sense of pressure, tension and awareness of failure by a variety of subterfuges. Teachers' strategies included making no overt reference to national assessment in the children's presence, asking parents to avoid mentioning the SATs, and presenting the tasks as 'fun' and a normal part of classroom life, in same cases turning the SATs into games and competitions, in which the teacher played the role of a quiz show host or master of ceremonies (Pollard *et al.*, 1994). The PACE interviews with children after the SATs had taken place suggested that these strategies were largely successful, since few 7-year-olds were aware that testing had taken place and many had actually enjoyed the activities. In Saint Anne's, an inner-city primary school in the North of England, for example, the Key Stage 1 teacher responsible for SATs said:

> We had many parents saying to us at the end of it [the SAT],
> 'When are they going to do their SAT?' thinking that it was all
> sitting in the Hall at separate desks! I'm sure the children have no
> idea they've done one. We just introduce them as puzzles or
> challenges or mysteries – 'We'd like to know what you know about
> ...' etc., etc.

For teachers, the central issue was to normalize the SATs and to integrate them as far as possible into day-to-day teaching, as the following extract from the same teacher's interview suggests:

> I found that the way we approached it and tackled it and we built
> it into our emergent work on multiplication, use of calculators ...
> the basic maths – addition, subtraction – were already there
> anyway. That was fine. The children just treated it like another
> activity which I regularly give them. Perhaps that was why it
> worked so well, when I think about it... is because I do take them
> off the textbook almost on a weekly basis to give them activities
> that we've created, or I've made, or which are parallel to how
> they're learning or what they're learning, and they just saw it as
> something else like that.

At Key Stage 2, protective mediation in relation to the SATs took a rather different common pattern. After the first full-scale SATs at Key Stage 2 in summer 1995, many class teachers of Year 6 children were dismayed to find how ill-prepared and ill-equipped children were to face what was only too clearly a test situation. Given the age of the children and the pencil-and-paper test nature of the majority of the SATs it was no longer seen as possible or appropriate to try to disguise the purpose and nature of the assessments. Many children experienced the SATs sitting in the school hall or in the classroom at separate desks in what was quite clearly a test situation and, in the autumn of 1995, Year 6 teachers often reported that at least some of their children had become anxious and stressed during the SAT period. In order to help children to deal with this in future, many argued that they planned to carry out regular mock tests during the year in order to teach the skills required, such as reading the questions carefully, allowing adequate time for each question, but also simply to provide general practice in taking tests in order to routinize the test situation.

Whereas some would limit this practice to Years 5 and 6 only, others argued that such practice needed to start lower down the school. As one teacher of a mixed Year 5 and 6 class put it:

> The SATs *are* affecting teaching and learning. We are having to start preparing for the SATs at the beginning of the year. We will be doing SAT like tasks regularly and making them aware of how to organize their time in the SATs; be aware of time limits. It all needs to start further down the school.

Another argued:

> The children need training for tests now. The situation is too foreign to them. The tests have implications for teaching in Year 5 as well as Year 6, and probably earlier on.

Some were reluctant to accept this but nevertheless felt that training for tests would be inevitable. As one Year 5 teacher put it:

> If you deliver the National Curriculum, you should have no need to do extra SATs work, but they do have an influence. There's a pressure to prepare the children for it – it's not teaching but training to take tests. It will be expected of me.

In one village primary school, the children had themselves asked for more formal testing to help them prepare for the SATs. Teachers were coming under pressure not only from their own desire to do their best for the children, but in some cases from the children themselves, from the parents, and from school policy, and the need to protect the reputation of the school when league tables of SAT results were published.

At both Key Stages 1 and 2 it was clear that a central concern of the teachers was to routinize the SATs so that they would be seen by the children as part of everyday practice. This common pattern of response adopted by teachers is of a kind which clearly contributes to assessment policy-making and changing classroom practice on a relatively large scale. Although each teacher is operating this protective mediation at an individual level, or at the most, at a school level, it will nevertheless have systematic effects, as similar actions by teachers aggregate across many primary schools.

INNOVATIVE MEDIATION

A second central concern of many teachers following the implementation of the National Curriculum and assessment has been to develop creative and innovative ways of working within a National Curriculum framework and of interpreting statutory requirements, as well as maintaining the freedom to go outside these when they felt it appropriate. In making these judgements about appropriateness, they often felt it necessary to first internalize the statutory requirements and make them part of their thinking, or, as one Year 5 teacher argued 'let it sink into the skin and come out as a professional judgement'.

Once again this common concern when faced with a similar situation has led numbers of teachers to respond by taking the aspects of the National Curriculum which most closely accorded with their beliefs and values as teachers and introducing creative ways of covering the attainment targets with children. Thus a Key Stage 1 teacher in the North of England argued:

> We've worked very hard at taking the National Curriculum and looking at our beliefs and philosophy and what we believe is good early years' practice and marrying the two. So we've worked very hard at not being swamped and panicking and rushing. For us to step outside our beliefs would be to rush into worksheets and have the children sitting at tables all day trying to cover attainment targets, but we've tried to make it part of our philosophy to give the children firsthand experience and the chance to discover things, and everything's kept very lively. We don't feel we've lost out.

These teachers often felt that the National Curriculum complemented and enhanced their skills, providing them with a focus and allowing them to concentrate on creative methods of covering the content. Sara, a Key Stage 1 teacher, felt in 1994 that she had emerged from the changes with a new sense of clarity and focus about her role and her practice. She could be seen as an innovative mediator who had taken active control of the changes in a creative, albeit selective way (Osborn, 1996a). Several other researchers have written detailed accounts of creative teaching taking place within a National Curriculum framework (Galton, 1995; Woods, 1995; Woods and Jeffrey, 1996). Common to all these accounts of creative teaching is the ability to make choices, to be adaptable and flexible, to see alternatives, although working within constraints, and to have the confidence and motivation to put values into practice. These teachers were able to resist pressures to become technicians carrying out the dictates of others. They worked hard to create new ways of working with children which were exciting and lively and yet covered what were perceived as important parts of the National Curriculum. As a teacher of a mixed Year 5 and 6 class put it in the autumn of 1995, being creative involves being able to take risks and to have the courage of your own convictions:

> You have to accept that you never know it all, be open to new things and go on learning. You need to be prepared to take risks and have confidence to do what you see is necessary in your class. A few years ago I had a very disruptive class and in that context my main priority was to create a happy work environment where learning could take place. It's that skill to have the power of your own conviction, to create the right environment and know where you want to go. What I got at the end of that year was phenomenal in terms of children's response, but I had to take risks, not just stick to papers and worksheets, and be prepared to follow the needs of the children at certain times.

Woods (1995), in his study of creative teachers, also found that such teachers often had in common holistic perceptions of children, of learning and of the curriculum, and were concerned with the affective as well as the cognitive. They 'possessed the ability and flair to formulate and act upon hunches, to "play with ideas", but within a disciplined framework' (Woods, 1995). To the extent that the teachers in the PACE sample were acting in common or similar ways as innovators and risk-takers, developing new forms of pedagogy, it could be argued that they were making policy in the classroom.

New teachers who had been trained within a National Curriculum framework and had come into schools in the last few years were also contributing to this process. Many saw the guidance and framework provided by the National Curriculum as a distinct advantage, although there was anxiety created by the 'shifting of goalposts' created by frequent changes in government policy, particularly in relation to assessment. However, many new teachers in the PACE sample had quickly gained confidence to experiment and adapt the National Curriculum framework, using it as a tool, rather than letting it govern their approach. As one Year 5 teacher, in her third year of teaching, put it:

> It's good to have a format to follow. Within that there is a lot of freedom. The curriculum can be personalized to suit the teacher and the class.

A Year 4 teacher, in his first year of teaching, pointed out that like most new teachers he was adapting his approach all the time as he gained experience. He argued that he felt 'very free' within the National Curriculum:

> It's easy to plan. I can plan around the National Curriculum, use it and work within it.

61

He did not feel, as some more experienced teachers did, that the National Curriculum had an effect on his relationship with the children:

> I'm still close to my class. We have good fun and have a laugh. I get loads of satisfaction. I have a smile on my face at the end of the day.

COLLABORATIVE MEDIATION

One of the unintended consequences of National Curriculum implementation was the unprecedented level of collaboration which emerged amongst primary teachers. This has been seen as a mainly positive outcome by teachers although with some reservations (Acker, 1990; Nias *et al.*, 1992; Pollard *et al.*, 1994). However, there is a particular sense in which collaboration by some groups of teachers has emerged as a practice which makes policy in the classroom. A major concern of teachers in Years 5 and 6 has been with the difficulties of covering the curriculum in the breadth required, and a lack of confidence in covering some of the subject areas in depth (Bennett *et al.*, 1992; Osborn and Black, 1994). A study of Year 5 and 6 teachers in 1993 found that some classroom teachers had made their own informal arrangements to mediate the effects of the overloaded curriculum (Osborn and Black, 1994). This involved teachers swapping and sharing the teaching of certain activities and subject areas in which one felt confident or had a particular expertise in an area where the other felt less confident. In one school a Year 5 and a Year 6 teacher made an informal arrangement, which they saw as building on each other's weaknesses and strengths, whereby one taught science for the other's class while the other taught PE and gymnastics. In another school it was higher language and reading skills which were swapped with maths by teachers who felt particularly strong in one area and weak in another. These arrangements, although supported by the headteacher, were largely instigated by the teachers themselves when they recognized that they had complementary skills, and consequently acted upon this, using their own initiative.

In the autumn of 1995, the first term in which the revised National Curriculum was implemented, a number of Year 5 and 6 teachers interviewed as part of the PACE sample reported that they had similar arrangements with colleagues. In spite of the 'slimming down' of the curriculum they found a greater degree of satisfaction in teaching what they knew they were good at, and leaving a colleague to do the same, although this in no way extended to a desire to give up responsibility for teaching the majority of subject areas to their own class. Examples of such swapping and sharing were music and drama swapped with technology, PE swapped with science and technology, and art swapped with music and science. Newer teachers were particularly likely to see themselves as having identifiable strengths in some subject areas and as being weaker in others. In 1995 most of the new teachers of Years 5 and 6 whom we interviewed felt that there was a place for some subject specialist teaching in the upper years of primary school. A number had made informal arrangements with colleagues to build upon each others' strengths in the classroom, particularly in areas such as PE, music, drama, science and technology.

To many of the teachers in the PACE sample, the details of such sharing were not so important as the general principle that collaboration was a survival strategy, as well as a source of increased job satisfaction. As one older, experienced teacher of a mixed Year 5 and 6 class put it:

> If someone likes doing something or has a particular interest you
> should give them a chance. There is no place in teaching now for
> prima donnas. You must work with others. If you don't share
> ideas, planning and practice you will go under. The teacher who
> can't share is no longer a good teacher.

CONSPIRATORIAL MEDIATION

In a few schools in the PACE sample, collaboration had taken a more subversive form, where teachers had worked together and supported one another to resist aspects of the National Curriculum that were felt to be particularly inappropriate for the children. This type of collaboration, which I have termed 'conspiratorial mediation', was strongly evident in one inner-city school where teachers, with the tacit support of the head, saw themselves as 'conspirators' working together to implement the National Curriculum selectively in a way they felt would protect the children and avoid overload. In this school, a decision had been made in 1992 to ignore the history and geography programmes of study, except where they 'fitted naturally' into topics planned for the core subjects.

In the same school in 1995, Year 2 teachers had decided, again with the support of the headteacher, not to carry out the SATs, although they had agreed to use SAT materials in their teaching and in their own teacher assessment of children. On this occasion they had the added support of their wider cluster of schools, all of whom had 'conspired' to refuse to implement the SATs in the same way. This form of mediating the SAT materials to what were deemed more acceptable professional ends, making use of them in their own teaching and assessment but not as the government had intended, could also be seen as a common action by a group of inner-city teachers which, if more widely adopted, would have a systematic impact on assessment policy.

There is evidence to suggest that some teachers may have adopted a form of conspiratorial mediation in relation to school inspections by OFSTED. While, in both form and content, such inspections represent one of the most stringent attempts to control teachers' work, teachers in some schools have 'conspired' to mediate this by strategic compliance and impression management both before and during the visit in order to be seen by the inspectors to be complying with OFSTED criteria (Jeffrey and Woods, 1995; Troman, 1995).

CONCLUSION

In this chapter I have identified some areas where teachers can be seen to have mediated policy through professional practice in ways which may amount to policy creation. I have outlined four strategies of creative mediation – protective, innovative, collaborative and conspiratorial – by which teachers can be seen to have formulated classroom policy by acting in common, although not necessarily collective ways.

As the revised National Curriculum is taken on board more fully, it may be that the potential for a margin of manoeuvre by teachers between centralized policy and its implementation may have been increased still further as a result of Dearing's attempt to restore room for professional judgement to teachers through the creation of 20 per cent of 'discretionary time'. However, in the short term at least, it appears that the availability of such increased time is largely illusory rather than real. In the longer term, the evidence presented here suggests that creative mediation by teachers is an important strategy which may have system-wide effects on policy and which will continue as long as there are teachers who feel sufficiently confident to adapt and develop practices that accord with their values and working situations.

REFERENCES

Acker, S. (1990) Teachers' culture in an English primary school: continuity and change. *British Journal of Sociology of Education*, **11**(3): 257–73.

Apple, M. W. (1986) *Teachers and Texts: A Political Economy of Class and Gender Relations in Education*. London: Routledge.

Bennett, S. N., Wragg, E. C., Carré, C. G. and Carter, D. S. G. (1992) A longitudinal study of primary teachers' perceived competence in, and concerns about, National Curriculum implementation. *Research Papers in Education*, **7**(1): 53–78.

Bowe, R. and Ball, S. J. with Gold, A. (1992) *Reforming Education and Changing Schools*. London: Routledge.

Broadfoot, P. and Osborn, M. with Gilly, M. and Brucher, A. (1993) *Perceptions of Teaching. Primary School Teachers in England and France*. London: Cassell.

Broadfoot, P., Osborn, M., Planel, C. and Pollard, A. (1994) *Primary Teachers and Policy Change*. Final Report to the ESRC.

Campbell, J., Emery, H. and Stone, C. (1993) The broad and balanced curriculum at Key Stage 2: some limitations on reform. Paper given at 1993 Annual Conference of the British Educational Research Association, University of Liverpool.

Cox, T. and Sanders, S. (1994) *The Impact of the National Curriculum on the Teaching of Five Year Olds*. London: Falmer Press.

Croll, P. (ed.) (1996) *Teachers, Pupils and Primary Schooling*. London: Cassell.

Croll, P., Abbot, D., Broadfoot, P., Osborn, M. and Pollard, A. (1994) Teachers and educational policy: roles and models. *British Journal of Educational Studies*, **42**(2): 333–47.

Darmanin, M. (1990) Maltese primary school teachers' experience of centralised policies. *British Journal of Sociology of Education*, **11**(3): 275–308.

Dearing, R. (1994) *The National Curriculum and its Assessment. Final Report*. London: HMSO.

Densmore, K. (1987) Professionalism, proletarianization and teachers' work. In T. Popkewitz (ed.), *Critical Studies in Teacher Education.* Lewes: Falmer Press, pp. 130–60.

Galton, M. (1995) *Crisis in the Primary Classroom.* London: David Fulton.

Hargreaves, A. (1992) Time and teachers' work: An analysis of the intensification thesis. *Teachers' College Record,* **94**(1): 491–505.

Jeffrey, B. and Woods, P. (1995) Panic on parade. *Times Educational Supplement, Primary Update,* 8 September, p. 13.

Krespi, A. (1995) *Greek primary teachers and the National Curriculum.* Unpublished poster presentation, British Educational Research Association, University of Bath.

Lawn, M. and Ozga, J. (1981) The educational worker: a reassessment of teachers. In M. Walker and L. Barton (eds), *Schools, Teachers and Learning.* London: Falmer Press.

Nias, J., Southworth, G. and Campbell, P. (1992) *Whole School Curriculum Development in the Primary School.* Lewes: Falmer Press.

Osborn, M. (1995) Teachers as adult learners: the influence of the national context and policy change. In G. Claxton, T. Atkinson, M. Osborn and M. Wallace (eds), *Liberating the Learner.* London: Routledge, pp. 59–73.

Osborn, M. (1996a) Teachers mediating change: Key Stage 1 revisited. In P. Croll (ed.), *Teachers, Pupils and Primary Schooling.* London: Cassell, pp. 35–52.

Osborn, M. (1996b) Identity, career and change: a tale of two teachers. In P. Croll (ed.), *Teachers, Pupils and Primary Schooling.* London: Cassell, pp. 53–68.

Osborn, M. and Black, E. (1994) *Developing the National Curriculum at Key Stage 2: The Changing Nature of Teachers' Work.* Birmingham: University of Bristol/NASUWT.

Osborn, M. and Broadfoot, P. with Abbott, D., Croll, P. and Pollard, A. (1992) The impact of current changes in English primary schools on teacher professionalism. *Teachers College Record,* **94**(1): 138–51.

Pollard, A., Broadfoot, P., Croll, P., Osborn, M. and Abbott, D. (1994) *Changing English Primary Schools? The Impact of the Education Reform Act at Key Stage One.* London: Cassell.

Troman, G. (1995) The rise of the New Professionals?: the restructuring of primary teachers' work and professionalism. Paper presented at the Annual Conference of the British Educational Research Association, University of Bath.

Vulliamy, G. and Webb, R. (1993) Progressive education and the National Curriculum: findings from a global education research project. *Educational Review,* **45**(1): 21–41.

Woods, P. (1977) Teaching for survival. In P. Woods and M. Hammersley (eds), *School Experience.* London: Croom Helm, pp. 271–93.

Woods, P. (1995) *Creative Teachers in Primary Schools.* Buckingham: Open University Press.

Woods, P. and Jeffrey, B. (1996) *Teachable Moments.* Buckingham: Open University Press.

Chapter 5

Creative Teaching in the Primary National Curriculum

Peter Woods and Bob Jeffrey

CREATIVE TEACHING

It has been argued that teachers' work is intensifying, and that teachers are becoming increasingly deskilled, proletarianized, alienated workers (Apple, 1986). With a closely prescribed National Curriculum and extensive national assessment, there would appear to be not much demand or time for teacher independence and innovation. Compared to a generation ago, they are faced with more work, less time to do it in, less time for leisure and for reskilling, an increase in administration, a narrowing of responsibility, and being required to concentrate more exclusively on the execution, as opposed to the conceptualization, of tasks – in other words, less opportunity to be creative (Campbell and Neill, 1994; Pollard *et al.*, 1994). There is hardly a teacher in the UK who would not identify with such a scenario. Yet, in some schools at least, there would appear to be a contrary trend occurring at the same time. This is toward 'creative teaching'.

We have been researching into this phenomenon for the past ten years, having been impressed during the 1980s, while engaged in some other research in primary schools, by the inventiveness of primary teachers. Following attempts to capture some of the character of this creativity in the classroom (Woods, 1990), the enquiry moved to examine and portray exceptional events in primary schools (Woods, 1993). Most of those events took place before the National Curriculum took hold. Clearly, no further study could ignore it. Consequently, our research since has followed two strands: (1) continuing to delineate the character of creative teaching; and (2) exploring how creative teachers cope with the National Curriculum (Woods, 1995; Woods and Jeffrey, 1996). It is upon this work that we draw in this chapter.

At all stages of the research, we have used qualitative methods of enquiry, consisting of unstructured interviews and classroom observation over periods averaging two years. Our samples have consisted of primary teachers judged particularly 'creative' by the criteria specified. Their schools have been drawn from both inner city and rural areas in the London and South Midlands areas. Most of these teachers were in mid-career, experienced, well-respected and generally highly regarded by their peers, inspectors, pupils and pupils' parents as successful, and with management as well as teaching responsibilities (see

Woods, 1993, 1995; Woods and Jeffrey, 1996, for further discuss
research methods used).

From our observations, we have identified four major components
teaching – innovation, ownership, control and relevance. Innovation r
the boundaries of the conventional. It can result from a new combination of
known factors, or from the introduction of a new factor. It may be planned or
serendipitous. There are broad aims certainly, but some learning outcomes are
unpredictable. The process is as important as the product, being concerned with
the generation of ideas, which, in interaction with others, then breed more.

The innovation belongs to the teacher concerned. It may be the teacher's own
idea, or it may be an adaptation, perhaps in new circumstances, of someone else's
(perhaps a pupil's) idea. It might be generated by an individual alone, or more
commonly as a result of collaboration with others. Some novel aspect of the
process is produced by the teacher concerned. Nias (1989, p. 99) illustrates the
personal satisfaction of teachers who reported 'You're the one who is making it
happen at first hand'. However, the teacher's efforts need to be attuned to the
values of the society in which they take place, and to their pupils' interests and
cultures. In other words they need to be relevant. Teachers can be extremely
innovative, but if not relevant, may have the morality of their teaching questioned, or be perceived as self-indulgent, or not be listened to by pupils (see
Jeffrey and Woods, 1996).

Creative teachers are able to see alternatives and to achieve analytical
distance from their professional role, continuously evaluating their own performance. They can, to some extent, affect the situations in which they work, applying
their talents to changing or modifying the circumstances and increasing the
range of opportunities. They cannot do this without a large measure of commitment to the values they espouse, and strong motivation, and indeed, on
occasions, inspiration, in seeing their values promoted. Creative teachers seem
guided by particular theories of pedagogy and of learning that cut across vague,
all-embracing, bipolar concepts such as 'traditionalism' and 'progressivism'.
They have holistic perceptions – of the pupil, of learning, and of the curriculum.
They are concerned with the affective as well as the cognitive. The pupil is
considered as the whole child, and knowledge is indivisible. They have a fund of
knowledge – of subject matter, pedagogy and pupils – on which to draw, and a
disposition to experiment in finding the optimum means to advance toward their
aims. They possess the ability and flair to formulate and act upon hunches, to
'play with ideas', but within a disciplined framework. They have adaptability and
flexibility to cope with ever-changing sets of circumstances (see Woods and
Jeffrey, 1996, for further discussion of 'creative teachers').

The National Curriculum is based on an objectives model of teaching,
focusing on ends to be achieved, bodies of information, codified facts, measured
products. It is divided into subjects, which in turn are compartmentalized into
sections to be taught. It contains a great deal of material that must be covered. It
is not, on the face of it, conducive to the process model preferred by the teachers

in our research (see Elliott, 1991, for a critique of the National Curriculum along these lines). The question of how creative teachers coped, therefore, was not just a matter of managing overload. Different educational philosophies were at work, making their task – and the demands on their creativity – even more complex. How did they fare?

CREATIVE TEACHERS AND THE NATIONAL CURRICULUM

We found a range of adaptations to the National Curriculum among creative primary teachers, which we have characterized as resistance, appropriation and enrichment (Woods, 1995). There was also failure to adapt in some cases, leading to stress and burn-out. We discuss each in turn.

Resistance

Resistance was the prevailing mode in a lower school with a large minority ethnic intake – the needs of these pupils, as speakers of English as a second language, had been overlooked in the National Curriculum. Their teachers were resisting the demotion of the issues of equality, multiculturalism and bilingualism, and the promotion of differentiation, centralism and ethnocentrism. Connected to this was a distinctive child-centred teaching approach, and they were also resisting any wholesale drift towards more traditional methods. Thirdly, they opposed any tendencies to turn them into rational-technocrats and to depro-fessionalize them as teachers. The resistance took three main forms:

1. A discourse of resistance, consisting of 'fighting talk'. The teachers' commitment to the cause of their children led them to talk of 'fighting to regain the high ground', and 'not being beaten'.
2. Collaboration. These teachers were in the process of developing a culture of collaboration. There was strong accord among them on basic values, on educational beliefs, and on teaching approach. In some important respects, these are at variance with the values and thinking behind the 1988 Education Reform Act. The collaborative culture thus had a political purpose.
3. A whole-school perspective. Over the two years of the research, the staff 'thought through' and articulated their beliefs about teaching, showing that the collaboration was strong at the level of ideas. There was support for the National Curriculum in some respects, but not with regard to its neglect of social issues and lack of relevance for their children. They held a child-centred view of learning based on autonomy, ownership and empowerment, concepts which applied also to the children's parents. These ends would be reached through collaboration, cooperation and

negotiation, designed to produce confidence and motivation. Their pedagogical approach was based on the cultivation of relationships; an emphasis on 'real learning' (Clayden *et al.*, 1994; Holt, 1970; Jackson, 1992), including assessment in context; 'scaffolding' – the concept derived from Vygotsky (see Edwards and Mercer, 1987); and balance, involving a variety of methods, managing constraints, and adopting a fitness-for-purpose approach.

A new professional discourse

Since this research, we have noted a number of teachers in different schools developing what we have termed a 'new professional discourse'. Managerialism is currently the 'dominant discourse', but there appears to be sufficient discursive space to allow resistance, and 'resistance to the dominant at the level of the individual subject is the first stage in the production of alternative forms of knowledge' (Foucault, in Weedon, 1987, p. 110). The main features of the new professional discourse involve firstly, reaffirmation of the principles that under-pin teachers' practice and a rehearsal of its successes, pitted against a critique of the new pretender. Teachers preferred a model which allowed for the creation of ends and knowledge within the process of classroom interactions, rather than one slavishly addressed to pre-specified objectives. They resisted elements that ran counter to those principles, such as increased bureaucracy and the over-loaded curriculum; and appreciated others that seemed to them to offer educational benefit, such as the new framework the National Curriculum offered for their teaching. They took the attack to the enemy, for example putting to the test the knowledge and capabilities of some of the inspectors who came to evaluate their work. They distanced themselves from what they saw as 'easy way out' options, such as too ready compliance. They transformed some of the main tenets of professional managerialism. Thus 'choice' became a matter of pro-fessional choice. 'Accountability' in the managerialist discourse became 'heavy duty', misplaced and counter-productive; they preferred an accountability located within their own professional values, involving judgement by peers. 'Quality' was not what was determined by standardized tests, but what emerged from 'teachable moments', those occasions that often happened by chance, when learning opportunities were maximized. Above all, perhaps, is the articulation of solutions, the finding of 'ways through', such as the finding that it *was* possible to do adventurous topics within the context of the National Curriculum, or the liberating effect that one teacher found in team teaching. In these various ways, teachers were constructing a new professionalism on the framework of the old, rather than being taken over by contrary forces.

The new professional discourse was not just a matter of substance. Its style was equally important, giving it strength and cementing the various elements together. We've mentioned the fighting talk and spirit of resistance. There was also a great deal of humour and laughter, notably irony, self-parody, joking, satire and a kind of rhythmic rhetoric, with which teachers built up effects through imagery and cadences which enveloped the researcher in a kind of conspiratorial and empathetic amusement. One teacher kept her records in a shoe cupboard. Why? Because 'she wanted to trample them to death!' Another gave thanks for the Dearing Report:

> Since the publication of the Dearing Report I see now we're only going to have to do the National Curriculum four days a week and we can do real education on the fifth day. 'And on the fifth day there will be civilization.'

Another, illustrating the 'getting done' approach, rattled off the treatment of the heart:

> So it was a case of 'right, here's the heart, this is what it does, goes in here comes out there, right the blood goes all round', and it was done in an hour because we'd got to move on because we'd got to do all the major organs in the body, and we'd got to do those quickly because we had to get on to the last bit of sex education and 'Oh crickey! There's only three weeks left of term'. So you do skim over a lot of it because you haven't got time to relax and really go into something. We'll do the brain in an hour tomorrow. That will be it, the brain. The whole of the workings of this wonderful brain, one hour and that will be done.

Laughter offers a way of coping, but more than that, of 'redefining power structures' and 'reclaiming a sense of collective identity' (McLaren, 1986, p. 161). It provides moral support, and boosts morale. It is a way of wounding enemies, making alliances, of drawing other, like-minded individuals into the struggle and winning them over to the discourse. In such ways do teachers seek to generate a form of power for themselves.

Appropriation

With a new professional discourse, we see resistance moving into 'appropriation'. One head viewed the National Curriculum

> as a baseline from which to grow, not to become slaves to it, but to actually use it and adapt it in the ways that suit our philosophy and don't perhaps narrow our outlook too much.

Submerged initially by overload and bureaucracy, they were finding that there were exciting things the school used to do which, with some ingenuity, they could still do, and which were 'completely justifiable in terms of the National Curriculum'. The head and deputy had produced two books on the teaching of science which both met specified attainment targets and preserved their vision of science as a living experience. The school was noted for the development of its school grounds, and this was proving a 'fantastic resource for the National Curriculum' across the whole range of subjects. The National Curriculum, in fact, 'has probably spurred us on to keep finding things out there to resource it'. This school was performing a difficult feat – accommodating a collection-code curriculum, consisting of compartmentalized contents, within an integrated philosophy. They had the advantage of a strong relational idea in their dedication to the environment, and a considerable power base in their distinctive ethos. This enabled them to take good advantage of the customary spaces in English education between the making and the implementation of policy (Vulliamy and Webb, 1993), widened further by the collective action of teachers which led to the Dearing modifications to the National Curriculum in 1994.

This school had a distinctive ethos, from which the teachers drew considerable strength. They were generating a focus of power from below – which involves a notion of 'power with' rather than 'power over' (Kreisberg, 1992). This is a strength based on 'relationships of co-operation, mutual support and equity' (Bloome and Willett, 1991, p. 208). Foucault has argued that power is a force that 'produces things, induces pleasure, forms knowledge, produces discourse' (Foucault, 1980, p. 119). In a school such as this one, the seat of power is the school ethos, established, compelling, legitimated and permeating every moment of the day. Individuals draw from it to sustain and develop their selves, and also contribute to it, thus consolidating and developing its power. Power is enforced through discourse – through the new articulation, and through continual reminders like 'That's what it's all about'. It would be a mistake to underestimate the power of the state, or to deny that in some respects teachers' work *has* become intensified. The collective resistance of all teachers is required if the general structures and policies are to be changed or modified. It was this that led to the concessions made by the government following the Dearing Review (Dearing, 1994). Into the spaces opened up by collective action individual schools can work to develop their own power base, and make their own appropriations.

Enrichment

It becomes possible, in some instances, to speak of 'enrichment' in creative teaching through the National Curriculum. One of our best examples of this was where one of our research team, an expert in the area, joined with a teacher to work collaboratively over the space of a term on teaching the prescribed subject, 'Ancient Greece'. The teacher was apprehensive about the history syllabus, since it was 'very much dictated from above', seemed to challenge her autonomy, and to preclude the 'wide-ranging topics' she was used to. What developed, however, was a typical 'critical event', with high levels of motivation, involvement, excitement, and educational gain for both children and teachers. The pupils were noted to have 'a fire in their eye, they do have excitement, they look forward to Thursdays'. The teacher felt they had 'sown the seeds of enthusiasm for history'. For the children it was 'Brilliant! The best topic we've ever done!' There was even a celebration at the end with a 'Greek Day', where the children experienced 'a kind of magic'. For the teacher, the collaboration made her 'a bit more adventurous'; it gave her 'a whole lot of extra insight'; made her 'look carefully at the way I teach, and think about it fairly hard'. It rekindled her enthusiasm after a less happy experience in the previous year's project. What this project told us was that there was nothing intrinsic in the government's legislation to preclude critical events or creative teaching. It was more a matter of resources – together with, of course, professional factors such as vision, ability and resolution. Given the right circumstances, these elements could transform constraint into opportunity.

Stress and burn-out

However, successful adaptation of one kind or another is not the total picture. We know, for example, that the number of teachers retiring early through ill-health or otherwise escalated sharply in the years following 1988 (MacLeod and Meikle, 1994). There were two such in our research. One had featured in the 'critical events' research. But if that event, celebrated in 1988, was the high point of his teaching career, the Education Reform Act, ironically of the same year, and its associated legislation, was the lowest. His strong aversion to the new head-teacher role, the burgeoning bureaucracy, a loss of confidence not only in the abilities but also the motives of those directing education, his time of life (57), and a strongly critical inspection, led him to review his position and conclude that there were better chances for self-fulfilment outside education. If he stayed within, there was the increasing, frightening prospect of self-ruination.

This is what happened to another head, who had led the fight for resistance in his school, and who, under the weight of his new responsibilities, his struggle for equal rights under the new arrangements and his own high standards, succumbed to burn-out at the age of 50. He commented:

> When you're trying to transform national orders to actually fit the needs of your pupils ... in the context of a single school that's a very fragile process, and one that can be knocked down very easily.

These cases remind us that creative teachers tread a very fine line. On the one side lies successful appropriation and enrichment; on the other, stress and burn-out (see Woods *et al.*, 1997, for further discussion of teacher stress in the National Curriculum). What makes the difference may be a delicate balance of factors attending the situation, notably school ethos and history, teacher culture, personal histories and careers and local support systems.

TEACHERS AS CARERS

At the heart of the approach of all these teachers is an ethic of 'care'. 'Caring' has featured prominently in primary education for some time, but some forms of it have come under strong criticism from several quarters in recent years. As enshrined in the child-centred ideology associated with the Plowden Report, it was condemned by the government and media in their 1992 assault on primary pedagogy (see Woods and Wenham, 1995) on the grounds of there being 'too much caring and not enough teaching' in our primary schools. This view received support from some academics. Alexander (1992), for example, argued that primary teachers were in the grip of a child-centred ideology which constrained their practice. Simon (1988) argued that there was an urgent need to prioritize the cognitive aspects of learning.

Caring is integral to the curriculum. It is not something reserved for 'off-task', informal interaction with pupils. As with the teachers observed by Acker (1995), our teachers used emotional connections with a view to extending, developing, encouraging and liberating the child, and to increasing choices. 'Caring' is one aspect of these emotional connections – an important but not the only one. Teachers saw the child as person, rather than as client or student as in the National Curriculum. They felt the National Curriculum left out many aspects of primary teachers' responsibilities, embracing the personal, social, emotional and intellectual development of children. They talked of 'mutual respect', being 'able to relate to other people', 'teaching children to be people', producing 'people who can cope', teaching 'the whole person'. A major complaint about the National Curriculum was:

> You can't overlay your plastic transparency ... tick it all off and
> say, there you are, sixteen, made a little person there, well done
> ... In many ways I've found it quite offensive to the art of actually
> teaching because it gives it a simplistic quality that it doesn't
> have.

The end product for them was not people 'filled full of facts', but 'reasonably well-educated, responsible, socially acceptable human beings'.

Some of their children in these inner-city schools were so 'battered and bruised emotionally when they came in that they don't ever have the feeling of being an emotional person'. Teachers wanted to 'bring out the best in each individual' so that they could feel a 'worthwhile person'. But such a person exists within a social context, and this valuing of individuals within the group sets up a tension, the handling of which one teacher described as a 'subtle art'. The central feature of this skill was to do with a group dynamic, generated by 'dealing with their feelings as individuals', a certain 'standard of discipline', the class 'feeling secure and happy'; and seeing learning as an emotional experience.

Berger and Luckmann (1967) conceive of children passing through two phases of socialization – primary and secondary. The first takes place under circumstances that are highly charged emotionally, involving strong attachment to significant others, such as parents. The latter involves the 'internalization of ... institution based "subworlds" ... the acquisition of role-specific knowledge' etc. (*ibid.*, p. 158). Consequently, some of the realities encountered by children at school are seen as 'artificial' in comparison to earlier ones they experienced as 'natural'. To counter this, teachers try to 'bring home' the content,

> by making [the realities] vivid (that is making them seem as alive as in the 'home world' of the child), relevant (that is linking them to the relevant structures already present in the 'home world'), and interesting (that is, inducing the attentiveness of the child to detach itself from its 'natural' objects to these more 'artificial' ones). (Berger and Luckmann, 1967, p. 163)

English primary schools have traditionally offered children a bridging experience between primary and secondary socialization, cultivating a caring, homely ambience as they enter the institutional world. Government policy in recent years, however, has made primary schools more like secondary schools, with the compartmentalization of the curriculum and vastly increased bureaucracy. For the moment, however, and certainly for the teachers in our study, the emotions are a major feature in learning situations. One way in which they are used is through establishing a common bond of humanity (Berlak and Berlak, 1981) to bridge the gap between primary and secondary socializations. A main feature of 'going with the flow' – a term we use to describe the teachers' process model of teaching – is its ability to capitalize on positive emotions. As one teacher commented

> A lot of it is to do with the children needing to bond with you or they don't care whether they work or not.

This can result in a lot of hard work, certainly, but also a great deal of 'fun' and 'enthusiasm'. But the common bond is not only related to emotional high points. Thus a teacher resolved a dispute within her class one day by drawing on experiences within her own family, making connections with the children through common feelings of distress, anger and anxiety.

Teachers constantly look for what one described as 'teachable moments', as when, for example, children discovered a toad on their way to school, which gave rise to many profitable activities and motivated some children who were usually difficult to control. Another teacher used emotional connections to good effect with a boy who had learning difficulties. He had found an injured cat and had taken it home to care for it. The teacher encouraged the boy to write about the cat and 'it was the first time he wrote sequentially – a significant marker of his development'. Children's knowledge, memories, feelings and experiences were frequently used as a basis, as when the children compared Bangladeshi and English homes, thus reflecting the ethnic composition of the class, during a science topic on homes.

During these 'teachable moments' and the establishing of 'common bonds', 'common knowledge' is produced. Edwards and Mercer (1987) refer to this as a contextual framework where the business of 'scaffolding' the children's learning development can take place. They deal with cognitive processes, but do not discuss the prominent part played by the emotions in generating 'common knowledge'. Our research has many examples of teachers generating excitement and interest, and using emotional connections to underpin children's work. One used the affective power of a poetic style to confirm the importance of what the children were doing. In this way, the cognitive 'scaffolding' is held together with emotional bonds.

The emotions have little place in the technical-rationalist, market-oriented reforms of the late 1980s and early 1990s; indeed, they are to be discouraged. But in a pedagogy dedicated to the development of the 'whole person', teaching is a moral business first and foremost, in the way Noddings (1992), Tom (1988), Elbaz (1992) and others describe. Quite apart from that, however, the child as student is seen as being dependent on the child as person. Teaching is a matter of communicating and connecting – through the emotions, through care, trust, respect, rapport. It features a great deal of fun, excitement and enthusiasm. Esteem is important – for self and for others. So is confidence and the removal of fear. Teachers have to 'unblock' children's barriers against the unknowns of secondary socialization before they can proceed, deploying a 'subtle art' in constructing or identifying 'teachable moments'. As with Acker's (1995, p. 33) teachers, therefore, these teachers are not to be seen as 'unthinking conduits of child-centred ideology or the requirements of the modern state, or as "caring too much" '. They 'made judgements based on experience and according to what worked' (*ibid.*). This is not a 'Mumsy discourse' (Burgess and Carter, 1992), but positive pedagogy. They are 'channelling into learning' and servicing 'going with the flow' in a moral enterprise that has a clear vision of the kind of society into which they would wish their pupils to progress.

CONCLUSION

Hargreaves (1994, p. 22) has argued that, 'without desire, teaching becomes arid and empty. It loses its meaning.' Unfortunately, desire, or teachers' and pupils' emotional involvement in teaching and learning, has not figured prominently in government educational policy, especially of late. Rather, during the 1980s and 1990s, the latter has been marked by an increasing emphasis upon rationality in teaching, the close delineation of ends to be achieved, summative assessment with which to measure success, and bureaucratic structures and processes with which to monitor the system. Teaching is in danger of losing its 'emotional heart', even more so since, in the preoccupation with cognition, it has never been properly identified. The same might be said for learning. However, some teachers, at least, are still managing to cultivate what they consider to be the 'subtle art of teaching'. It is in this area that teachers give an 'aesthetic form to their existence through their own productive work' (Foucault, 1979). What is it that enables these teachers to cope in this way when so many other teachers are labouring under the effects of intensification? Personal factors clearly play a large part, such as commitment, values and beliefs, experience, life history, personal qualities (for example, skill, knowledge, degrees of care); but there are strong support factors also, in the form of headteacher, colleagues, school culture and history generally, governors, parents – and especially pupils (see Jeffrey and Woods, 1996). We have tried to indicate the potential fruitfulness of this area, and of the qualitative approach to its study, in seeking to understand some of the more intangible, but highly significant, constituents of the art of teaching, still alive and well in some areas, despite the National Curriculum.

REFERENCES

Acker, S. (1995) Carry on caring: the work of women teachers. *British Journal of Sociology of Education*, **16**(1): 21–36.

Alexander, R. J. (1992) *Policy and Practice in Primary Education*. London: Routledge.

Apple, M. W. (1986) *Teachers and Texts: A Political Economy of Class and Gender Relations in Education*. New York: Routledge.

Berger, P. L. and Luckmann, T. (1967) *The Social Construction of Reality: A Treatise in the Sociology of Knowledge*. Harmondsworth: Penguin.

Berlak, A. and Berlak, H. (1981) *The Dilemmas of Schooling*. London: Methuen.

Bloome, D. and Willett, J. (1991) Towards a micropolitics of classroom interaction. In J. Blase (ed.), *The Politics of Life in Schools*. London: Sage.

Burgess, H. and Carter, B. (1992) Bringing out the best in people: teacher training and the 'real teacher'. *British Journal of Sociology of Education*, **13**(2): 349–59.

Campbell, R. J. and Neill, S. R. St J. (1994) *Curriculum Reform at Key Stage 1 – Teacher Commitment and Policy Failure*. Harlow: Longman Group.

Clayden, E., Desforges, C., Mills, C. and Rawson, W. (1994) Authentic activity and learning. *British Journal of Educational Studies*, **42**(2): 163–72.

Dearing, R. (1994) *Review of the National Curriculum: Final Report*. London: HMSO.

Edwards, D. and Mercer, N. (1987) *Common Knowledge: The Development of Understanding in the Classroom*. London: Methuen.

Elbaz, F. (1992) Hope, attentiveness, and caring for difference: the moral voice in teaching. *Teaching and Teacher Education*, **8**(5/6): 421–32.

Elliott, J. (1991) *Action Research for Educational Change*. Buckingham: Open University Press.

Foucault, M. (1979) *A History of Sexuality*. Harmondsworth: Penguin.

Foucault, M. (1980) *Power/Knowledge: Selected Interviews and other Writings* (ed. C Gordon). New York: Pantheon.

Hargreaves, A. (1994) *Changing Teachers, Changing Times: Teachers' Work and Culture in the Post-modern Age*. London: Cassell.

Holt, J. (1970) *The Underachieving School*. Harmondsworth: Penguin.

Jackson, P. W. (1992) *Untaught Lessons*. New York: Teachers' College Press.

Jeffrey, R. and Woods, P. (1996) The relevance of creative teaching: pupils' views. In A. Pollard, D. Thiessen and A. Filer (eds), *Children and their Curriculum: The Perspectives of Primary and Elementary School Children*. London: Falmer Press.

Kreisberg, S. (1992) *Transforming Power: Domination, Empowerment and Education.* Albany: State University of New York Press.

MacLeod, D. and Meikle, J. (1994) Education changes 'making heads quit'. *Guardian*, 1 September, p. 6.

McLaren, P. (1986) *Schooling as a Ritual Performance.* London: Routledge and Kegan Paul.

Nias, J. (1989) *Primary Teachers Talking.* London: Routledge.

Noddings, N. (1992) *The Challenge to Care in Schools: An Alternative Approach to Education.* New York: Teachers' College Press.

Pollard, A., Broadfoot, P., Croll, P., Osborn, M. and Abbott, D. (1994) *Changing English Primary Schools? The Impact of the Education Reform Act at Key Stage One.* London: Cassell.

Simon, B. (1988) Why no pedagogy in England? In R. Dale, R. Fergusson and A. Robinson (eds), *Frameworks for Teaching.* London: Hodder and Stoughton.

Tom, A. (1988) Teaching as a moral craft. In R. Dale, R. Fergusson, R. and A. Robinson (eds), *Frameworks for Teaching.* London: Hodder & Stoughton. (See also Tom, A. (1984) *Teaching as a Moral Craft.* New York: Longman.)

Vulliamy, G. and Webb, R. (1993) Progressive education and the National Curriculum: findings from a global education research project. *Educational Review*, **45**(1): 21–41.

Weedon, C. (1987) *Feminist Practice and Poststructuralist Theory.* London: Basil Black-well.

Woods, P. (1990) *Teacher Skills and Strategies.* Lewes: Falmer Press.

Woods, P. (1993) *Critical Events in Teaching and Learning.* London: Falmer Press.

Woods, P. (1995) *Creative Teachers in Primary Schools.* Buckingham: Open University Press.

Woods, P. and Jeffrey, R. (1996) *Teachable Moments: The Art of Teaching in Primary Schools.* Buckingham: Open University Press.

Woods, P. and Wenham, P. (1995) Politics and pedagogy: a case study in appropriation. *Journal of Education Policy*, **10**(2): 119–43.

Woods, P., Jeffrey, R., Troman, G. and Boyle, M. (1997) *Restructuring Schools, Reconstructing Teachers: Responding to Change in the Primary School.* Buckingham: Open University Press.

Chapter 6

Teachers' Subject Cultures: Accommodating the National Curriculum in Maths and Technology

Murray Saunders and Terry Warburton

INTRODUCTION

This chapter is based on interviews with maths and technology teachers conducted as part of the ESRC-funded project on the Professional Culture of
Teachers and the Secondary School Curriculum (PCT project, see Helsby *et al.*,
1997). The analysis illustrates the way in which teachers' experience of the
National Curriculum differs markedly within these two subject groups. On the
one hand we can typify the experience of maths teachers as one of continuity and
relative stability, while on the other hand that of technology teachers is one of
change and instability. We argue that these differences are due in part to the
nature of 'subject culture' (Siskin, 1994) as it has evolved over recent years.

We have noted elsewhere (Saunders, 1995) that 'culture', in the context of
education, has been described using a collection of terms. Hargreaves, for
example, in an overview of the way in which the notion of culture might inform
our understanding of teachers' practices, suggests a distinction between the
'form' and 'content' of culture. The content of culture he describes as existing
attitudes, values and ways of doing things whilst the form of culture is embodied
in patterns of relationship and association between teachers who demonstrate
particular sets of cultural content (Hargreaves, 1992). This approach to culture
points to the way in which subject teachers share knowledge and beliefs about
teaching a particular subject, as well as a consciousness of how their collective
identity intersects with the legislative changes in the position and internal
structure of their subject promoted by the National Curriculum. Early work in
the sociology of the curriculum (see, for example, Young, 1971) suggests other
potential differences in the experience of teaching maths and technology which in
turn affect the way the evolution of the National Curriculum has made an impact
on teachers' work.

The different curricular structures and practices which are associated with
the two areas have grown up through custom and have produced a 'teacher
experience' of contrasting continuity and clarity of subject boundary. Maths, on
the one hand, has a subject matter which, while not static, has a long and
comparatively stable history. The more unstable dimension of its subject practices has been in the ebb and flow of different teaching and learning strategies

(see Cooper, 1984). This stability of subject matter, however, is not an absolute, but should be understood in relation to the way the content of other subjects might change over time and be constructed differently across cultures. At the same time, metaphorically, its subject 'persona' is highly distinguishable from other subjects and what counts as maths knowledge has remained relatively non-negotiable as far as the learner is concerned. Therefore debates have tended to be in the domain of teaching and learning method rather than on what constitutes the maths knowledge base.

Technology, on the other hand, has a very different profile. In an important sense it was not until the advent of the Technical and Vocational Education Initiative (TVEI), after Margaret Thatcher's surprise statement in the House of Commons in November 1982, that technology as part of the school curriculum entered the general discourse of UK teachers. Up until then, there was a collection of subject areas in the school curriculum, for example metalwork, woodwork, craft, art, home economics, textiles and technical drawing, which had more or less discrete and agreed approaches. Alongside these areas were the emerging business and office practice courses which included some information technology (IT) elements. The TVEI emphasized and promoted the development and discussion of a wide range of curricula which attempted to reconstruct an approach to technology which integrated, recast and reformed the relationship between the cluster of curricular areas we outline above. However, these developments were uneven and hugely varied in scope (see Barnes *et al.*, 1987; Dale 1985; Saunders, 1990) Further, the TVEI promoted the deconstruction and problematization of the idea of technology beyond the confines of those areas on which it drew in practice (see, for example, the work of Layton *et al.*, 1989). With the publication of continuously revised versions of the technology curriculum through National Curriculum orders, overlaying the more positive school-based explorations and negotiations emanating from the TVEI, we have a subject area characterized by the highest levels of change, still active debates about its parameters and constitutive elements, and a group of teachers who have been engaged in a long struggle to cohere and legitimate their work in relation to other areas of the curriculum.

These differences are embodied in interviews with teachers of maths and technology. Maths teachers suggest the way their position in the curriculum has been confirmed, indeed affirmed, by National Curriculum guidance. They seem imbued with a consensus on what the maths curriculum is and how it is distinguished from other areas of the curriculum. In contrast, the continued sense of instability, change and debate on what the technology curriculum is, expressed in many of our interviews with technology teachers, predates the National Curriculum and is axiomatic of a curriculum area for which it is difficult to determine a clear sense of boundary and definition. The evolution of these contrasting subject areas we believe has produced differences in subject preoccupations which form a shared internal agenda for the way teachers have responded to the National Curriculum.

We will extend the notion of the culture of teaching, identified by Little and McLaughlin (1993), in which teacher–teacher interactions might be the basis of subject-based 'professional communities'. Thus the intensity of the ties between teachers of the same subject, the inclusivity of teachers within subject cultures and the common orientation of their values and beliefs about the teaching of the subject are indicative of the strength of a subject culture. The data presented here support the argument that the differences between the two subjects in the evolution of their subject boundaries, and the way the National Curriculum has been accommodated by teachers, results in differences in the basis on which inclusivity and orientation of the subject cultures in particular has developed. In this way maths and technology teachers differ substantially in their responses to the intervention of the National Curriculum. However, as our data suggest, alongside the broad differences between the two subjects are different cultural nuances or threads within the subjects, what we have called oppositional threads. Little (1993) describes how teachers of different subjects might constitute sub-communities of practice in schools. Her analysis focuses on the distinctive cultures associated with teaching vocationally oriented subjects in comparison with those conventionally identified as 'academic'. These cultures are influenced greatly by perceptions of relative status and provide a cultural frame for action and belief. Our data echo these broad tendencies but also suggests that, even within subjects, cultures evolve and compete but the *constitutive elements* of the debate are understood and recognizable by the community of subject practitioners. More specifically, comparative analysis shows stronger *sub*-communities amongst technology teachers than maths teachers resulting in greater diversity in technology teachers' response to the National Curriculum. In these circumstances, how might teachers, in the two contrasting areas, talk about their strategic responses to the National Curriculum?

The approach we develop in this analysis is to depict 'teachers' talk' as *'narrative'*. The nature of their responses to prompts and questions during interview, particularly in the context of the style of interviews adopted in the project, was discursive and conversational, and was analogous to *recounting* experience and feelings about curriculum matters. We suggest that the way teachers structure and form narrative within subjects has a commonality regardless of subject subdivisions or the gender of the teacher. When asked to talk about topics and dimensions of teaching their subject, clearly teachers within a subject area do not make identical responses. But they do choose to engage in versions of a *narrative theme* which may be multilayered within an interview. In our example, a narrative theme might concern, for example, the values attached to subject expertise or levels of subject knowledge. Narrative themes are *resonant* and form what Weber and Mitchell (1995) call the 'cumulative cultural text' of the teacher. Part of the cumulative cultural texts for teachers are resonant narratives about the National Curriculum and its impact. This point is important because it is the recognizability or resonance of a theme which forms the basis of a common language of experience within a subject culture. Narrative themes form a thematic agenda which binds a practitioner group together. Just as a debate on agenda items contains diverse and contrasting positions, so do expressions of narrative themes. The point is that participants recognize and understand the agenda, thus forming, as Little (1993) has it, its orientation and degree of inclusivity. One final introductory point about the form narration takes is to emphasize that teachers' conversations may take up quite oppositional stances within a narrative theme. In this sense, while still resonant, a particular value or interpretation expressed by one teacher within a narrative theme might completely contradict another. The point is that both views are thematically bounded.

For the purposes of this chapter, we have chosen to analyse interviews which formed a large part of the PCT database. In summary, the interviews were semi-structured and attempted to establish an understanding of the term 'professional' with the teacher, and to apply this notion to issues associated with the teaching of their subject area and the changes they had experienced in their working lives (for an account of this methodology see Saunders, 1995).

The analysis of the maths teachers' interviews is based on an inspection of the notes and interview transcripts of 55 interviews with maths teachers, of whom 30 are male and 25 female. The analysis of the technology teachers' interviews is based on interviews with 52 technology teachers, of whom 27 are male and 25 are female.

The differing histories of maths and technology in terms of subject identity and the evolution of respective subject boundaries has resulted in different patterns of, and sites for, practitioner solidarity. We contend that this is demonstrated in terms of both the public process of defining, consenting to and contesting what is inclusive within subject cultures and the public/private orientation of values and beliefs. Consequently, teachers' narrative discourse about how the National Curriculum affects them and continues to shape and re-form their sense of subject identity, provides evidence, in mediated form, which charts these sites, preoccupations and values. Teachers' narratives indicate where useful connections are made between the individual, the National Curriculum and subject culture. They also allow insights about how habitual practices or more novel and reforming activity can enable or disable accommodation of the National Curriculum as a mechanism for defining subject boundaries and teachers' sense of place.

TECHNOLOGY TEACHERS

Within the general domain of technology curriculum design are three narrative themes which are particularly worthy of note. The expression of the first, which is about *consultation*, is resonant across subject culture boundaries. The other two are distinctive to technology teachers and fall into two broad categories, the *philosophy underpinning the subject* and *managing integration*.

Consultation

Teachers' feelings about the consultation process in the implementation of the National Curriculum is a theme which is resonant with many teachers, not just technologists, and is expressed by a number of technology teachers of both sexes. Thus a narrative theme which refers to the issue of 'consultation' is linked to a view that consultation was lacking but also presents the notion that the outcome would have been better had teachers been consulted. For example, narratives are developed concerning 'policy-makers having no recent experience in the class-room' (teacher 005). The same teacher argues that, as a consequence of this, rewriting material is a constant task and 'makes for "intensification" and "depro-fessionalization" ' (see below). Teacher 090 cites a further consequence of 'teachers not being talked to' as the production of 'unwieldy documents of 90 per cent drivel and 10 per cent quality'. Those compiling the National Curriculum are seen as 'bigwigs' (teacher 162) and curriculum content is described as 'unrealis-tic'. Teacher 028 develops this theme with several resonant strands. She states that technology is 'the subject that the government has made the most mess of. We haven't had any stability for five or six years.' She goes on, 'All the changes and upheaval has [*sic*] lowered the status of the subject.' Concluding that 'the old orders for technology have now thankfully turned full circle', she remarks that the National Curriculum has been 'developed by ex-teachers or those loosely connected to education'. The whole concept was 'a good idea' but the practical implications have not been 'thought through'.

Underpinning philosophy

It is widely perceived that there is a 'conflict of interests' (teacher 044) between the craft philosophy and the design-and-make philosophy, and that the National Curriculum has 'chopped and changed' the notion of technology it wants to promote. This is of fundamental concern to technology teachers as it determines the way they think of, plan and execute ideas and actions about how to imple-ment the National Curriculum and accommodate its imperatives. Put simply, the craft philosophy promotes the acquisition of skills related to a particular craft. This process centres upon the use of specific tools to make a range of traditional artefacts within a distinct craft discipline such as woodwork, metal-work or textiles. Alternatively, the design philosophy promotes the acquisition of principles involved in the design-and-make process which are thus applicable to and transferable between, both traditional craft disciplines and more novel technological subject identities.

How this argument is conceived by technology teachers is typically repre-sented by teacher 049. As the manufacturing base of the economy has been eroded, then 'craft' is perceived as of 'less status'. He is firm in the belief that 'skills should precede design' but describes the aim of technology as 'making children fit, able, multi-skilled and adaptable'. Articulating this theme differently, teacher 110 states of this aim that 'Technology is about using tools to provide solutions to problems'. Teacher 165 depicts this as 'the thinking is the same, the materials are different'. Many teachers emphasize the link between curriculum subject and the wider economy, though there is some ambivalence about the 'rightness' of this approach:

> There isn't the concentration on depth of knowledge and
> understanding. There is less emphasis on craft skills. Students are
> now allowed more scope. There is more emphasis on products
> industry and planning, I have my doubts about the commercial
> dimension. It is difficult expecting students to apply things
> without background. (female home economics teacher 181)

Such ambivalence is shared: teacher 088 remarks, 'I'm not sure we are in the business of training people for jobs or not.' Even within narrower subject distinctions this is represented: for example, one female home economics teacher relates 'the problem of home economics is understanding where we are going'. This though is mitigated by a very strong sense of purpose. A resonant narrative strand for home economics teachers, particularly for those operating in areas of social deprivation, is that 'Food has a very strong part to play. Children from poor backgrounds are not well fed.'

Recently, however, the perception that technology teachers are working with shifting emphases in the underpinning philosophy of National Curriculum is expressed by the experience of yet further change. Teacher 162, a female food teacher and head of department, feels that the emphasis on a particular philosophy has 'come full circle' and that now 'technology is very workshop oriented'. Similarly, teacher 070, a home economist with 25 years' experience, states that the 'philosophy has reverted' and that she is now 'less confident' about the place of her specialism and her identity relating to it. This feeling of return to a more traditional stance is not, however, shared to the same degree by the male technology teachers associated with particular craft identities, who still perceive an appreciable loss of status. For example, in the opinion of a male head of department, with 25 years' experience,

> Hard technology has been watered down. We now have a more
> design-centred population – skills take a bashing.

Indeed, this perceived slippage in status can be expressed in various resonant ways, as teacher 145 says: 'Craft gives technology a banging in nails mentality.'

Teachers hold different opinions and values about their identity and work. In their talk it is culturally coherent to both hold and represent these differences, providing they are expressed within unwritten socially constructed boundaries. For example, in talking about the philosophy underpinning the way technology as a subject is conceived, teachers make several points concerning how it is taught, how it is valued and how teachers' sense of identity is affected. In the following extract, teacher 049, an experienced male deputy head, relates the following concerning his reaction to teachers' general lack of recognition by others and elaborates an interesting balance between the losses and gains of the broader design and business emphases in the National Curriculum and the previous stable but low status position of the 'craft teacher':

> [Technology teachers] ... were probably deemed far less a professional teacher then than they are now. Well that's one thing that's shifted in the opposite direction in a way, in that at that time you were a craft teacher, which was looked down upon in a way, but upon reflection, being able to transmit a craft to people was in fact something to be quite proud of and that's one of the things that's missing now, because you're not able to do that.

This teacher values highly his own sense of skill and his ability to transmit it. Alternatively, teacher 005 expresses the same theme with the following narrative thread:

> My headteacher wants my department to deliver woodwork and metalwork. I am resisting that based upon my professional judgement. My professional judgement is that the skills and disciplines of traditional woodwork and metalwork are inappropriate for the needs of my students when they go out into the wider community. The argument formulated is that he... his concept of CDT is a very traditional one and in my professional opinion out of date. My argument with him is if I worked next to a shipyard that required welders, metalworkers, carpenters and so on, I would be able to legitimate my curriculum being traditional. I don't. I work in an area where my students will leave to work on computers; they will work for electronics firms, they might work in lightweight engineering firms, so they need a whole range of skills, knowledge and understanding.

So, both teachers express the same theme differently. However, the theme is resonant in both depictions and refers to a sense of professional values and worth obtaining in technology as a consequence of subject culture evolution peculiar to technology teachers. On the one hand is an expression of the subject culture broadly compatible with the broadening of emphasis in the National Curriculum, on the other is the sense of loss associated with the de-emphasis on craft skill. Such a latitude for oppositional values and beliefs would not be as appropriate in the more inclusively bounded and less contested value orientation of the mathematics culture.

Managing integration

As we note above, the National Curriculum reinforced the movement towards the integration of disparate subjects within the framework of 'technology'. In teacher narratives about managing integration two particular themes predominate. The first takes the form of a general commentary about the process of integration encompassing its pros and cons. Descriptive organizational terms such as 'merry-go-round', 'circus' and 'rota system' frequently act as a prelude to complaints about lack of time, lack of training, increased stress and pressure, and feelings of being undervalued. Food studies teachers in particular (in our sample all women, which is not uncommon more widely) relate narratives which indicate the insecurity they felt as their 'subject' came under threat as various expressions of technology were published in National Curriculum orders. One home economics (HE) teacher comments, 'I felt "home ec" was going to be wiped out but now it's part of design technology.' Another remarks, 'They tried to cut Food out three times. But it's a basic requirement of life.'

When talking about how integration has been managed, in general opinion tends to be in a fairly negative vein. Such comments as 'It's a disaster' (male IT teacher 011) and 'It's been an unnatural evolution – It's all about the balance of power in schools' (male teacher 067) are not uncommon. The fact that teachers feel they have been 'forced to adopt different teaching styles and change their ways of working' as they attempt to accommodate the demands of the National Curriculum, leaves some teachers with a sense of resentment.

However, when talking more specifically, there emerges a second, strong and resonant thread concerning how the process activity of integrating National Curriculum technology has imposed a sense of discipline and teamwork. It has, in fact, played an important role in reforming the identity of technology teachers in respect to their subject. While, on the one hand, most teachers feel that 'Technology has become a general term for several subject disciplines', actually making the subject 'happen' coherently, as part of the National Curriculum, has been a major source of achievement and something to be proud about and has created a sense of subject solidarity. As teacher 083 puts it, 'organized chaos takes a good deal of organizing'. This sense of working together through chaos, instability, disorder and indeed adversity, to create a working and useful curriculum is a solid foundation. 'What we have in common is a necessary alliance', is how teacher 145 puts it.

These patterns of association and collaboration are valued by teachers as important signs of shared identity and professional worth. Teachers utter many such commentaries, for example:

> We have worked together. There are regular meetings. (teacher 165)
> We work as a team while respecting others' opinions and beliefs. (teacher 090)

> This has made the department 'gel' as a team. (teacher 154)
> We help each other 'troubleshoot' to develop expertise. (teacher 090)

One female food technology teacher, with 16 years' experience, sums up the results of the process succinctly:

> The National Curriculum has changed how you perceive yourself in two ways. First, the way you see yourself and second the way the school sees you. (teacher 131)

By this mechanism, more technology teachers are defining a sense of 'professional identity' in the emergent boundaries of technology as a subject in action. Knowing how to make the subject 'work' is receiving greater status as a unifying catalyst for inclusivity and orientation of 'professional' values amongst technology teachers than the sense of knowing what in relation to subject identity and content. In this way the ties which bind teachers of technology into a 'professional community' with a subject-unique curricular understanding are in the domain of organizing and integrating diverse knowledge and skill bases. One food technology teacher relates a sense of place that could equally well have been depicted by any teacher for any other technology sub-discipline:

> The National Curriculum has affected HE teachers as it has located their role in technology. (teacher 093)

MATHS TEACHERS

It is interesting to note that the agenda of themes from the maths teachers' interviews differs markedly from the technology teachers. The collection of publicly accessible and resonant themes reflects the more stable position of maths within the changes and pressures which characterize the period since the Education Reform Act of 1988. In the first theme we analyse ways in which maths teachers talk about the values that frame the broadest aims of their maths teaching, values that seem to both predate and transcend the demands of the National Curriculum.

Subject values

Within the theme of curricular design there were several references in the interviews to 'subject values'. The first of these concerns maths teachers as subject experts or having a 'feel' for the subject . The theme of 'maths teacher as subject expert' yields a number of contrasting threads within individual interviews. This notion of expertise is linked to being able to operate effectively in the classroom but perhaps more importantly helps to define a sense of identity in the teacher of maths which somehow sets them apart from other subject teachers. This thread is expressed by a female teacher (001) as she describes how she sees herself first as a maths teacher with a 'prime aim' of producing numeracy. She feels that maths underpins many of the other subjects. She expresses this sense of subject identity strongly by saying

> I suppose deep down I possibly do [feel more professional] to be honest, in other words I'm a bit elitist about maths. I would try not to let it show but I see it as a subject which some people can't tackle and I also see myself as being a woman tackling maths.

Male teacher 019 goes on to describe his sense of values and the subject identity of maths and maths teachers: 'There is something more difficult about maths.' This perception is graphically illustrated by a contrast he draws between teaching maths and the less framed and classified area of personal and social development (PSD):

> One assumes that 55 out of 60 members of staff are comfortable teaching PSD. But if I went and told them they had to teach maths next week the reaction would be different. They would say 'I don't like doing it', 'I haven't been trained'.

Female teacher 013 similarly separates maths from other subjects by saying to us that

> there are enormous differences between the subjects; maths is considered rightly so to be very important, therefore we *have* to get them through it. Parents come to a parents' evening, they will never miss out the maths teacher.

While this notion of maths teacher as expert and the nature of maths as a 'hard' subject was celebrated, thus confirming its high status (see Little, 1993, p. 140), the theme was not shared by all our interviewees. Female teacher 084, for example, considers that

> You've got to like maths , I'm not sure you have to be absolutely brilliant at maths. You've got to be one step ahead of whoever you're teaching.

She considered pedagogy as probably more important than deep subject knowledge:

> you've got to make it more interesting and find more exciting ways to put it across, there's lots of times when you can actually make it more relevant.

We will return to the idea of relevance later. What all these teachers suggest in their comments is that the subject matter of maths is 'known' to them and to their colleagues as a relatively stable body of knowledge, and familiarity or sympathy with it constitutes an important value.

Linked to the observations made by teachers 019 and 084 above is the narrative theme concerning the personal traits of 'patience' and 'explanatory competence'. For example, female teacher 013 talks about this characteristic in the light of maths having the status of a core subject and thus conferring extra pressure on the maths teachers:

> I suppose very importantly in mathematics is giving the time to explain, I mean it, what makes maths a very difficult subject to teach is that everything has to be explained.

Similarly, male teacher 076 observes that after a clear knowledge of maths

> there is nothing special about mathematics teaching, you need generic qualities of patience and an ability to relate to pupils not to alienate them, which is a particular danger in maths because it can be seen as girl unfriendly; people have maths phobia.

The perception of maths as a 'difficult' subject prompts another narrative theme, which is to counteract stereotypical views of what learning maths is like, particularly the idea that it is dry and unenjoyable. The following teachers, for example, aimed to make maths 'enjoyable':

> I want children to enjoy maths but I want as a responsible professional for them to be able to cope with it adequately in outside life, so I want to give them enough mathematical knowledge to survive outside. (male teacher 112)

> There is pressure for our department to change, our first aim is for pupils to enjoy maths and for it to be accessible, also to maximize results for all pupils ... That is the target, that pupils enjoy doing maths, spend time doing areas that they enjoy that aren't necessarily directly exam focused. (male teacher 092)

The imperative which prompts these teachers to 'make maths fun' might result from the explicit nature of the criteria for inclusion of specific knowledge as an essential part of the curriculum and is accompanied by the perception that it is a conceptually difficult subject which might in turn produce a negative response from the pupils. Some teachers saw this response as derived from low motivation often through repeated failure. Another outcome of this perception is a narrative theme which identifies an imperative to make maths 'relevant'. This imperative is also supported by the perception of maths promulgated in the Cockcroft report, developed through initiatives such as TVEI and to some extent in the National Curriculum. There is an interesting tension in the culture of maths teachers between the identification of maths as a 'hard' subject – an important dimension of the celebratory sense of subject identity discussed earlier – and an egalitarian value, supported by the National Curriculum, which stresses the need for all young people to have access to the same core elements irrespective of their inclinations. This latter imperative puts the onus on teachers to come up with appropriate pedagogy which, in the following extract, is represented by the term 'relevance'. In effect, the reference to relevance is about the attempts by these teachers to undermine the abstract nature of maths by making it more 'concrete' and connected to day to day practice:

> You need to have a knowledge of maths but this is not sufficient; you need to show its relevance, which means good communication skills. It's more than just teaching your subject, isn't it? There's a caring side to teaching children maths. (female teacher 052)

Perhaps the most important point about this extract is that for this teacher at least, content, justification and prescription about the teaching of maths transcend National Curriculum directives in the maths area and are not tied to a temporal context. They embody a perception of the nature of maths as a stable, almost irrefutable body of knowledge and to some extent as a set of practices.

We have discerned four interlocking themes at the heart of maths subject values. The first theme is the relationship between the teacher and maths as a subject for study. While the narrative threads we have included differ on the extent to which teachers need to be mathematicians or maths experts, there is continuity in an agreement that there is a need to have some empathy or 'feel' for the subject in order to respond to pupils' needs and to use creative pedagogic styles.

The second, third and fourth themes concern the way maths as a subject values concerning the relationship between pupils and teacher. The second theme concerns the qualities or personal characteristics of the maths teacher who, according to the perception of maths as conceptually difficult, has to display patience and high degrees of explanatory capability in order to 'put it over' to the pupils. The third theme forms not only an antidote to the negative stereotypical expectations teachers feel pupils have of the maths area, but also a pedagogical value which asserts that pupils having a positive experience are more likely to learn, particularly in intellectually demanding subjects – i.e. maths can be 'fun' and enjoyable. The final theme is strongly associated with the pedagogic value identified above and a sense of the 'use value' of maths in that it should furnish young people with resources to pursue everyday life effectively. In other words maths should be 'relevant'. All these themes constitute a subject cultural agenda on which the National Curriculum has made little impact.

What counts as Maths

There was a strong theme in the interviews which concerned the stability of the maths curriculum. We note above the theme of strong subject identity in maths teachers. We may add to this a sense of solidity and confidence in the boundary of maths, particularly in relation to other areas of the curriculum. To use Bernsteinian terms (Bernstein, 1971), the maths curriculum continues to be perceived by teachers, despite the National Curriculum guidelines both pre- and post-Dearing, as highly framed (as a given non-negotiable knowledge area) and classified (clearly distinguishable, recognizable and bounded in relation to other subjects). What counts as maths has remained relatively constant despite high levels of policy activity; it is clearly distinguishable from other subjects, and teachers prescribe, through the schemes of work, what counts as maths knowledge *in the classroom*. This theme yields some interesting threads, which articulate a sense of 'subject confidence' and fidelity:

> If they start cutting down on the National Curriculum, which is what's in focus at the moment, it wouldn't ever be mathematics. (female teacher 013)

> In the classroom I don't feel affected at all, it's outside where you feel the pressures ... with reporting and recording ... Syllabus content is very little different than we've had before, it's just the peripherals that seem senseless, because we are so short of time in some areas. (female teacher 123)

These extracts illustrate a theme of continuity of content or maths knowledge. We might say that the National Curriculum impact on the subject knowledge of maths has been minimal. To some extent this is predictable and reinforces a strong sense of subject certainty maths teachers might already have, particularly when they compare themselves with colleagues working in other areas of the curriculum. The identification of maths as a core National Curriculum subject further emphasizes the solidity of the position of maths in a school curriculum and *de facto* the position of maths teachers. As one teacher puts it,

> the National Curriculum has affected the different status of different subjects with making maths and English and science the core subjects and the other subjects non-core subjects. (male teacher 153)

What counts as teaching Maths

While the subject content of the maths curriculum might be seen as stable overall, a narrative theme emerged in which the decision-making 'space' on maths content might lie not on *what* to teach but on *when* and *how*. It would be a mistake to assume that what counts as maths knowledge in the context of the school curriculum has always been characterized by a high level of consensus, as the work of Cooper suggests (Cooper, 1984, p. 51). In his discussion of the development of the Schools Mathematics Project (SMP) he describes the way in which modern algebraic approaches were attacked by commentators as ' the enfeeblement of mathematical skills'. There was no evidence in our interviews that the 'paradigm wars' of the 1950s and 1960s between what Cooper calls classical/pure and modern/applied perspectives were still simmering under the surface, although our general line of questioning may have precluded such considerations. However, while the boundaries and content of the maths curriculum might be 'given' and not subject to teacher debate, we might find a site for considerable decision-making and variance with the *when and the how* of maths teaching, as this interchange demonstrates:

> *Can you picture or somehow describe the sorts of decisions you can make and the sort you can't?*

> Well I can't make the decision on what to teach, I can't make the decision to teach Pythagoras, but I can make the decision about whether we'll teach it as an investigation or whether we will teach it as bookwork and this is how you do it.

> *Right.*

> Yes, yes, but each teacher will teach it differently. We don't have, our schemes of work don't say, you must teach using this method. (female teacher 180)

We are faced then with a situation in which the National Curriculum may have confirmed a knowledge base which already had tacit agreement amongst the key stakeholders. An enforced curriculum to which maths teachers could not agree is clearly *not* the problem. For some, the offence might be in solidifying, by central dictat, agreement already enforced by exam boards and shaped by syllabuses, which had been for some time a matter of tacit consensus, a *de facto* National Curriculum within the domain, on which maths teachers built their sense of 'professional' expertise and identity. As one teacher put it with reference to the maths curriculum in Years 10 and 11:

> the content in mathematics has always been there, it was just called an exam syllabus (male teacher 033).

However, while some teachers echoed this, other narrative threads view the National Curriculum in a more positive light, particularly those who did not share this sense of tacit subject consensus. Their perception was that the framework provided by the National Curriculum *gave* a curriculum structure within which flexibility and choice of approach was still possible, indeed that it was enhanced. Female teacher 180, cited above, considered, for example, that the National Curriculum had increased decision-making by asking teachers to make more judgements about *how* they teach elements of the maths curriculum by using a wide range of resources rather than plodding through a textbook. In her case these considerations had been undertaken in association with her colleagues. In providing a broad frame, her view was that National Curriculum guidance could not be addressed by reference to a single source but provided an imperative for teachers to cast a wider net in search of resources for planning schemes of work:

> I think this one [post-Dearing guidance] has some major
> advantages. When I started teaching, now this may not be true of
> all schools, we worked through SMP and we worked through them
> from chapter 1 in book A to chapter whatever it was in book Z
> without missing anything out at all – we just worked through
> them from the beginning to the end and we did everything and we
> panicked if we didn't. I actually think there is more imagination in
> teaching now because we specifically don't have a set textbook so
> we can sit around our table at lunch time and say 'Well, I am
> teaching Pythagoras and I thought I'd do it by investigation; does
> anybody have a good idea of a book we could use?' So I think that
> maths teachers talk more about maths now than they ever used
> to. (female teacher 180)

The theme which identified *structure* or *guideline* as a useful contribution
from the National Curriculum is expressed variously by our interviewees. This
theme often contained narrative threads based on a distinction between pre- and
post-Dearing versions of the idea of structure. The former structure was understood as more restrictive and prescriptive than now. The present structure was
described by one teacher as 'formless' in comparison. Another teacher (female
teacher 063) makes a similar point but senses a remaining stricture:

> No I don't think it [the National Curriculum] is as rigid as it used
> to be. I think things have slackened off a little bit and it's not so
> much 'you will do this' it's more 'these are the possibilities, take it'.
> I still don't think we get quite as much choice as we did, say, ten
> years ago in how and what we teach. There's this guideline all the
> time that you can't really go too far outside.

The sense of structure and prescription and corresponding support or resistance
is of course expressed differently from teacher to teacher depending on the
specific circumstances of their experience. The nuances in these threads are
illustrated in the following extracts:

> I think maths lends itself to something like the National
> Curriculum because it is a cumulative subject. There are certain
> things you've got to understand before you can go onto a next
> stage ... it also lends itself to the recording and it certainly eases
> transition from one school to another. (female teacher 147)

> We have to make sure that we cover it because we've got an
> obligation to do that and in a way it doesn't allow us the licence to
> select topics and lay on the topics that maybe we would have
> selected to give more time to. (female teacher 163)

> I welcome the National Curriculum; it does enhance my
> professionalism. To be able to turn to the booklet or the sheet or

> whatever that we produce from the National Curriculum, as I say,
> at this time of year this is where we should be using the targets
> that we should be aiming at and these are the levels we should be
> getting towards. (male teacher 136)

These extracts are illustrative of the way maths teachers have been able to make useful connections between the National Curriculum and their own work and practice. It suggests that there was a strong sense of continuity and recognizability in the maths guidelines which enabled these teachers to accommodate the structure relatively unproblematically.

SYNTHESIS

This chapter has focused on themes associated with the way in which maths and technology teachers' narratives depict the impact of National Curriculum guidelines on their sense of subject culture and identity. In focusing on this general theme we note that technology and maths teachers have rather different pre-occupations. The emphasis of the extracts from interviews with technology teachers tends to reflect the process of reformation and reconstruction they have experienced during the last decade or so. For example, the threads which reflect a concern with the fundamental composition of the technology curriculum have an oppositional flavour. While one approach over another may be favoured in the various guidelines, there are still curricular factions concerning justification of emphasis on specific skill over process or theory over experience and so on. The boundaries and purposes of technology as a subject lack consensus, are contested and remain a site for continual debate. These debates have been fuelled and encouraged by the focus on technology provided by the TVEI and, we argue, are reflected in the diverse interpretations, both in writing and in practice, which emerged during the 1980s. The debate about the knowledge domains which should be included in the technology curriculum as well as the degree of emphasis on specific rather than generic skills associated with project design and implementation predates the publication of the various National Curriculum guidelines. With the intervention of an externally derived and shifting framework which technology teachers have been forced to accommodate, we have a cultural environment in which central debates, of the kind we identify above, are left unresolved and have resulted in a subject culture typified by schism and diversity. However, despite the dislocated nature of technology's present subject identity, its position is enshrined as a foundation subject within the National Curriculum (see Goodson, 1994), which may well have effects on its relative status within the curriculum and produce a strong subject identity in technology teachers in the longer term. In comparison with maths, its history as a subject in the curriculum is relatively short.

How to manage the integration of the 'subject' elements brought together under National Curriculum technology and the competition for resources and curriculum time between previously discrete subjects typify the subject cultural preoccupations of the area. Establishing coherence and squaring individual teachers' notions of structure with the imposed structure from the National Curriculum is demanding enough, but this process of accommodation has taken place in an environment of diminishing resources. This context has produced individual narratives which embody a crisis of authority in the source of the guidance on the one hand, and a pragmatic acknowledgement of the present framework for action on the other. The latter theme has produced some interesting narratives which chart the way the demands of the situation have led to new and effective teams developing within schools.

While the existence of a 'meta framework' for action in the form of the National Curriculum, has enabled some maths teachers to trawl in a collective way for interesting ways to teach the maths curriculum, in general the preoccupations have been rather different from those of the technology teachers. While the themes are within the domain of curriculum design and justification, we could find little evidence of uncertainty or even debate about the structure or composition of the maths curriculum. There were oppositional threads concerning the value placed on subject knowledge, but overall there was consensus on the 'mission' that should guide maths teachers. Given this base of 'subject confidence' it is interesting to note the way debate has drifted to questions of decision-making opportunity in the areas of pacing and learning methodology. In other words, we might say that the National Curriculum has done little to offend or challenge the existing expectations maths teachers had of the maths knowledge base. Indeed, we might say that the status and position of maths and maths teachers has been affirmed and even consolidated through the intervention of the National Curriculum and its status as a core subject, guaranteeing its claim for resources and key specialist staff. At the same time it has produced an emphasis on the pedagogic demands of the maths curriculum and increased recording and assessment activity. In sum we can discern relative continuity in maths teachers' subject values and in their perceptions of curriculum structure. It is teaching strategy and pacing which continue to be areas in which considerable 'expert' demands are placed on them and in which they can display considerable pedagogic judgement.

REFERENCES

Barnes, D., Johnson, G., Jordan, S., Layton, D., Medway, P. and Yeomans, D. (1987) *The TVEI Curriculum 14–16. An Interim Report Based on Case Studies in Twelve Schools*. London: Manpower Services Commission.

Bernstein, B. (1971) On the classification and framing of educational knowledge. In M. F. D. Young (ed.), *Knowledge and Control*. London: Collier-Macmillan, pp. 47–69.

Cooper, B. (1984) On explaining change in school subjects. In I. F. Goodson and S. J. Ball (eds), *Defining the Curriculum*. London: Falmer Press, pp. 45–63.

Dale, R. (1985) *Education, Training and Employment: Towards a New Vocationalism*. Oxford: Pergamon Press.

Goodson, I. (1994) *Studying Curriculum: Cases and Methods*. Buckingham: Open University Press.

Hargreaves, A. (1992) Cultures of teaching. In A. Hargreaves and M. G. Fullan (eds), *Understanding Teacher Development*. London: Cassell, pp. 216–40.

Helsby, G., Knight, P., McCulloch, G., Saunders, M. and Warburton, T. (1997) *Professionalism in Crisis?* Lancaster: C.S.E.T.

Layton, D., Medway, P. and Yeomans, D. (1989) *14–19 The Range of Practice: Technology in TVEI*. Sheffield: Manpower Services Commission.

Little, J. (1993) Professional community in comprehensive high schools: the two worlds of academic and vocational teachers. In J. Little and M. McLaughlin (eds), *Teachers' Work: Individuals, Colleagues and Contexts*. New York: Teachers' College Press, pp. 137–63.

Little, J. and McLaughlin, M. (eds) (1993) *Teachers' Work: Individuals, Colleagues and Contexts*. New York: Teachers' College Press.

Saunders, M. (1990) Control and influence: recent government policy on technical and vocational education in British education. In P. Summerfield and E. Evans (eds), *Technical Education and the State since 1850*. Manchester: Manchester University Press, pp. 171–89.

Saunders, M. (1995) Researching professional learning. *Journal of Computer Assisted Learning*, 11(3): 231–8.

Siskin, L. S. (1994) *Realms of Knowledge: Academic Departments in Secondary Schools*. London: Falmer Press.

Weber, S. and Mitchell, C. (1995) *That's Funny, You Don't Look Like a Teacher*. London: Falmer Press.

Young, M. F. D. (ed.) (1971) *Knowledge and Control: New Directions for the Sociology of Education*. London: Collier-Macmillan.

Chapter 7

Reconstructing the Geography National Curriculum: Professional Constraints, Challenges and Choices

Margaret Roberts

INTRODUCTION

From September 1991 state-maintained secondary schools in England and Wales had to start teaching the Geography National Curriculum (hereafter referred to as the GNC). It appeared that central control would replace teacher autonomy and that conformity would replace variety. My research into the GNC suggests a more complex process. The huge variety of practice which existed in geographical education in 1989 for pupils aged 11–14 (Roberts, 1991) was replaced not by standardization but by continued diversity (Roberts, 1995). Certainly, there have been changes in secondary schools following the introduction of the GNC (Roberts, 1992); however, continuing differences between schools suggest that central control has its limitations and that there is still scope for professional choice or 'space for manoeuvre' (Bowe and Ball, 1992, p. 84).

This chapter sets out to explore differences in professional choices in relation to geographical education using data mainly from three case study departments. In this introduction I will firstly examine some ideas which have contributed to my understanding of difference. Then I will give some details of the research on which this chapter is based. Lastly, I will outline areas of professional concern to be considered in this chapter.

Differences in professional responses to the GNC can be related to: (1) the scope given within policy documents for different interpretations; (2) different views and commitments of teachers; and (3) different school contexts. Some limits were intended by the legislation of the 1988 Education Reform Act. In 1987 the government had stated that 'pupils would all have access to broadly the same good and relevant curriculum' (DES, 1987, p. 4). Rawling (1992), writing about the creation of the GNC from her own perspective as a member of the geography working group, stated that 'the theorists had had their day, geography was not the property of school teachers and educationalists' (p. 299). Limitation of what Hewitt (1989) had termed 'rampant institutional autonomy' (p. 104) was intended. How these limitations were interpreted, however, depended on how the GNC texts were perceived. Bowe and Ball (1992, p. 11), drawing on concepts developed by Roland Barthes in relation to literature, distinguish usefully between 'readerly' texts, for which there appears to be little opportunity for interpretation, and 'writerly' texts, which seem to invite readers to make sense of the text for themselves. It could be argued that, officially, the statutory orders for geography were intended as 'readerly' texts, with one meaning.

Yet research has shown that teachers have read the GNC texts differently (Fry and Schofield, 1993; Lambert, 1994; Roberts, 1995). Bale (1995) has argued that the scope for different interpretations was inherent in the 1991 Orders: 'the entire document could be read as a strange mixture of geographical paradigms and an equally eclectic mix of educational philosophies – from utilitarian to reconstructionist' (p. 294). He wonders whether the scope for different readings of the text was intentional: 'the wording of the statements of attainment were sufficiently (and deliberately?) broad (bland?) to allow teachers to interpret the numerous "pupils-should-be-able-to-explain" . . . statements in various ways' (*ibid.*).

How teachers interpret texts has much to do with how they conceptualize the curriculum. Grundy (1987), basing her work on categories devised by Habermas, identified three ways of thinking about the curriculum: in *technical* terms, in which the teacher wants to control what is taking place so that predetermined outcomes can be achieved; in *practical* terms, in which the teacher, knowing the situation in which the curriculum will be applied, has 'not only the right, but also the obligation, to make his/her own meaning of the text' (p. 69); and in *emancipatory* terms, in which teachers negotiate their courses with pupils and in which knowledge is subject to critical reflection.

Teachers with these different views of curriculum would 'frame' the challenge of the GNC differently. Schön (1983) developed the concept of practitioners 'framing' their professional problems so that 'they bound the phenomena' to which they paid attention: 'Their frames determine their strategies of attention and thereby set the directions in which they will try to change the situation, the values which will shape their practice' (p. 309). Schön distinguished between practitioners who were unaware of their frames and the way they constructed reality and those who were 'aware of the possibility of alternative ways of framing the reality of his practice' (p. 310). If this concept is applied to teachers' interpretations of the GNC it would suggest that some teacher action is unconsciously limited by particular ways of 'framing' the situation, whereas other teachers' decisions are made with greater awareness of choice.

Rizvi and Kemmis (1987) also stressed the importance of teachers' understandings in their report of the Victoria Participation and Equity Programme in Australia:

> those who participate in a program at the school level will
> interpret it in their own terms, in relation to their own
> understanding, desires, values and purposes, and in relation to the
> means available to them and the ways of working they prefer. In
> short, all aspects of a program may be contested by those involved
> in a program, moreover, a program is formed and reformed
> throughout its life through a process of contestation. (p. 21)

Rizvi and Kemmis see contestation as a process in which teachers struggle over status, resources and territories – territories of ideas, practices and forms of organization. They emphasize not only the understandings of teachers but also 'the means available to them' and 'circumstances': 'they were obliged to confront a variety of practical and moral dilemmas about the best courses of action to pursue in difficult circumstances' (p. 39).

Teachers have to resolve their dilemmas in their 'circumstances', in their own unique context. Bowe and Ball (1992, p. 117), writing about teachers' response to the National Curriculum, emphasized the importance of four aspects of context: *capacity*, which referred to the skills and experience of members of the department; *contingencies*, which included staffing and facilities within the school; *commitments*, which related to strongly held views within a department and/or school; and *histories*, particularly related to past experience of curriculum innovation.

The research on which this chapter was based took place between 1989 and 1995. Initially, in 1989 and 1990, I interviewed heads of geography and/or humanities in twelve case-study comprehensive schools, chosen for their variety of practice and not as a representative sample. The interviews suggested that different practices were underpinned by fundamentally different ways of conceptualizing curriculum and pedagogy. Three categories of heads of department emerged: those who conceptualized the curriculum as content to be transmitted to pupils; those who conceptualized the curriculum in terms of a framework of ideas explored through practical activities; and those who conceptualized the curriculum more in terms of pupils' development. I chose one department from each category for further study and carried out in-depth interviews with heads of geography and/or humanities during the summer terms of 1991, 1992 and 1994. These interviews were supplemented by interviews with other members of the department, by occasional lesson observation and by substantial documentary evidence. Although the schools were very different in terms of Bowe and Ball's 'capacities', 'contingencies', 'commitments' and 'histories', the range of socio-economic backgrounds of the pupils was similar. Results in public examinations were slightly higher than the national average in all three schools, both generally and for geography. Issues arising from data collected in the case-study schools were further investigated in questionnaire surveys of all state-maintained secondary schools in South Yorkshire in 1990, 1992 and 1995, for each of which there was a response rate of over 80 per cent.

The Statutory Orders did not arrive in a vacuum, but in particular schools and departments with accepted ways of working. The heads of department in the case-study schools were confident in what they were doing. The next part of the chapter will explore this professional confidence. This will be followed by a discussion of three issues of professional concern which emerged during interviews: the subject structure of the National Curriculum; problems of curriculum planning for the GNC; and prescription of content.

PROFESSIONAL CERTAINTY

All the interviews with heads of department (HoDs) in the case-study schools were underpinned by notions of what constituted a good teacher and good classroom practice. Before the introduction of the GNC all the HoDs in the case-study schools – denoted A, B and C – considered their existing practice to be 'good':

> They are successful courses. Children find them interesting.
> (A, in 1989)
> Ideally, we'll hang onto the good practice that operates now.
> (B, in 1989)
> a lot of the good work that we think we've done in this school over
> the years ... might be in jeopardy. (C, in 1989)

The authority for such *professional certainty* was provided by statements about length of classroom experience and about knowledge of children:

> over the years we have thought long and hard ... (A)
> when you've been teaching for 18 years you have a really good idea
> about children's abilities and what they are doing, based on years
> of experience ... (B)
> I have taught for 25 years. (C)
> it is teachers at the chalk face who know what kids are interested
> in. (C)

The feeling that their department was already doing good work made HoDs initially resentful of the National Curriculum:

> an unnecessary intrusion. (A)
> the criticism here is that the National Curriculum is devised by
> people who have long since had any experience in the classroom.
> (A)
> I can see the advantage of trying to standardize what's done ...
> but people feel resentful about not being able to choose. (B)
> this is rubbish because it has not built on what teachers have
> done. (C)

These teachers thought that professional expertise came from teachers, not from people outside schools. They felt that decisions should be based on 'experience in the classroom' and 'what teachers have done'.

Their notions of what constituted 'good' were, however, totally different. The interviews revealed the importance of personal biographies in influencing professional thinking. Although the schools in which the HoDs were working were part of their personal biographies they had also all been influenced by previous schools, by people they had encountered in their professional lives, and by professional work outside their schools. Their professional certainties had been shaped and modified over the years as they adapted to the constraints and opportunities provided by the contexts in which they had worked. A few details of each case will indicate some of the influences.

The HoD in school A had years of experience of examining a traditional O-level geography syllabus. He had chosen not to adopt any of the innovative Schools Council projects during the 1970s and 1980s, partly because his own examining expertise was able to help pupils succeed in other syllabuses. His teaching experience had been entirely within traditional schools. He conceptualized the geography curriculum in terms of content and basic skills:

> I think we have a duty to teach children things like map work and use of an atlas. They should have a basic knowledge of weather and climate and so on. I certainly believe that all the youngsters should know some geography when they leave school. I think we put in the basic input in the first, second and third years. (A, in 1989)

He favoured formal classroom approaches in which the authoritative knowledge of the teacher was transferred to pupils. His view was, in Grundy's terms, relatively 'technical'.

The HoD in school B had taken part in piloting two Schools Council geography projects. She and other members of the department had published magazine articles and textbooks. She conceptualized the geography curriculum in terms of concepts and a broad range of interpretative skills, which would be developed through a wide range of resource based learning activities:

> we try to make it a skills-based, resources-based, enquiry-based type of course. (B, in 1989)

Her view was, in Grundy's terms, relatively 'practical'.

The HoD in school C had worked in the 1970s in a school which was developing an integrated humanities course. His collaborative work with teachers from a range of humanities subjects had influenced his thinking ever since. He conceptualized the curriculum in terms of pupil investigations across subject boundaries, through which important concepts would be explored and through which independent and cooperative learning skills would be developed:

> A lot of the work we do stems from the kids, from their knowledge that they bring to the classroom ... In the classroom the kids in a sense are in charge, they're in charge of their own learning. We're all learning together. (C, in 1989)

His view had characteristics of Grundy's 'emancipatory' category.

The HoDs had developed confidence in their judgements from their own experiences and through collaboration with teachers who had worked with them for years in their present schools. In addition to having a localized 'situated certainty' (Hargreaves, 1994, p. 59), they had developed a more broadly based confidence through work in other schools and outside the school in examining and publishing.

Confidence in their opinions and 'firmly held and well entrenched subject' and 'pedagogic paradigms' (Bowe and Ball, 1992, p. 118) made them 'frame' the National Curriculum differently. The National Curriculum documents were read differently; different aspects of the documents were noticed, overlooked or ignored (Roberts, 1995). The GNC provided a different challenge for each department, not only because the changes needed to meet GNC requirements were different, but also because of differences in the ways HoDs conceptualized what was required.

Throughout the period from 1991 until 1995, their professional certainties were constantly challenged. The introduction of the GNC was not a discrete event, taking place wholly in September 1991, but a long process during which the legislation had to be gradually implemented and during which there were changes in the legislation, culminating in the replacement of the original 1991 Geography Orders with revised orders in 1995 (DFE, 1995).

The next part of the chapter will examine how three very different departments responded to the challenges in three areas in which their professional actions seemed to be limited by the legislation: integration; curriculum planning; and selection of content.

PROFESSIONAL DECISIONS ABOUT INTEGRATION

Before 1991, schools had freedom to decide how geography should be incorporated into the curriculum, i.e. as a separate subject, as part of an integrated course of study, or not at all. From 1991 onwards secondary schools had, by law, to include geography in the curriculum, but officially it was up to the school whether to teach it within or across traditional subject boundaries: 'The use of subjects to define the National Curriculum does not mean that teaching has to be organised and delivered within prescribed subject boundaries' (DES, 1989, para. 4.2). Government action, however, contradicted this: the geography working group was discouraged by its chairman from having any contact with the history group or from adopting its approach. Whilst the history group had based its attainment targets on processes of historical investigation, the geography group had based them on content. No consideration was given to linking the content of the two subjects. The geography working group was cautious about integration: 'we believe that great care must be exercised in developing formal links between history and geography, especially in the context of combined courses' (DES, 1990, p. 74). Clarke (1992), then Secretary of State for Education, suggested that integrated humanities courses weakened 'the rigour and integrity of the contributing disciplines' (p. 28).

For the geography/humanities departments in schools A and B, central government had not 'reinstated' traditional subjects as Goodson (1994, p. 18) suggests. On the contrary, both had strong commitments to geography as a subject and as a medium for education and had resisted local initiatives encouraging integration. They already 'framed' the curriculum in terms of subjects and were pleased that geography was included in the National Curriculum as a subject in its own right. Integration of history and geography was, however, an issue for the department in school C, whose HoD struggled to resolve the conflict he saw between the statutory requirements and his commitment to integration. He felt that the government's intentions were clear and that his own professional choices were being criticized:

> you can't integrate them any more . . . because one is process-oriented, the history one, and this is content-based and there is just no connection between the two . . . it sort of criticizes teachers for putting history and geography together. We realize they don't want to have history and geography integrated. (C, in 1990)

> it was obviously designed that way so they don't intend the two subjects to be integrated at all. We could find very little overlap. (C, in 1991).

At first, however, he had remained committed to integration and challenged what 'they', the government, had intended:

> we had two Baker days and we sat down as a department and we said 'right, we're going to integrate, we're going to carry on as we were' and we got history together and geography together and we just looked through it at the places of contact. We looked through it for concepts that we could integrate . . . we couldn't . . . we could find very little overlap . . . so what we've done is we've set up two very different departments. (C, in 1991)

Resistance was restricted by several contextual factors. The fact that the HoD was a geographer, rather than a historian, made integration less acceptable:

> we couldn't . . . put together a proper integrated course. It would've had to have been history driven, because that has to be done chronologically, and geography would have been the poor relation, just sort of feeding in here, there and everywhere. It would have been very contrived. (C, in 1991)

The headteacher's views on integration also supported a change to separate subjects:

> the head's cock-a-hoop . . . he's supported the integrated approach for 20 years, but . . . he is a traditional geographer and his heart's never been in it. (C, in 1991)

Also, the strength of integrated humanities in the school had depended on teachers with specialisms in geography, history and sociology all being confident to teach the integrated course. The demands of the GNC removed this confidence:

> the historians were looking at this [the 'Final Report' of the
> geography working group, DES, 1990] and they are absolutely
> horrified, saying 'I can't teach this. It is too specific, it is too
> detailed'. I have this fear at the back of my mind that what we are
> going to have to do is say, 'OK the geographers are going to be
> teaching geography and the historians are going to be teaching
> history'. (C, in 1990)

By September 1991, the process of contestation in this department ended in acquiescence rather than acceptance. The revision of the GNC in 1994 made no difference:

> I don't think that humanities will come back. That was a decision
> by the head. When the National Curriculum came in, it was an
> opportunity to split it. I don't see it coming back. (C, in 1994)

The decision to separate subjects was not taken without a struggle. It had, however, been carefully considered within the constraints of both the legislation and the 'contingencies' of the school.

The National Curriculum did not prevent integration since other schools in the country continued to develop integrated courses. However, the South Yorkshire surveys suggest that these are in a small minority. The proportion of schools combining geography in some way with other subjects declined in Year 7 from 40 per cent in 1990 to 22 per cent in 1995, and in Year 9 from 16 per cent to less than 2 per cent. In most of the schools where humanities continued to be on the timetable, it meant little more than pupils being taught separate history and geography by the same teacher. The 1994 revision of the National Curriculum did not encourage a reversal of this pattern; geography remains a separate subject with its content distinct from history. None of the survey schools planned to reintroduce integrated courses in 1995. The National Curriculum has restricted the opportunities for integration. However, only 3 per cent of the HoDs (geography and/or humanities) completing the 1995 survey preferred geography to be taught as part of an integrated course. The subject structure of the National Curriculum coincides with the way many teachers continue to frame the curriculum.

PROFESSIONAL DECISIONS ABOUT CURRICULUM PLANNING

The starting point for curriculum planning for Key Stage 3 geography was not of the three departments' own choosing; the content and the emphases within the subject had been decided for them. Yet although the 1991 GNC was highly prescriptive in terms of content, it was flexible in terms of how skills, themes and study of places could be integrated to produce a course. Far from controlling what was required from teachers in terms of planning, the 1991 Orders made huge demands on professional skills of curriculum development. The departments responded in different ways.

The HoD of Department A initially welcomed the flexibility:

> you can generate your own course as to whether you want it to be
> regionally based or thematically based. (A, in 1990)

However, by 1991 the reality of constructing a curriculum plan in a few months was thought to be 'an impossible task' and one which was not made easier by the prolonged illness of a member of the department. The solution was 'to buy a package', a series of textbooks written by an author whose previous books had suited the departmental approach. The willingness of the department to hand over decisions about course structure to a textbook author was little different from what already happened for courses in the upper school. The department had chosen public examination syllabuses which required little in the way of curriculum planning and had based the teaching for them on textbooks. The lower-school syllabus had been constructed piecemeal over the years. Generally, therefore, the school had no experience of large-scale curriculum planning. They thought about planning for the GNC in technical terms:

> he's [the textbook author] done his work in making sure that it fits
> all the statements of attainment ... and there's a checklist, so
> we're off to a good start. (A, in 1991)

The HoD justified his decision in terms of 'responsibility for colleagues' and not wanting to 'impose another burden on them'. In 1994, they were pleased with their decision:

> we are very conscious that we are only using this book ... you
> could sit down and try to brainstorm, but I don't think you would
> come out with anything better. (A, in 1994)

Professional input into curriculum planning had been limited more by their views and past experience than by central control.

Whereas department A had treated the GNC text in a 'readerly' way, seeing little scope for their own interpretations, department B, working co-operatively as a team in a series of planning meetings, read it in a 'writerly' manner. They did not feel compelled to take geography orders literally, but saw possibilities for developing their own meaning from the text, to reconstruct it for themselves:

> we can work it out so that it is not that desperately different from
> what we do and what we want to do. (B, in 1990)

> some schools seem to have taken it literally saying, 'we've got to do
> everything within the National Curriculum'. We've felt that wasn't

the approach that we were going to take. Obviously, we're going to fulfil our requirements as far as we can, but there were also other priorities, like geography has got to still be the subject which we want to teach. (B, in 1991)

we've made a course which we think is making sense. (B, in 1992)

The teachers in department B took the 1991 Geography Orders apart and reassembled them to produce their own curriculum plan. They did this confidently, supported by their previous experience of curriculum innovation. The 'hours and hours' of time they spent cooperatively enhanced rather than restricted their professional development. The structure of their final plans owed more to their previous professional experience than to the National Curriculum.

Department C worked in a similar way, spending their own time to construct a three-year course of study, in spite of having no commitment to separate geography. They felt they had no choice:

we said, if this is what is on the statute books, then we will put our hearts and souls into it and work to try to make the impossible work. (C, in 1994)

They felt the pressure of the statute book through the expectations of the headteacher and the local education authority humanities adviser. They also took pride in producing well-planned courses:

over the years we've put together countless courses and we're recognized in the school as being sort of authorities on this. (C, in 1991)

Although they worked with as much energy as department B to produce curriculum plans, they were unable to put together a course which matched their own principles. They did not like the subject-specific content of the GNC but felt obliged to include it in their plans. They did find opportunities, however, to include units of cross-curricular work, for example a study of settlement included work on medieval settlements and a visit to Lincoln.

All three departments welcomed the revisions proposed in the Dearing review of the GNC (DFE, 1994):

it will give us a bit more flexibility, a bit more time and a bit more choice. (A, in 1994)

I like the idea of more professional judgement. You are your own boss and you do what is best. We see it as a framework for building the elements we want because it is no longer prescriptive ... I think we will hold on to what we have got, modify it, and pull out the things we don't need. We will still end up with a course we like, based on what we wanted to do. (B, in 1994)

> we are hoping it will create some space, some time ... we will then
> be able to get back to more group work, more experiential learning
> and more how we used to run things. (C, in 1994)

The revised GNC gives teachers more flexibility in planning their curricula than the 1991 Orders, but the interviews suggested that this would not be fully exploited. Department A planned to continue basing its course on textbooks. Department B planned to base its revised curriculum on its 1991–4 curriculum. Department C planned to introduce into their 1991–4 curriculum *more* of what they had done before, but not revert totally to what they had previously. The starting points for planning the new curricula in these departments were, because of time and resource restraints, the curricula devised for 1991–5, which in turn were framed by previous practice. It seems likely that differences in curriculum plans would persist and be magnified as the departments used the new more flexible 'spaces for manoeuvre' differently.

PROFESSIONAL DECISIONS ABOUT CONTENT

The aspect of teacher autonomy most threatened by the GNC was the freedom to select *what* was taught. The Education Reform Act of 1988 required National Curriculum subject orders to specify 'the matters, skills and processes which are required to be taught'. Geography teachers in secondary schools were unused to such specification. Before 1991, they had had freedom to decide what was taught to pupils aged 11–14, although they would clearly be influenced by current views on what constituted geography or humanities. Departments also had a wide choice of examination syllabuses, each giving emphasis to different aspects of geography. The content of many syllabuses was defined by key ideas, leaving teachers free to select appropriate examples.

From 1991 onwards, for pupils aged 11 to 14, there was one prescribed course, the GNC. If teachers did not like the emphasis given to any aspects of geography they could not choose another syllabus as they could for public examinations. In the 1991 GNC the content was set out in great detail in 114 separate statements of attainment at Key Stage 3 (DES, 1991) and teachers had to choose countries to study from a prescribed list. The scope for decisions about content was limited, but the departments responded differently.

Before 1991, department A had had a lower-school syllabus structured by content, and considered choice of content to be a professional matter:

> I still feel that they don't trust the professional judgement of the
> teacher to choose case study examples and to use the expertise of
> teachers, and the resources of departments that have been built
> up over many years. I don't understand why in the developing
> world you have got to do Nigeria when you can't do Ghana or any
> other that you choose to do. (A, in 1990)

By 1990, Ghana had been included in the GNC and content was no longer mentioned as a cause of concern:

> it is mainly rejigging from what we did before. I don't see any major departures from what we've taught before. (A, in 1990)

> A high percentage of what we do is what we did before. We just had to rearrange it. (A, in 1992)

Acceptance of GNC content was an extension of the willingness of the HoD to accept content prescribed by examination boards, in the syllabuses he chose. Where the GNC gave the department an opportunity to use its own expertise and resources on Ghana, the HoD, strongly supported by the second in department, who was also interviewed for the research, chose not to. Instead they studied Egypt from the new textbook. Gradually, from 1991 onwards, textbooks replaced their previously accumulated subject knowledge. Far from contesting the GNC the department accepted the new content, being concerned only about the amount 'to get through'.

Department B was accustomed to making all its own decisions about the details of content; since the late 1970s it had chosen public examination syllabuses where choice of case studies was left to the teacher. HoD B was far more critical of the documents:

> It seems fairly limiting. You might know something about South America and not a lot about the sort of concept that you can apply to the whole world. (B, in 1989)

> There is too much emphasis on factual information. One way of cutting down on content is to look at process and ideas and concepts and that just seems to be given lip service. (B, in 1990)

At an early stage they became aware of the impossibility of covering everything. Instead of accepting the content as given, they made decisions about what to include and what to omit. Initially this was done with caution, but later with confidence:

> We will not leave things out, but I think we'll give them a bit lower key. (B, in 1990)

> I don't think we are going to be able to do the USA, USSR and Japan. I'm feeling more confident now ... whereas last year I was thinking 'are we going to be a slave to this document?' (B, in 1992)

> It was time the lower-school curriculum had a revamp, although we didn't like being told what had to be included. We didn't include everything ... we never did Japan, CIS, USA or energy supplies. (B, in 1994)

Department B also reacted differently to the few choices available. Instead of handing over the choice of country to a textbook author, they chose to study Peru, because of specialist knowledge of some members of the department. They saw this as an opportunity of involving younger colleagues in curriculum development.

Department C, with its more emancipatory approach to the curriculum, had, before 1991, left the detailed choice of content to pupils. It was the pupils, not the teachers, who would collect data, e.g. from libraries, the BBC Domesday Disc or from interviews. The pupils' investigations, guided by teachers, were open ended. The prescriptive content of the GNC challenged this and was considered to be 'a straight jacketing of the educational system' in which pupils were 'going to be told what they have to learn'. The head of department disapproved of the GNC:

> what can pupils do with their knowledge? I think it is highly questionable. I would rather be able to say there are intellectual skills which geography is about ... it is wrong, totally, wrong, it has taken away that flexibility, the autonomy we had in deciding what we wanted to teach. (C, in 1990)

In spite of resentment of 'all that content' being 'imposed' on them, the department fitted the content onto their own curriculum grid:

> it's the law and we'll do it. We've just got to get on with it. (C, in 1990)

> we've been told by the government that you have got to do this so we do it. (C, in 1994)

Although there were differences of *details* of content on the curriculum plans in departments A, B and C, what was more significant was *how* the content was taught. For example, the topic 'settlement' was included in the Year 7 plans of all three departments. Pupils in department A studied urban patterns from the textbook and completed the textbook exercises. This work was supplemented with a visit to Victorian houses, where pupils were told about the history of the area and completed worksheets. Pupils in B studied settlement mainly from photographs and maps. Pupils in C had to conduct land-use surveys in local villages and design questionnaires to find out about the villages from local people. Although the content – settlement – had been prescribed, the pupils in these schools were learning very different things. In A they were learning new terms, facts and concepts, with the aim of being able to recall this information. In B they were learning how to interpret resources to find out information, with the main aim of learning transferable skills. In C they were constructing knowledge from their own investigations, with the main aim of learning *how* to investigate. The reality of *what* the pupils were learning was related more to the methods of teaching and learning than to the centrally prescribed curriculum. Although this example gives a fair representation of how A and B translated the content into practice, it would be misleading to suggest that C was able to use investigative methods for most of the time:

there is far more talk and chalk than there has ever been before. People are saying we haven't got time for group discussion, we haven't got time to wait for kids to discover this, that and the other. We haven't got time for computer simulations, we haven't got time even for watching videos, and so there is a panic feeling. People are saying we must get through the syllabus. (C, in 1992)

Department C felt that

you can't have open-ended learning any more, not when you've got a list of things they've got to achieve. (C, in 1991)

Yet in 1994 there was evidence that pupils in C still had opportunities for investigative work in which they could select the content. C was the only one of the three departments in which pupils studied one of the prescribed countries through their own questions and interests. It was also the only department in which fieldwork was based largely on investigating the pupils' hypotheses.

The 1995 revisions to the GNC substantially reduced the volume of content and the amount of prescription. These two changes were the features of the revised GNC most welcomed by respondents to the 1995 survey. However, the way the departments were likely to use the increased opportunity for professional choice was likely to vary. Department A expected to 'slim down' their curriculum, but seemed likely to continue to select content from textbooks and to continue to teach in formal ways. Department B was concerned that the change might reduce the time for geography. Geography had to compete for timetable space with modern languages, to which the headteacher, a modern linguist, attached particular importance. During the period 1991–4 department B had been given additional time for geography and this had enabled them to adapt the 1991 GNC to what they wanted:

We have experimented a bit more. I introduced some flexible learning where the kids did some research themselves. I think basically there haven't been any major changes to the style of teaching within the department other than trying to be a bit more adventurous with a bit more time. (B, in 1994)

Paradoxically, the slimmer more flexible curriculum to be introduced in 1995 could prove more constricting, because of possible changes in time allocation, than the more prescriptive GNC of 1991.

Department C suggested that they would use the opportunities offered by the revision of content:

If we have the opportunity to go back to what we were in the late 80s before all this was imposed on us ... we will be off ... you remove the imposition of all that content on us and we will go back to where we were using our old teaching style. Our fundamental philosophy about the way the kids learn hasn't changed. (C, in 1994)

How each department constructed the new 1995 GNC would depend on practices established before and during the implementation of the 1991 GNC, on professional commitments and the way the HoDs resolved professional dilemmas in their particular contexts.

CONCLUSIONS

Before the introduction of the GNC the case-study departments had established their own ways of working through which they had developed their own professional confidence. The National Curriculum challenged what they were doing and created a tension for heads of departments between preserving what they valued from previous practice and meeting the statutory requirements. There was a conflict between continuity and change.

The years 1991–4 were difficult, as evidenced by quotes such as

> This is not the only thing that is going on. We are just in the business of day-to-day survival. It is very stressful. (A, in 1992)

> The last three years have been hell and it hasn't been self-imposed. It has been imposed by the government. (C, in 1994)

The research indicates that the tensions and conflicts were different for the three departments, both because of differences in previous curricula and because of differences in previous professional behaviour. Where the previous curriculum was similar in content to the GNC and where previous subject and pedagogic paradigms seemed to be still tenable, the challenge was less. The space needed for professional manoeuvre was small. There were fewer professional dilemmas. A limited process of contestation could take place within the department. Where, however, subject and pedagogic paradigms to which the head of department was committed no longer seemed tenable, then a very large space was required for manoeuvre. There were many professional dilemmas to be resolved, and the process of contestation involved struggles of power beyond the department.

The teacher autonomy which existed prior to 1991 had been used in totally different ways. Where some of this autonomy had already been surrendered by choosing highly prescriptive examination courses and by basing courses on textbook series, imposition of demands from outside was less of a problem. Acceptance of new restrictions on professional choice was an extension of earlier acceptance. Teachers had already defined their professional role in fairly instrumental terms, implementing curricula planned by others.

On the other hand, where teachers had used their autonomy to the full, devising their own unique courses, even in relation to examination syllabuses, and in some cases going beyond subject boundaries, there was a tendency for teachers to continue to define their professional role in pro-active ways. They saw a need to criticize, to analyse the GNC, to interpret it in their own ways and to reconstruct it.

Persistent differences between schools can be understood, it seems, not only in terms of different *responses* to the National Curriculum in particular contexts but in terms of *continuities* of professional action, which are underpinned by persistent ways of thinking about curriculum, pedagogy and professional roles.

REFERENCES

Bale, J. (1995) The challenge of postmodernism. In M. Williams (ed.), *Understanding Geographical and Environmental Education*. London: Cassell, pp. 287–96.

Bowe, R. and Ball, S. J. (1992) *Reforming Education and Changing Schools*. London: Routledge.

Clarke, K. (1992) Geography in the national curriculum. *Teaching Geography*, **17**(1): 28–30.

DES (Department of Education and Science) (1987) *The National Curriculum 5–16*. London: HMSO.

DES (1989) *From Policy to Practice*. London: HMSO.

DES (1990) *Geography for Ages 5 to 16*. London: HMSO.

DES (1991) *Geography in the National Curriculum*. London: HMSO.

DFE (Department for Education) (1994) *Geography in the National Curriculum: Draft Proposals*. London: HMSO.

DFE (1995) *Geography in the National Curriculum*. London: HMSO.

Fry, P. and Schofield, A. (1993) *Teachers' Experiences of the National Curriculum in Year 7*. Sheffield: Geographical Association.

Goodson, I. F. (1994) *Studying Curriculum*. Buckingham: Open University Press.

Grundy, S. (1987) *Curriculum: Product or Praxis?* London: Falmer Press.

Hargreaves, A. (1994) *Changing Teachers, Changing Times: Teachers' Work and Culture in the Post-Modern Age*. London: Cassell.

Hewitt, M. (1989) Accentuate the positive. *Teaching Geography*, **14**(3): 104–5.

Lambert, D. (1994) The national curriculum: what shall we do with it? *Geography*, **79**(1): 65–76.

Rawling, E. (1992) The making of a national geography curriculum. *Geography*, **77**(4): 292–309.

Rizvi, F. and Kemmis, S. (1987) *Dilemmas of Reform*. Geelong: Deakin Institute for Studies in Education.

Roberts, M. (1991) On the eve of the geography national curriculum: the implications for secondary schools. *Geography*, **76**(4): 331–42.

Roberts, M. (1992) A case of information overload. *Times Educational Supplement*, 20 November.

Roberts, M. (1995) Interpretations of the geography national curriculum: a common curriculum for all? *Journal of Curriculum Studies*, **27**(2): 187–205.

Schön, D. A. (1983) *The Reflective Practitioner*. London: Temple Smith.

Chapter 8

Legislating Philosophy and Practice: Teaching and Assessing Scientific Investigation

Edgar Jenkins

INTRODUCTION

'Scientific investigation' (Sc1) was the first of the four Attainment Targets which prescribed the science component of the National Curriculum in England and Wales in 1991. This chapter explores the response of science teachers and of their professional organization, the Association for Science Education, to this attempt by central government to define and implement a philosophy of scientific inquiry for the purposes of teaching and assessment. In particular, it examines how science teachers, while initially sympathetic to investigation as a central component of science education, came to regard Sc1 as a fundamentally flawed and externally imposed policy initiative which ignored their expertise and undermined their professional autonomy. Since engagement with the policy and curriculum issues presented by Sc1 requires some understanding of the wider context of school science teaching, the chapter begins with a historical outline of the origins of scientific investigation as a curriculum objective. This is followed by a brief consideration of a number of philosophical issues relevant to the scientific endeavour. The chapter concludes by challenging the notion, held by the teachers themselves, that they were simply respondents to an external curriculum initiative, suggesting instead that they played an active and substantial role in originating and sustaining policy in teaching and assessing Sc1. The corollary, at least as far as Sc1 is concerned, is that policy itself can be regarded as a function which, far from being centrally controlled, is delocalized, differentiated and actively constructed by teachers.

TEACHING SCIENTIFIC INVESTIGATION: A HISTORICAL PERSPECTIVE

Teaching something of the nature of science as an investigative activity has long been an important element of the rationale of school science since the subject was first schooled in the mid-nineteenth century. When a committee of the British Association for the Advancement of Science (BAAS) reported in 1867 *On the Best Means of Promoting Scientific Education in Schools*, it suggested that the case for teaching science in schools rested upon several distinct grounds. Drawing a distinction between scientific information and scientific training but acknowledging that both were important in science education, the authors of the report had no doubt about the principal benefit of teaching science in schools. This was the inculcation of 'the scientific habit of mind', a habit described as of 'incalculable value, whatever ... the pursuits of after life' (BAAS, 1868, p. xxxix).

In according this primacy to mental training and the scientific habit of mind, the BAAS report reflected the role which scientific method had come to occupy in the ideology of science itself, which the BAAS had so assiduously and successfully sought to cultivate. The proper application of this method generated knowledge which was 'objective', 'value free' and useful, although, as the BAAS was at pains to emphasize, utility was not the yardstick against which such knowledge should be measured. The case for scientific education presented in the report in terms of the scientific habit of mind was, therefore, more than an elegant means of meeting the requirements of a liberal education, i.e. a mental training distanced from utilitarian concerns. It was designed to encourage the future well-being of science and was an integral part of the tacit 'social contract' developed in the mid-nineteenth century between the rapidly developing scientific community and the society within which it was acquiring an increasingly powerful and influential voice (Layton, 1982, p. 103).

Despite the unqualified reference to schools in its title, the BAAS report was principally, and often explicitly, concerned with the position of science in the curriculum of the public schools. The case which it presented for a liberal education in science was not readily transferable, therefore, to other types of school designed to serve different social purposes and within which science might be taught with different ends in view, e.g. public elementary schools, classes supported by the Department of Science and Art, or trade schools with explicitly vocational curricula. Although the BAAS made repeated attempts in the last quarter of the nineteenth century to promote the teaching of science in the public elementary schools, little real progress was made and the 1904 Code of Regulations, along with its annual successors, effectively constrained most elementary school science education to little more than nature study. This situation was to prevail until well after the Second World War when a coalition of pedagogic, economic and scientific concerns prompted a number of primary science curriculum initiatives (Richards and Holford, 1983). The teaching of scientific investigation, therefore, has a different history in elementary and post-elementary education and this difference reflects, among much else, wider assumptions about the form, content and purpose of different types of schooling.

In the public schools, and in other institutions which came to model themselves upon them, science education was cast firmly in an instrumental and pre-professional role and, even as early as 1870, a consensus had begun to emerge about the content of what was to become the secondary science curriculum. Central to that consensus was the teaching of scientific method, a cause espoused with remarkable zeal and vigour by Henry Edward Armstrong (Brock, 1973). Armstrong's heuristic method significantly strengthened the pre-professional dimension of secondary-school science and provided it with a powerful, beguiling, and explicit rationale founded upon the teaching of scientific investigation.

There was, of course, reaction to Armstrong's heurism, much of it reflected in the report of the Thomson Committee, which concluded in 1918 that 'in many schools more time is spent in laboratory work than the results can justify'. Yet even the Thomson Committee, hostile as it was to the excesses of heurism, was convinced that 'the spirit of inquiry should run through the whole of the science work, and everything should be done to encourage it' (Thomson Committee, 1918, para. 42). This conviction was to be expressed on many subsequent occasions. During the so-called science curriculum development era of the 1960s, training in scientific method was strongly reasserted as a curriculum objective. Supported by references to investigative, open-ended or discovery learning, science curriculum projects in many parts of the world emphasized scientific procedures and attitudes. Students following *Chem. Study* programmes in the USA were promised that they would 'see the nature of science by engaging in scientific activity' (Pimentel, 1960, p. 1 and preface). On this side of the Atlantic, the intention was to get 'pupils to think in the way practising scientists do' or, as the organizer of the Nuffield O-level chemistry project expressed it, 'to learn what being scientific means to a scientist' (Halliwell, 1966, p. 242). 'Scientific Investigation' was one of the assessment categories deployed by the Assessment of Performance Unit during the 1980s, and when the Department of Education and Science published its policy statement in 1985, the essential characteristic of school science education in England and Wales was stated officially to be that 'it introduces pupils to the methods of science' (DES, 1985, para. 11).

This commitment to teaching scientific investigation is reflected in the form, contents and titles of many recently published science texts for use in schools, e.g. *Process Science*, *Science in Process* and *Active Science*. The last of these texts states with particular clarity 'what it takes' for a pupil 'to be good at science', namely 'communicating and interpreting, observing, planning investigations, investigating and making', together with such basic skills as an ability to 'follow instructions for doing experiments' (Coles, 1989, pp. 4–5). The firmest possible commitment, however, is manifest in the science component of the National Curriculum in England and Wales, introduced following the passage of the 1988 Education Reform Act. The original Statutory Order for science, laid before Parliament in March 1989 after public consultation, consisted of seventeen Attainment Targets, of which two (AT1, *Exploration of Science*, and AT17, *The Nature of Science*) are of particular significance in the present context. This large number of Attainment Targets, coupled with a complex ten-point scale of assessment, proved unworkable, and, in 1991, the science component of the National Curriculum was reviewed. The revised Order, laid before Parliament in December 1991, reduced the number of Attainment Targets from seventeen to four, and combined elements of the former AT1 and AT17 into a new first Attainment Target, entitled *Scientific Investigation*, and commonly referred to as 'Sc1'. Overall, Sc1 absorbed the emphasis in the former AT1 on investigating the relationship between variables, and rejected most of AT17, which projected an image of science as historically, culturally and socially contingent. Sc1 legitimized an identifiable and universally applicable method of generating scientific knowledge and stressed the relationships between this method and the scientific content prescribed by the remaining three Attainment Targets. Following the most recent review of the National Curriculum, the first of the four science Attainment Targets has been renamed *Experimental and Investigative Science*, and changes have been been introduced in the former ten-level scale of assessment. However, the commitment to scientific investigation as fundamental to school science education remains essentially unchanged.

SOME PHILOSOPHICAL CONSIDERATIONS

The nature of science and, in particular, the nature of experimentation within the scientific endeavour, are problematic and contentious matters, and attempts to understand them span several domains of scholarship, notably history, philosophy and sociology. Writing of the history of science in the USA during the first half of the twentieth century, Thackray has commented that it 'displayed the heroic achievements of great scientists of the past' and constituted a 'possible basis for confidence in the continuation of the achievements of the scientists in the future' (Thackray, 1980, p. 450). This characterization, which is equally applicable to the UK, reflected the widespread acceptance of a positivistic philosophy which promoted and sustained the notion that science offered a unique route to objective and benevolent truth, derived by the proper application of scientific method. Despite the difficulties caused for this traditional philosophical understanding of the nature of science, notably by the development of relativity and quantum theory, the logical positivism of the Vienna circle dominated the philosophy of science during the interwar years.

However, even during this period, there were significant challenges to both the philosophy and the historiography of science. There were attempts to develop a philosophy of science anchored in historical understanding, rather than derived from the dictates of logic, with the work of Bachelard (1958) foreshadowing Kuhn's ideas about 'revolutionary' and 'normal' science. The events of the First World War also prompted an attack on the Rankean notion of 'scientific history', with the ideas of Butterfield and, later, of Collingwood, helping to create a new intellectual framework for the construction of the past. Within the past 30 or so years, that framework has had to accommodate not only the 'internalist–externalist' debates among historians of science but also the radical contextualist approach, which has raised the important question of the extent to which the formulation of scientific knowledge, and not simply the use to which it is put, is determined by developments taking place in the wider social context. It has also had to respond to the ideas encompassed by the so-called 'New History and Sociology of Science' (NHSS), which offer important insights into the generation, validation and replication of scientific knowledge.

As for the philosophy of science, the mixture of Popperian idealism, Kuhnian pragmatics and its logical extension, Feyerabend's *Against Method* (Feyerabend, 1975) has done more than highlight the fallibility of science or relativize scientific knowledge, and, thereby, help to diminish the standing and authority of the scientific endeavour. It has also contributed to the revolution in empirical philosophy, marked by the turn from logical models to historical models of understanding (Hesse, 1980). Of more immediate consequence in the present context, it has rendered antique 'the sort of ideology of science which, explicitly or implicitly, has provided coherence and security for generations of [science] teachers' (Ravetz, 1990, p. 20), and left those with a concern to promote an understanding of the nature of scientific investigation with no agreed replacement. There is now

> no well-confirmed general picture of how science works, no theory of science worthy of general assent. We did once have a well-developed and historically influential philosophical position, that of positivism or logical empiricism, which has now been effectively refuted. We have a number of recent theories which, while stimulating much interest, have hardly been tested at all. And we have specific hypotheses about various cognitive aspects of science, which are widely discussed but wholly undecided. If any extant position does provide a viable understanding of how science operates, we are far from being able to identify what it is. (Laudan *et al.*, 1986, p. 142)

The task facing those charged with prescribing scientific investigation for the purposes of teaching and assessment within a National Curriculum was, therefore, formidable. Perhaps inevitably, however, multiple meanings and scholarly insights yielded to the pressing demands of curriculum construction within a framework designed for accountability, and, as far as Sc1 is concerned, science teachers were advised that their pupils 'should develop the intellectual and practical skills which will allow them to explore and investigate the world of science and develop a fuller understanding of scientific phenomena, the nature of theories explaining these and the procedures of scientific investigation' (DES/WO, 1991). Such development was to take place through progressively more systematic and quantified activities which encouraged the ability to plan and carry out investigations in which pupils:

(1) ask questions, predict and hypothesise;
(2) observe, measure and manipulate variables;
(3) interpret their results and evaluate scientific evidence.
(DES/WO, 1991, p. 3)

These three strands were amplified at each of ten levels of attainment. For example, at Key Stage 3, pupils achieving at Level 4 could be

> asked to investigate variables which affect the rate at which water cools, identifying temperature as the variable to be measured, the thickness of material as the variable to be changed, and (to) choose appropriate instruments to measure quantities such as the volume of water used, water temperature and cooling time.

At Key Stage 4, Level 6, pupils could be expected to consider the factors affecting the rate of a chemical reaction, identify the variable to be controlled, conduct an appropriate investigation, present the results graphically and account for them in molecular terms.

TEACHERS' RESPONSES TO Sc1

Except where otherwise indicated, the responses referred to in the following paragraphs are derived from data collected as part of a wider study of Sc1 as a policy initiative (Donnelly *et al.*, 1993). The data were obtained from a variety of sources. Written sources ranged from statutory publications (DES/WO, 1989, 1991) and official but non-statutory publications (NCC, 1989), through professional journals for teachers, to documents produced at school or local authority level. Observations were made and recorded at a number of different sites. These included school science laboratories, where teachers were engaged in teaching 'scientific investigation' or assessing their pupils' competence at it, and both formal and informal meetings held to discuss Sc1, the former organized by a variety of organizations, notably local education authorities and Examining Groups. Finally, semi-structured interviews were used to collect data from pupils, teachers, professional subject officers within national organizations and Examining Groups, and from some of the science educators involved in the development and assessment arrangements for Sc1. Thirty-one teachers, drawn from ten schools in different parts of the country, were interviewed between October 1993 and March 1994. The teaching and assessment of Sc1 in schools was also closely observed, the schools themselves being chosen partly at random and partly upon the advice of science educators invited to locate high-quality work in this aspect of the National Curriculum. The teachers' responses at interview proved to be consistent with the opinions widely expressed by the much larger numbers of their professional peers attending in-service and other meetings concerned with Sc1. Data were also obtained from a subsequent round of interviews (including some re-interviews) conducted in June/July 1994. This introduced additional schools and teachers to give a total sample size of 38 teachers and 23 pupils.

The incorporation within the National Curriculum for England and Wales of an Attainment Target concerned with scientific investigation can be regarded as a statutory codification of a long-standing rhetorical commitment to science education as an activity concerned with 'finding out' or discovery, based upon experimentation as a means of generating new knowledge and understanding of some aspect of the natural world. To this extent, therefore, science teachers in England and Wales might be expected to have welcomed scientific investigation, if not necessarily its interpretation as Sc1, as reflective of a fundamental and established feature of their professional practice. There is some evidence that this was the case: a survey conducted by the Association for Science Education (ASE) in 1993 concluded that many of the respondents were very positive about investigations and regarded them as lying at the heart of all good science education (ASE, 1993a).

However, the attempt to translate a rhetorical commitment into the successful teaching and satisfactory assessment of Sc1 within the framework of the National Curriculum was bound to present severe difficulties. As noted above, there is a lack of agreement about a number of fundamental aspects of the nature of scientific investigation. In addition, science teachers had no previous experience either of engaging all their pupils in 'whole investigations' or of assigning their competence at scientific investigation to one of ten levels of attainment, as required by the Statutory Order. To this extent, therefore, Sc1 was a radical departure from existing practice and science teachers were left to explore the feasibility of teaching and assessing this Attainment Target while simultaneously seeking to give effect to the legal requirement to 'deliver' this and other components of the National Curriculum. These difficulties were compounded by the fact that only a small minority of science teachers had any direct experience of involvement with scientific investigation as a research activity. Most, therefore, were called upon to teach a curriculum component which, despite its rhetorical resonances with investigative pedagogy or discovery learning, was unfamiliar to them.

> Basically, none of us understood [scientific investigation], so we had to go away and find out all about it.[1]

> [Scientific investigation] is as much a learning process for teachers as it is for children.

In seeking clarification of what the authors of the National Curriculum intended by 'scientific investigation', science teachers looked to the Statutory Order itself and, in particular, to the assessment framework elaborated for Sc1. Further clarification was sought from the variety of training days, in-service courses and publications about Sc1 that collectively soon came to constitute a minor industry. Quasi-official guidance from the School Examinations and Assessment Council (e.g. SEAC, 1992, 1993a, b) was supplemented by other material generated principally by local education authorities, the Association for Science Education, the Examination Boards responsible for assessment at Key Stage 4, some institutions of higher education, educational consultants and, in the later stages, commercial publishers. The time devoted at the Annual Meeting of the Association for Science Education to lectures, symposia, workshops, etc. concerned with Sc1 rose, as a proportion of the overall programme, from 2.8 per cent and 2.7 per cent in 1991 and 1992 respectively to about 8 per cent in each of the following two years (Buchan, 1995). The anxiety of teachers and others about what was being asked of the teaching profession in teaching and assessing 'scientific investigation' was also reflected in correspondence in the professional press, where critical letters or articles sometimes prompted eccentric and defensive responses at a time when what was needed was informed professional debate, e.g. 'Too many voices shouting too soon about aspects of Sc1 being unworkable are more likely to endanger the very position of practical investigation in science education' (Revell, 1993) and 'Negative messages about scientific investigation could have damaging effects on science education' (*Education in Science*, 1993)

For many science teachers, in-service courses and much of the published material concerned with Sc1 initially enhanced, rather than diminished, their concerns about teaching and assessing this component of the National Curriculum. In the absence of a substantial body of experience of such teaching and assessment upon which those offering training programmes or providing exemplar material or advice might have been able to draw, significant differences in interpreting aspects of an innovative curriculum component were inevitable. The frustration of many science teachers attending in-service courses concerned with Sc1 has been well captured by Buchan (1995). She refers to 'heated exchanges' between teachers and trainers at sessions organized by the Examining Groups and to the teachers' sympathy with some of those trying to assist them: 'They [the Examination Group] have been stumbling their way like everybody is stumbling their way through to try and generate material' (Buchan, 1995, p. 94). Some of the teachers' frustration touched upon matters of a more fundamental kind: 'All you tell us is basically against everything we have learnt' (Buchan, 1995, p. 93).

Examining Boards, responsible for assessing pupils' work at Key Stage 4, undertook work jointly with the School Examinations and Assessment Council to 'provide exemplification of the standards for assessing coursework in GCSE science' (NEAB, 1993, p. 3). However, teachers did not always find it easy or possible to reconcile this exemplification with the understanding of Sc1 which they derived directly from the Statutory Order or from other sources. These sources included local education authorities, some of which worked with teachers in their employ to produce appropriate curriculum materials. These materials were often highly derivative, both in terms of their suggestions for investigation and in their reference to the terminology (suitably reworded for pupils to read) of the National Curriculum, e.g.

> Asking questions in science:
> *At Level 2*, I can ask why something happens. I can *predict* what might happen in my investigation.

> *At Level 3*, I can use my own ideas about things I have seen to
> think up investigations.
> *At Level 4*, I can use some ideas I have learnt in science to think
> up an investigation.

Although materials of this kind were often well produced, they were not always well received – one teacher (who abandoned them after a first attempt to use them) compared the sheets produced for pupils to record their work in Sc1 with 'social security benefit claim forms', the pupil spending hours trying to fill them in. The large-scale generation at school or local authority level of tightly structured worksheets to teach and facilitate the assessment of scientific investigation is, of course, only one of a number of organizational responses to the assessment requirements of the National Curriculum.

The Order itself was also not without uncertainties and ambiguities. The requirement that pupils distinguish between generalizations and predictive theories was difficult to interpret, and the distinction itself, presented in the National Curriculum as unproblematic, is the subject of much debate among epistemologists. There were also difficulties within the assessment structure of the Attainment Target, notably at the upper levels. At Level 8 of Key Stage 4, pupils were required to 'use scientific knowledge or theory to generate quantitative predictions and a strategy for investigation'. This is not easily distinguished from the corresponding Level 9 requirement that pupils 'use a scientific theory to make quantitative predictions and organise the collection of valid and reliable data', although a distinction might be made on the ground that the Level 8 statement entails no judgement about the quality of the strategy which a pupil develops. Equally, however, it might be claimed that any approach properly described as a 'strategy' involves much more than the collection of valid and reliable data, with the consequence that performance at Level 8 represents a higher level of achievement than at Level 9 in the supposed hierarchy.

Difficulties of this kind were dealt with in a Circular, sent to headteachers and addressing the key features of investigations at the higher levels. Produced by the School Examinations and Assessment Council (SEAC, 1993a), the Circular carried a status that might be described as quasi-official. It could not supplant the Statutory Order but it was perceived as another layer of 'government interpretation' of the legal definition of Sc1. Interestingly, the Circular ignored the three strands of Sc1 identified in the Order and offered specific differentiating features between adjacent levels of attainment. For example, Level 8, referred to above, was said to require the investigation of 'more than one aspect of a question or problem', an interpretation far from obvious in the Order itself. It is, of course, acknowledged that any written statement must under-determine practice and that the meaning of the remaining three Attainment Targets of the science component of the National Curriculum also needed to be negotiated. However, Sc1 differed from these other Targets in several important respects. It was largely a construct of the National Curriculum and it lacked an adequate foundation in the professional training and practice of the science teachers who were responsible for its entirely school-based assessment. In addition, it was meant to be integrated with the other Attainment Targets for assessment purposes. In these circumstances, the need for clear guidance, adequate training and time for professional discourse was overwhelming, and the concern of teachers was understandable, as they sought to reshape their professional practice in response to the demands being made upon them. The notion of 'accountability' was also important for some teachers:

> I want to know exactly what it is you want me to teach ... because someone, some day is going to say to me 'Have you done it?' and I want to be able to show that I have.

Equally understandable, although not sitting entirely comfortably alongside the claim that 'Investigative work is seen as an important part of students' science education' (ASE, 1993a, p. 5), was the strong sense among science teachers that the burden of responsibility for, and knowledge in relation to, Sc1 lay elsewhere than with them. Typically, the generation and definition of the Attainment Target was seen as having been done by 'mysterious figures', 'a professor or somebody who had been sent away for a weekend to do this', 'people up there' (i.e. in government) or 'those in authority'.

> We were suddenly presented with a whole new framework for practical science   and told to get on with it.

The implication of comments such as these was that:

> if this whole thing had been our idea, it would have been different.
> None of it was our idea, not any of it, it was all government
> decision and they appointed people to do this. What they have
> done is ... come up with paperwork with fantastic ambitious ideas
> and they have not managed to put any of it into schools in a usable
> form. They can't because we are not on the same wavelength.

A corollary was that curriculum development was shifted 'away from teachers, who are the ones who should be managing the development themselves'. Science teachers found themselves 'desperately trying to make Sc1 work for them', instead of confronting government at an earlier stage and saying: '[This] is rubbish. Go back and change it until it is something we can implement.'

Comments of this kind from teachers about the origins, ownership and practicality of Sc1 were often coupled with an abiding commitment to the importance of investigation in science education. For some science teachers, what was at issue was control over their own professional practice:

> I can't understand ... why science teachers have allowed the wool
> to be pulled over their eyes ... We didn't take a professional
> stance.

121

> Structures of responsibilities have changed ... Some people are
> seen as providers and others as deliverers.
>
> Who said we were still professionals?

Some science teachers speculated on the motives of those responsible for the inclusion of scientific investigation as an Attainment Target in the National Curriculum. The lack of agreement about motives among the science teachers is itself of some significance:

> I think it is ... an encouragement for people to do more practical
> work.
>
> When I was teaching in the '60s and '70s ... there was quite a lot
> of practical work but it was all recipes ... Never did the [pupils]
> make their own hypotheses.
>
> I think it's because we are trying to teach people to be scientists
> and this is one way of measuring a person as a scientist.

These perceptions by teachers should be set alongside the following comments from members of the Working Party which had, in effect, constructed Sc1:

> To us on the Working Party, skills of investigation was a main
> signal about the flavour of what science was about ... We tried to
> see ... investigatory science as really fulfilling several functions
> ... [developing] the skills needed to do science, motivating
> learning and as an example of what we believed to be ... the best
> aspects of learning in general.
>
> Everybody knew in principle [scientific investigation] was
> important, but no one knew how to describe it, and so it nearly
> didn't exist at all ... but in the end we got a version ... Looking
> back, it was rather a sort of Pandora's box of bits and pieces.

It was some time before the concerns and perceptions identified above came to be acknowledged and discussed openly within the science teachers' professional organization, the Association for Science Education (ASE). When the plans of central government for a National Curriculum were first announced, the ASE might have challenged the competence of those appointed by government to legislate the professional practice of most of its members, and/or it might have sought to distance itself from the National Curriculum and adopt the role of informed professional critic as events unfolded. The close involvement of a number of prominent members of the Association in the first Science Working Party set up in 1987 to advise government upon the content of the science component of the National Curriculum perhaps made direct criticism of that component more difficult but members of the ASE were alerted to the wider issues involved in a letter published in the Association's bulletin, *Education in*

Science. Chapman, writing in 1990, commented that the ASE seemed 'through the involvement of its leading members and officers, to have allowed itself to become too closely identified with approving ... the inherent totalitarianism of centralised curriculum control'. For Chapman, the National Curriculum threatened to reduce science teachers to 'curriculum postpersons', charged with 'delivering whatever is put in their postbags by those employed to do the government's bidding' (Chapman, 1990, p. 39). However, Chapman's view seems to have commanded little in the way of support, although the correspondence pages of the ASE bulletin are necessarily a limited and selective indication of wider opinion. Responding to Chapman's letter, Martyn Berry advised that the 'ASE must ... speak out far more loudly and more often about the true aims of science education and the need for an independent, fully professional teaching force' (Berry, 1990, pp. 38–9). Another member of the Association, lamenting that he had 'felt increasingly distanced from the ASE editorially, and in the content of many of the articles published', commented that 'At long last the ASE is publishing, albeit only in its correspondence column, something which reflects the concern of the majority of teachers' (Hennessy, 1990, p. 37).

The Association did not respond publicly to these opinions expressed by individual members and subsequent action suggests that they were ignored. Its stance, which might be summarized as 'assisting members to deliver the National Curriculum', was one which was to cause the ASE and its members some difficulty when the revised Order, incorporating Sc1, was published in December 1991 and given effect from 1 August 1992.

At the Annual Meeting of the Association in January 1993, dissatisfaction surfaced among the membership over this stance. Comparison was made with the National Association of Teachers of English (NATE), which had confronted the government over both the content of the English component of the National Curriculum and the associated testing procedures. Unusually for an ASE Annual Meeting, a resolution was prepared by eleven members, circulated to those attending the Meeting and placed before the Annual Business Meeting on the Sunday morning. The resolution called upon the Council of the Association to 'take urgent steps to assess the damaging impact of the rushed implementation of KS3 and KS4 and to advise members of the action required to prevent further damage to students' learning and enjoyment of science' (Calton and Kinsman, 1993).

Although this motion was unsuccessful, it prompted the ASE to seek the views of its members about the development of the science curriculum. Using a double-sided A4 questionnaire, members were invited to comment upon a wide variety of issues, including the use ('seen, read/used, helpful, unhelpful') which they made of official and ASE publications and how the latter might further assist them in their work. There is uncertainty about the size and composition of the sample of members who completed the questionnaire but it is likely that less than 1 per cent of the membership expressed an opinion. Nonetheless, among the responses, concern about Sc1 was a dominant feature. The ASE was urged to give greater prominence in both its journal, the *School Science Review*, and the more-frequently published *Education in Science* to 'samples of pupils' work for Sc1 with marks', 'advice on interpreting Sc1 criteria', and 'short, snappy articles giving practical advice'. Although the centrality of scientific investigation in the science component of the National Curriculum attracted some support, most ASE members emphasized the pedagogical and assessment difficulties of implementing Sc1 and drew attention to the stress and uncertainty experienced by both science teachers and their pupils. Some identified 'more time', 'more training' and 'better support material' as ways of easing their difficulties. Others urged reform or even the abolition of Sc1. Overall, the attitude of the ASE members who responded to the questionnaire was strongly negative, with over half the respondents classifying this Attainment Target as a problematic curriculum initiative (ASE, 1993b).

In May 1993 the ASE acknowledged that the 'majority of concern' expressed in the questionnaire related to Sc1 and undertook a further survey to identify more specific ways of helping its members. More particularly, the survey sought to gather detailed views from teachers 'regarding the problems they perceived in delivering Attainment Target 1 of the National Curriculum for Science', and to 'gain a clearer understanding of how science teachers thought science education in schools might be supported more effectively by the scientific industries'. The questionnaire was designed and printed by British Nuclear Fuels which also undertook to analyse the data and prepare the report. The questionnaire, sent by the ASE to 2500 primary- and 2500 secondary-school teachers, generated a 23 per cent response by the end of the summer term of 1993. Of the 1145 respondents, 698 and 413 members were teachers in secondary and primary schools respectively. Asked whether 'Sc1 is the most important of the 4 Science Attainment Targets', 80 per cent of the primary teachers agreed that this was so, with half of these expressing 'very strong agreement'. Among the 698 secondary-school science teachers, only 25 per cent supported the privileged status of Sc1. Unfortunately, the survey did not explore respondents' reasons for their opinions and the report could only conclude, rather lamely, that 'it is interesting . . . that teachers mostly qualified in core science subjects feel Sc1 to be less important than those with mostly other teaching qualifications who may be having difficulty in delivering this area of the curriculum'. In the absence of firm data, it is perhaps legitimate to speculate that the difference between the primary and the secondary teachers, while it may be related to qualification, also derives from the greater emphasis in primary pedagogy upon skills, processes and 'child-centred learning', at the expense of scientific knowledge acquisition. It is also interesting to note that both primary and secondary teachers in the survey found Sc1 'more difficult' than the remaining three Attainment Targets and judged that science teaching would 'deteriorate' if 'Sc1 were not delivered satisfactorily' (ASE, 1993c, p. 6).

This greater difficulty is reflected in the opinions recorded by schools' inspectors following their inspection of science lessons. In 1992–3, standards in scientific investigation were said to 'remain lower than for other Attainment Targets' at Key Stages 3 and 4, although some high standards of investigative work were 'beginning to emerge' (OFSTED, 1993, p. 2). The following year, the Office of Her Majesty's Chief Inspector of Schools again reported that 'In Key Stages 3 and 4 levels of achievement in Attainment Target 1 are lower than in the other Attainment Targets', adding that there was also greater variation between schools in this aspect of their work (OFSTED, 1994, p. 3).

EDUCATIONAL POLICY AND THE RECONSTRUCTION OF PROFESSIONAL PRACTICE

The centralized, 'top-down' approach to educational policy represented by the National Curriculum in England and Wales has received attention from scholars working within a number of different research perspectives. Some (e.g. Ball, 1990; Kogan, 1975, 1983) have focused their attention on the shaping of educational policy as a political response at national level to a variety of social, economic or other interests. There is a corresponding and complementary literature concerned with the 'implementation' of national policy at some appropriate level (e.g. Gleeson, 1989; Saunders, 1985). However, two assumptions are noteworthy in these approaches. The first is that policy-making and policy implementation can be sharply distinguished. The second is that it is possible to determine a central educational policy relating to the curriculum or assessment that is unequivocal and unproblematic. Both of these assumptions present difficulties and both have important consequences, not least for those with research interests in educational policy. For example, by presenting policy as an essentially linear process, the distinction between policy-making and policy implementation promotes a dichotomy between 'theory' and 'practice' and privileges the former over the latter. It also encourages the notion of 'policy subversion' in which teachers, or others, 'subvert' policy, for example, by appropriating it for purposes very different from those intended by the policy-makers. Such subversion/appropriation is much in evidence in the literature concerned with the response of schools and local education authorities to the Technical and Vocational Education Initiative (e.g. Dale *et al.*, 1990; McCulloch, 1986; Saunders, 1985).

In the case of Sc1, the evidence presented above suggests strongly that it is inappropriate to regard policy, formulated as a central government directive about the nature, teaching and assessment of scientific investigation within the school context, as something centrally promulgated and then subject to drift or, depending upon one's perspective, appropriation and subversion. Arguably, the greater role in originating and sustaining policy in teaching and assessing Sc1 lay not with central government but with schools, Examining Groups, the Association for Science Education and the teachers themselves. In these circumstances, policy becomes a function that, far from being centrally controlled, is delocalized and differentiated. From this perspective, much of the data cited above is indicative of science teachers actively constructing policy by continuously drawing upon their professional experience and 'teacherly knowledge'.

More is involved here than the observation that 'Practitioners do not confront policy texts as naive readers' (Bowe *et al.*, 1992, p. 22) and its corollary that curriculum or assessment policy is contested, negotiated and realized by diverse individuals functioning in different contexts, each with its own legacy of experience, interests, values and sense of purpose. Central to the understanding of policy realization presented here is the professional practice of science teachers and, in particular, the notion of 'professional judgement'.

This notion was frequently invoked when teachers sought advice on how to deal with the many uncertainties with which Sc1 presented them. Such invocation seems, at first sight, to challenge the sense of deprofessionalization and deskilling to which reference has been made above, since it recognizes both the independence of science teachers and the indeterminate elements within their practice. However, two key aspects of the implementation of Sc1 contradict this. The first was the insistence that the activities undertaken by pupils for assessment purposes must meet specific and centrally defined characteristics, pre-eminent among which was the requirement that these activities involve self-generated entire investigations. There was no general recognition by policy-makers that teachers might have views on the value and practicability of this requirement, and where such views were acknowledged, they were dismissed. The negative judgements made by teachers about Sc1 came to be represented as, or were assumed to be, wrong or misdirected, rather than valued as contributions to a professional debate. The second aspect which indicates a thrust towards deprofessionalization was the stream of *ad hoc* guidance, addressing specific issues within Sc1 and illustrated above. This was a consequence of widespread uncertainty and ignorance, among teachers and others involved in science education, about the structure of Sc1 and what could or 'ought' to be taught and assessed within it. It was when such guidance failed, as it frequently did under the weight of the self-imposed task of seeking to construct a codified, bureaucratized version of 'the processes of scientific investigation', that the rhetoric of teachers' professional judgement came into play.

An associated claim that the emphasis on investigation represented by Sc1 merely reflected a widespread element within the existing practice of science teachers is untenable. Sc1 involved not a consolidation of existing practice but an attempt to impose curricular change by statutory means. It also involved a contradictory and fractured perspective on the role of teachers, within which it is possible to see their putative professional status and their competence to decide matters of educational practice simultaneously exploited and dismantled. Ultimately, however, the difficulties underlying teachers' responses to trying to teach and assess scientific investigation within the context of the National Curriculum reflect the lack of a coherent and common perspective on their professional relationship to, and authority over, their own practice in laboratories and classrooms.

NOTE

1 Throughout this chapter, quotations derived from those interviewed as part of the research study are unattributed in order to preserve anonymity.

REFERENCES

ASE (Association for Science Education) (1993a) *The Place of Investigations in Science Education: A Report from the Investigations in Science Task Group*. Hatfield: ASE.

ASE (1993b) *Developing the Science Curriculum*. Hatfield: ASE.

ASE (1993c) *Sc1 Survey by the Association for Science Education with the Support of British Nuclear Fuels Education Unit*. Hatfield: ASE.

BAAS (British Association for the Advancement of Science) (1868) *Report of the Thirty-Seventh Annual Meeting, Dundee 1867*. London: Murray.

Bachelard, G. (1958) *Le nouvel esprit scientifique* (6th edn.; first edn. 1934). Paris: Presses Universitaires de France.

Ball, S. J. (1990) *Politics and Policy Making in Education: Explorations in Policy Sociology*. London: Routledge.

Berry, M. (1990) Letter. *Education in Science* **138**: 38–9.

Bowe, R. and Ball, S. J. with Gold, A. (1992) *Reforming Education and Changing Schools: Case Studies in Policy Sociology*. London: Routledge.

Brock, W. H. (ed.) (1973) *H. E. Armstrong and the Teaching of Science, 1880–1930*. Cambridge: Cambridge University Press.

Buchan, A. S. (1995) Realising a policy: INSET provision for a problematic Attainment Target. *British Journal of Inservice Education*, **21**(1): 1–15.

Calton, P. and Kinsman, J. (1993) Resolution proposed to the Annual Business Meeting of the Association for Science Education, submitted under Rule 55(1) section (v).

Chapman, B. R. (1990) Letter. *Education in Science* **137**: 39.

Coles, M. (1989) *Active Science*. London: Collins Educational.

Dale, R., Bowe, R., Harris, D., Loveys, M., Moore, R., Shilling, C., Sykes, P., Trevitt, J. and Vasecchie, V. (1990) *The TVEI Story: Policy, Practice and the Preparation of the Workforce*. Milton Keynes: Open University Press.

DES (Department of Education and Science) (1985) *Science 5–16: A Statement of Policy*. London: HMSO.

DES/WO (Department of Education and Science/Welsh Office) (1989) *Science in the National Curriculum*. London: HMSO.

DES/WO (1991) *Science in the National Curriculum*. London: HMSO.

Donnelly, J. F., Buchan, A. S., Jenkins, E. W. and Welford, A. G. (1993) *Investigations in Science Education Policy. Sc1 in the National Curriculum for England and Wales*. Leeds: Centre for Policy Studies in Education, University of Leeds.

Education in Science (1993) Highlights of February Council EIS, **152**: 7.

Feyerabend, P. (1975) *Against Method: An Outline of an Anarchistic Theory of Knowledge*. London: New Left Books.

Gleeson, D. (1989) *The Paradox of Training: Making Progress out of Crisis*. Milton Keynes: Open University Press.

Halliwell, H. F. (1966) Aims and action in the classroom. *Education in Chemistry*, **3**: 5.

Hennessy, A. (1990) Letter. *Education in Science*, **140**: 37.

Hesse, M. B. (1980) *Revolutions and Reconstructions in the Philosophy of Science*. Brighton: Harvester Press.

Kogan, M. (1975) *Educational Policy-making*. London: Allen and Unwin.

Kogan, M. (1983) The case of education. In K. Young (ed.), *National Interests and Local Government*. London: Heinemann, pp. 58–75.

Laudan, L., Donovan, A., Laudan, R., Barker, P., Brown, H., Leplin, J., Thagard, P. and Wystra, S. (1986) Scientific change: philosophical models and historical research. *Synthese* **69**(1): 142–223.

Layton, D. (1982) Science education and values education – an essential tension ? In J. Head (ed.), *Science Education for the Citizen*. London: British Council and Chelsea College, pp. 101–8.

McCulloch, G. (1986) Policy, politics and education: the Technical and Vocational Education Initiative. *Journal of Education Policy*, **1**(1): 35–52.

NEAB (Northern Examinations and Assessment Board) (1993) *Science Framework: Guidance on the Assessment of Sc1*. Manchester: NEAB.

NCC (National Curriculum Council) (1989) *Science: Non-Statutory Guidance*. London: NCC.

OFSTED (1993) *Science. Key Stages 1, 2, 3 and 4, Fourth Year 1992–3*. London: HMSO.

OFSTED (1994) *Science. A Review of Inspection Findings 1993/94*. London: HMSO.

Pimentel, G. C. (ed.) (1960) *Chemistry: An Experimental Science*. San Francisco: Freeman.

Ravetz, J. R. (1990) New ideas about science, relevant to education. In E. W. Jenkins (ed.), *Policy Issues and School Science Education*. Leeds: Centre for Studies in Science and Mathematics Education, University of Leeds, pp. 18–27.

Revell, M. (1993) Test-tube baby. *Times Educational Supplement* (Extra Science), 21 May p. 2.

Richards, C. and Holford, D. (eds) (1983) *The Teaching of Primary Science: Policy and Practice*. Lewes: Falmer Press.

Saunders, M. (1985) *Emerging Issues for TVEI Implementation*. Lancaster: University of Lancaster.

SEAC (School Examinations and Assessment Council) (1992) *School Assessment Folder (Part 3), Materials to Support the Assessment of Sc1: Scientific Investigations. Science 1992 National Pilot*. London: SEAC.

SEAC (1993a) *Scientific Investigation and GCSE in '94 and '95*. Letter from Hilary Nichols to all headteachers, dated 27 September 1993. London: SEAC.

SEAC (1993b) *School Assessment Folder – Assessing Sc1*. London: SEAC.

Thackray, A. (1980) The pre-history of an academic discipline: the study of the history of science in the United States 1891–1941. *Minerva*, **18**(3): 448–73.

Thomson Committee (1918) *Natural Science in Education*. London: HMSO.

Chapter 9

Careers Under Threat? Careers Teachers and the National Curriculum

Susan Harris

INTRODUCTION

The Education Reform Act of 1988 (ERA), which included the introduction of a National Curriculum in England and Wales, marked a significant change in educational policy from what had gone before. The previous concern over relevance in the curriculum, which had been dominant in the early 1980s (reflected in, for example, the introduction of the Technical and Vocational Education Initiative), was superseded by concern over standards and accountability.

On the eve of the introduction of the National Curriculum careers education had, for a brief moment in time, reached a high point in its history only to find itself first of all omitted altogether from the National Curriculum Consultative Document of 1987 and then included in the final document in 1989, but only as a mere 'cross-curricular theme', subordinate to the core National Curriculum subjects.

The stated rationale for the introduction of a National Curriculum was to increase standards of teaching and learning and provide greater standardization across schools. It is on these two points that its impact on careers education and therefore on careers teachers will be examined in this chapter. However, it is important to first say something about the origins of careers education and to establish its position in the curriculum prior to the upheavals brought about through ERA and the imposition of a National Curriculum.

THE EMERGENCE OF CAREERS EDUCATION

'Careers guidance' emerged at the beginning of the twentieth century as a response to a growing concern for youngsters who were leaving school for the workplace in a period of high unemployment and social upheaval following World War I. The concern of educators as well as welfare organizations was shared by a government fearful of the possibility of social unrest. As a result, in addition to labour exchanges set up to help workers find work, juvenile employment bureaux were targeted specifically at youngsters because of their more vulnerable position in the labour market (Harris, 1990; Roberts, 1971). A dual system of vocational guidance slowly developed with education authorities responsible for advising school leavers, and the juvenile employment bureaux responsible for finding them suitable work. However, although guidance represented a new aspect of work for both schoolteachers and for officers of the juvenile employment service, there was little contact between the two and no effective division of labour negotiated. In practice, schools provided very limited careers information for youngsters, while employment officers generally 'fitted' youngsters into whatever jobs were available.[1]

In the early decades of careers work, careers teachers primarily provided information about local jobs, although they had little in the way of resources other than pamphlets and brochures. They were unlikely to have a specific 'careers' library for pupils to access. It was not until the 1960s (a period marked by educational expansion and optimism) that careers guidance came to be seen as an important aspect of the curriculum, involving skills that pupils could and should be taught, instead of being seen simply as an adjunct to the main academic curriculum (Harris, 1990). This change was signalled in the new terminology of 'careers education'. However, although a more sophisticated form of careers education developed in schools, there was little change in the marginal position and status of careers teachers, a point to which I shall return.[2]

By the 1970s, when careers education began to 'take off', the country was plunged into a deep economic crisis which had profound implications because it exposed the underlying tension between education's ability to meet the needs of the individual and the needs of the economy. (Examples of this unresolved tension were the Black Papers and Prime Minister Callaghan's Ruskin College speech, which stimulated the 'Great Debate' on education.) Instead of practitioners and professionals setting the agenda, economic and political interests dominated the educational debate, including the development of vocational elements in the school curriculum during the 1970s and 1980s.

THE POSITION OF CAREERS TEACHERS IN SCHOOLS[3]

Careers teachers come into careers work for different reasons and by different routes because careers education is not a subject in which student teachers can specialize during their initial teacher training. Some careers teachers are highly committed to careers education whilst others may simply have been designated a responsibility for careers (Harris, 1990, 1992a). Careers teachers are not conventional classroom teachers with their own subject specialism; most retain a large subject teaching commitment, with little time allocated specifically for their careers work.

Historically, the position of the careers teacher has not been one of high status, and careers work has operated on the periphery of school life. A number of factors can be identified which help explain this marginal position. The first is the academically oriented curriculum that has been a significant characteristic of the English education system, which has meant that subjects or activities deemed non-academic have traditionally struggled for curriculum time and status (Goodson, 1983; Goodson and Ball, 1984). In addition to this lack of subject status, careers teachers, unlike other colleagues, are not part of a traditional department and this places them at a disadvantage when it comes to securing resources, timetable time, and influence. A third factor is that few careers teachers can draw on claims to having had specialist training for careers work. There has been no accepted or uniform remuneration specifically for teachers' careers responsibilities, and many have in the past and continue to carry out their careers work with little or no recognition (Harris, 1990, 1992a, b).

Moreover, in addition to their disadvantaged situation the actual position and standing of careers teachers differs across schools, depending largely on the level of support of the headteacher (who has the power to sponsor or ignore certain curricular areas or particular teachers); the level of support from staff; the ethos and culture of the school; and the commitment of the careers teacher to careers education. Irrespective of their credentials or commitment to careers education, those careers teachers who enjoy the active support of their head-teachers are in a much more influential position than those who do not (Harris, 1992b).

THE RISE AND FALL OF CAREERS EDUCATION, 1986–9

During 'Industry Year' in 1986 the government published its White Paper, *Working Together – Education and Training* (DES, 1986), which encouraged education to become more responsive to the needs of industry. This document suggested a more prominent role for careers education and guidance in schools, and indeed careers education appeared to have become a key point in the government's thinking. In the following year a Joint Initiative of the then Department of Education and Science and the Department of Employment, *Working Together for a Better Future* (DES/DE, 1987), was published in which emphasis was given to the need to prepare young people for adult life. It was recommended that careers education should be given a central role in the curriculum as a means by which schools could prepare young people for their transition from school to work. The document also outlined a way of moving towards a more integrated policy for education and training. Although there was little that was new in either document, careers teachers generally welcomed both documents for the attention they drew to their 'specialist' work and because they appeared to indicate that careers education and careers teachers should have a much higher profile than hitherto.

However, in the same week as the Joint Initiative was launched, the government issued its proposals for the National Curriculum, and thereby significantly reduced the impact of its schools' Careers Initiative because all attention was drawn to the National Curriculum. More remarkably, the National

Curriculum 5–16 consultative document made no mention at all of careers education. Not surprisingly, the response of the National Association of Careers and Guidance Teachers (NACGT) was one of disbelief and anger.[4] At its Annual Conference the Association passed a resolution demanding that in future statements about the National Curriculum, the then Secretary of State for Education, Kenneth Baker, should ensure that careers education was included as an 'essential element'. Different explanations for the absence of careers education were given depending on which spokesperson was questioned (*NACGT Journal* 1987). For example, Angela Rumbold, the then Minister of State for Education, explained to an NACGT delegation that the government had not wanted to prescribe too much of the curriculum. Baroness Hooper, then Parliamentary Under-Secretary of State, commented that while careers education had not been mentioned it would form an integral part of the entire curriculum.

These developments demonstrate the way in which careers education *per se* had become a secondary consideration of the government, whose main concern was that schools should be encouraging positive attitudes to work and that the Initiatives were a response to a much broader economic and political discourse than the merits of careers education. That the government was able to blow hot and cold over careers education was, in part, possible because of the weak bargaining position of the NACGT but also because the government was not at the time, as one NACGT council member explained, 'in listening mode'. The eventual White Paper on the National Curriculum, *From Policy to Practice*, published in 1989, highlighted the vulnerability of the careers teacher: although careers education re-emerged, it did so as one of five 'cross-curricular themes'. The distinction between National Curriculum subjects and cross-curricular themes strengthened the already dominant position of traditional subjects in terms of, for example, timetable time and resources *at the expense of* other curricular areas. Moreover, given the curriculum overload resulting from the implementation of the National Curriculum, careers education was, once more, on the periphery.

THE RE-EMERGENCE OF CAREERS EDUCATION

Between the National Curriculum consultation document (DES, 1987) and the final blueprint, *National Curriculum: From Policy to Practice*, two years later (DES, 1989), some hope was given to careers teachers by the publication of *Careers Education and Guidance from 5 to 16* (DES, 1988). This document was 'intended as a contribution to the deliberations of the National Curriculum Council and its working groups' (Preface). It suggested that careers education and guidance was needed by all pupils in years 9 to 11 although groundwork for it needed to be carried out in primary schools. However, it is questionable how much notice the National Curriculum Council (NCC) took of this document.

During the first year of National Curriculum debate, when the Whole

Curriculum Working Parties (and their subgroups) were set up to discuss different subject areas, there was a great deal of anxiety expressed by the NACGT Executive Council about the future of careers education not least because there was, initially, no one on the working parties with particular expertise in careers (*NACGT Journal*, 1988). But by the following year the Interim Whole Curriculum Working Party eventually recognized that careers education had a specific role within the curriculum, a point which had not been acknowledged when the working party had been first set up. In addition, the NACGT president had been appointed to the Careers Working Party subgroup. Both developments were welcomed enthusiastically by the NACGT:

> At last I am pleased to report, I think some advances have been
> made. The reference to careers education in 'The National
> Curriculum: From Policy to Practice' *clearly and unambiguously*
> puts careers education on the curriculum map. (*NACGT Journal*,
> 1989; italics added)

Although the Association was now more optimistic there was still cause for concern. For example, there were reports of cuts in training budgets for careers teachers, raising fears that the staffing demands in schools brought about by the National Curriculum might affect the availability of teachers for careers work.

The influence of NACGT on the final *Curriculum Guidance 6: Careers Education and Guidance* (NCC, 1990) is questionable. Although two of the leading names in the guidance field, Tony Watts and Bill Law, acted as consultants to the working party, NACGT was not involved in the early discussion and planning stages and indeed it has been suggested by some NACGT members that NCC discarded a lot of the input by the guidance professionals. According to one NACGT council member, quoted in June 1995, this was because the government was not really interested:

> Cross-curricular themes booklets were a mishmash ... I know Tony
> Watts wrote the careers one but a lot of the stuff put in was cut out.
> There was no real interest in it so it began to fall into disrepute.

CAREERS TEACHERS' VIEWS OF THE NATIONAL CURRICULUM

This chapter draws on data gathered from in-depth interviews with careers teachers from eight comprehensive schools in a Midlands town in June and July of 1995. These teachers had previously been part of a larger study I carried out between 1986 and 1988, which examined the position and status of careers teachers in secondary school.[5] Additional data are drawn from discussions held with careers teachers and practitioners from other parts of the country.

The careers teachers interviewed – here denoted CT1, CT2, etc. – were unanimous in their view that the National Curriculum had not improved the position and status of careers education in the curriculum and had, in some cases, actually been detrimental.

> National Curriculum did nothing for careers, in fact in many ways it was a very negative move, very negative. (CT1)

> I wouldn't say that the National Curriculum had played much of a part in developments in careers education here. (CT2)

In contrast to their scepticism of the National Curriculum, most of the careers teachers felt that careers education had been given a substantial boost by the various financial incentives from the government aimed at improving the quality of provision in schools and colleges, for example the Careers Libraries Initiative (1992–3) and the Enhanced Guidance for Years 9 and 10 announced in the 1994 Competitiveness White Paper.[6]

> All I would say is that the profile (of CE) has been raised because of the financial initiatives ... but I don't think it is anything to do with the National Curriculum. (CT5)

Some of the comments made by the careers teachers reflected a wider concern among educationalists of the impact of the radical change brought about by the Education Reform Act. With the introduction of such measures as open enrolment, local management of schools, grant-maintained status, league tables and the National Curriculum, schools have been forced to compete against each other, with the result that differentiation within and between schools has increased (Bowe and Ball, 1992; Harris, 1994; Harris *et al.*, 1996). The more competitive climate raises concern for careers teachers in particular because traditionally careers education programmes have been focused around the individual and their personal and social needs, rather than primarily upon academic performance and achievement. For example, one careers teacher who worked in a school which had prided itself on its pastoral work and where there was a well-established careers programme operating, felt that teachers no longer had the same flexibility in their teaching that they had enjoyed prior to the National Curriculum because of the demands of the new Subject Orders. Moreover, the emergence of a competitive school ethos worked against the more open and pupil-centred approach developed over the years in many areas of the curriculum, including careers education:

> ...there's been a change of emphasis generally in schools away from the general helping and social care of children to the development of examination results and league tables and competition between schools and fighting for kids and marketing schools. And you know, it's the real commercial world, which really doesn't put the emphasis on the pastoral development of individual kids and the care of individual kids in the same way that the [careers education] programme used to. (CT6)

When asked if this happened even in his own school, which had had such a strong pastoral base, he replied:

> Yeah ... The National Curriculum has become the priority of the school for the last three or four years. And because it's been the priority of the school then the emphasis on in-service training and the allocation of resources, the allocation of time, time on timetable, everything has been focused on developing the National Curriculum really at the detriment to everything else, so a detriment to the PSE programme, a detriment to careers education and guidance, and a detriment to the pastoral system of the school. (CT6)

Another careers teacher interviewed, who had been appointed in 1991, argued that for her school, which had a poor academic track record but had established a good reputation for its social education programme, the National Curriculum had been 'disastrous' because the non-academic traditions of the school were no longer seen as a strength but had become a weakness:

> I actually think it's [the National Curriculum] had a disastrous effect on this school because this school had a sort of knee-jerk reaction about it ... and that coupled with the fact now the government expects all these league tables ... and we're not an academic school and the kids don't perform very well. (CT1)

The external pressure on the school to shift its traditional stance was substantial. Despite the careers teacher's strong views about the need for the school to move towards vocational courses to cater for its pupils, she felt that it was very unlikely to happen because:

> heads like ours are still too frightened to move onto that area, and so many of our kids need it, but it would affect our exam statistics. And that's a big worry in an 11–16 school. (CT1)

Nor were schools with a proven academic track record immune to the new competitive climate. For example, one careers teacher in a school with a strong academic reputation remarked that all headteachers were now under a great deal of pressure to maintain and improve their results and outperform their 'rivals':

> I think there's pressures on all schools now to get the results ... so it's getting the kids through the exam subjects [which] is I suppose any head's priority. (CT2)

It was also evident from the data that in schools where careers education was firmly established, enjoyed the support of the headteacher and had a committed careers teacher, the National Curriculum had offered no guarantee of holding on to such a secure position. For careers teachers who were less established and less secure of management support, the National Curriculum had made their struggle for timetable time, resources and status even harder.

Reflections of two careers teachers about their experiences during the introduction of the National Curriculum illustrate this point. The first quotation is from a careers teacher who prior to the National Curriculum enjoyed the support of his headteacher and had a committed team of teachers to help him in careers education; the second is from a careers teacher who was, at the time, quite new to careers work, did not have similar support from her headteacher, and had no staff support.

> Initially when National Curriculum came on line, or when it was first proposed and the initial documents came out, I thought it was lip service being paid to [careers education] . . . it was important to do this and it was important to do that in schools, and there seemed to be no provision for careers . . . If you took science and maths and English and those subjects that were seen as being important and put them next to PSE, it looked as if PSE was being eased out and it was going to be under a lot of pressure. I felt then and still feel that in some schools where they didn't have PSE under way in some form, it would be difficult to actually get it on to the timetable with pressures from National Curriculum time. (CT7)

> I felt threatened, yes, I felt very threatened by it and I felt that I could have decisions made that could totally alter my working life and my role in school. I almost felt like schools were being given the opportunity to ditch the subject if they wanted to, and I did feel very uneasy about it. (CT3)

CAREERS EDUCATION AS A CROSS-CURRICULAR THEME

In 1989, the NCC published *The National Curriculum and Whole School Planning* (NCC, 1989), which summarized the core and foundation subjects and laid out its plan for various types of cross-curricular provision in terms of 'dimensions', 'skills' and 'themes'. Dimensions were concerned with promoting personal and social development and were to be met through the curriculum as a whole; skills were to be developed through subjects; and themes were described as 'elements that enrich the educational experience of pupils'– these included education for economic and industrial understanding; health education; careers education and guidance; environmental education; and education for citizenship.

Two points need to be made about the cross-curricular themes because they further illustrate the vulnerability and inability of careers teachers, as a professional group, to impose their views of the importance of careers education on the curriculum. The first concerns the status of the 'themes'. Dufour (1990) has drawn attention to the absence of public deliberation over the cross-curricular themes compared with that surrounding the public and legal requirements of the National Curriculum 'subjects'. The implication of this is that 'subjects' have a greater status than 'themes', which are not contentious and can be imposed with little discussion or negotiation with the various interest and pressure groups.

The second point is the way in which the five themes were chosen by the NCC. There were a large number of themes to choose from, including media studies and aesthetics, but the five themes which came to be adopted were those which seemed to have the strongest backing from interest groups (Dufour, 1990). The fact that careers education had the support of employers most probably explains the reason for its inclusion in the five. Without such backing it is doubtful that the NACGT's voice alone would have been listened to.

Although not prescriptive of how careers education as a cross-curricular theme was to be incorporated into the school curriculum, the underlying rationale was that permeation was the best method. This approach was not new and many careers practitioners had been unconvinced by it in the past, believing it to have been unsuccessful because of the tendency for careers to get 'lost'. Indeed the NICEC Careers Guidance Integration Project (Evans and Law, 1984) came to the conclusion that it was difficult to make cross-curricular careers actually work. Moreover, the proposals went against the views expressed in the *National Curriculum 5–16* (DES, 1987), which in effect argued that careers education could not be totally permeated. It is also interesting to note at this point that although there had been very little consultation with NACGT over the NCC's *Curriculum Guidance 6*, it had been asked to provide case studies to accompany the document. These never appeared and although no official reason was given, it is widely thought, within NACGT, that it was because the studies had not shown careers education permeating the curriculum as NCC had hoped they would. This episode reinforces the general view among careers practitioners that there were serious questions about the validity of the cross-curricular model.

Careers teachers' earlier scepticism of the permeation model remained when it reappeared in the National Curriculum. Many believed it was not the most appropriate way of providing for careers education, and that an integrated approach simply meant a downgrading for careers education *and* less of it. They also feared that most subject departments would be preoccupied with fulfilling the Subject Orders and would, therefore, have little time for the cross-curricular themes.[7] As one careers teacher interviewed explained:

> they've come and gone, haven't they. Where are they now? And the idea on paper was good but in reality with all the other National Curriculum Orders that were coming through, it was a wish-list quite honestly. Staff were more interested in delivering what they had to. (CT4)

Or, as another careers teacher argued, teachers had more pressing concerns than ensuring cross-curricular work was going on:

> I think staff are terribly bogged down with the National
> Curriculum and they're always keeping their things in order and
> then with inspections and statistics and league tables, there aren't
> many cross-curricular things going on. (CT8)

There is evidence to suggest that the views of careers teachers were well founded. Whitty *et al.* (1994) report that cross-curricular themes have been marginalized by National Curriculum Subject Orders, whilst other research suggests that this failure is not at all surprising:

> Whilst the NCC requires schools to take whole school curriculum
> planning seriously there has been little useful guidance as to how
> schools can begin this process ... It is difficult to expect schools to
> take such a challenge seriously when it clearly comes as an
> afterthought, as a way of producing coherence and wholeness in a
> curriculum which is increasingly fragmented and narrowly subject
> led. (Buck and Inman, 1993)

In addition to lack of status, schools have faced severe restraints in delivering cross-curricular themes because of pressure on school timetables, lack of funding and lack of staff expertise (Saunders *et al.*, 1995). Findings from a national survey conducted for the NACGT in 1993 also suggest that careers education has been badly affected by the National Curriculum. Of the five ways of organizing careers education mentioned in the NCC's *Curriculum Guidance 6*, only one way (through personal and social education) was found to be used to any great extent, and less than a quarter of schools had careers education permeating the whole curriculum, except in Years 7 and 8 (Cleaton, 1993, p. 35). While there had been an increase in the number of schools providing careers education in Years 7 and 8, there were still schools which did not provide careers education for certain students.[8] Cleaton's report (made on behalf of ICG and NACGT) concluded with the following: 'careers education has suffered a setback since the 1987 Survey ... schools are now delivering careers education in accordance with the National Curriculum' (Cleaton, 1993, p. 84).

It was claimed that the National Curriculum was introduced to improve the quality of teaching and learning and also as a means of achieving greater uniformity of provision. In the case of careers education neither has happened. There has been a great deal of confusion about the status of the NCC's 'guidance' to schools regarding the cross-curricular themes and this has resulted in a wide variation across schools in their interpretation and implementation. As Watkins suggests: 'The influence of pieces of paper which are centrally published as guidance on the curriculum is as weak as it has ever been. It is frequently difficult to find these guidance publications in a particular school' (Watkins, 1995, p. 126).

Because of the lesser status of 'themes', coupled with the confusion about what was statutory and what was guidance, schools with little support for careers education have been able to ignore or pay lip-service to the themes, whilst other schools supportive of careers education have been left in a weak bargaining position to face struggles with National Curriculum subjects. Such confusion has undoubtedly been exacerbated by the fluctuating views of education ministers. For example, during Kenneth Clarke's period as Education Secretary little guidance was given on cross-curricular elements because he felt that schools should be allowed to concentrate on the core subjects and statutory obligations. Consequently, from 1992 to 1994 there were few public pronouncements on the cross-curricular themes. Currently, it appears to be the case that while some schools still talk about cross-curricular themes and cross-curricular careers work, others have abandoned this and instead refer to 'integrated careers work', which is defined in terms of their own school's curriculum.[9]

Whilst careers teachers were very sceptical about the cross-curricular themes, there was perhaps some consolation to be drawn from the recognition in the NCC's *Curriculum Guidance 6* of the important role of the careers coordinator:

> Careers teachers/co-ordinators will need a job description,
> sufficient status, resources, support and the skills required to
> undertake the job, i.e. skills of staff management, curriculum
> development and management, liaison with outside agencies,
> employers, further and higher education. (NCC, 1990, p. 6)

Unfortunately, although it comes as no surprise to careers teachers and practitioners, such positive statements have not been realized. As the 1993 survey of careers education and guidance shows, the level of specialized training for careers teachers has not significantly improved since the first national survey in 1987 (Cleaton, 1987). Another worrying trend is that there appears to have been a fall in the number of teachers involved in careers education (Cleaton, 1993). Perhaps more significantly, careers teachers' involvement in school management decision-making has not greatly improved since 1987. Such findings are echoed in the more recent 1995 OFSTED survey of careers education and guidance in almost 200 schools in England. This OFSTED survey painted an all too familiar picture with little evidence found of senior management promoting or coordinating careers education and guidance, and few institutions with a coherent and developmental careers education and guidance provision across the key stages; moreover, in about half the schools in the survey timetable time for careers education had declined (OFSTED, 1995c).

CONCLUDING COMMENTS

One of the main reasons given for the introduction of the National Curriculum in schools was to raise standards and improve the quality of teaching and learning. In the case of careers education, data from the research presented in this chapter would suggest that this goal has not been achieved. The position of careers education in the National Curriculum was clearly an afterthought. In 1986 and 1987 it had been given a central role in preparing young people for adult life. By the time the National Curriculum consultative document appeared careers education had disappeared, only to reappear as a cross-curricular 'theme'. As such, it remains subordinate to National Curriculum 'subjects', in particular those making up the 'core curriculum'.

Schools' careers education programmes have historically reflected careers teachers' perspectives on the needs of their pupils in their particular school and have, therefore, varied enormously in orientation and underlying rationale as well as in content and method of delivery. There has been no uniform improvement or standardization in careers education since the National Curriculum was introduced. NCC guidelines, which were not statutory, have been interpreted in very different ways by schools, with no uniform response, and in some cases schools have ignored the guidelines altogether. Provision and delivery of careers education remains varied and variable across schools.

Similarly, neither the position nor the status of careers teachers in schools has been enhanced as a result of the National Curriculum. The National Curriculum did not provide any mechanisms by which those careers teachers in the least influential positions prior to its introduction could enhance their status, nor did it offer any guarantee to those who had fought and won battles for timetable time, resources and management support. The status of careers teachers and careers education remains dependent (even more so than prior to the National Curriculum) on the ethos of the school, the support of the headteacher, the commitment of the careers teacher and the support of colleagues.

The review of the National Curriculum by Sir Ron Dearing in 1993/4 has done little to redress the continued vulnerability of careers education and careers teachers. Although some curriculum time has been freed, teachers of National Curriculum subjects are in a stronger position to argue for this (newly found time) because the success of schools depends so much on league table performance and identifiable signs of predominantly academic achievement.

However, since the National Curriculum there have been some encouraging signs which may help improve the position of careers teachers. For example, in the revised OFSTED Framework (OFSTED, 1995a), which took effect from May 1996, careers education has been included in the section dealing with the curriculum (and assessment) instead of being placed under a section relating to pupils' support and guidance, a move which should raise its profile and therefore that of careers teachers also. There is also more detailed guidance provided for inspectors, (OFSTED, 1995b), which should, in theory at least, move towards a more consistent reporting of careers education and thereby provide a more reliable picture of current practice.

Another important publication is *Looking Forward: Careers Education and Guidance in the Curriculum* (SCAA, 1995), which is designed to bring up to date earlier NCC guidance on careers education. This document is significant because it is the first time that SCAA has considered non-core curriculum subjects. However, despite its optimistic and supportive tone, some of the very real problems which careers teachers face are not adequately addressed. For example, the National Curriculum referred to careers teachers as careers 'coordinators' and as such should have an overview of the curriculum, involvement at whole-school planning level and a position of authority (SCAA, 1995, p. 11). But, what is clear from the research discussed here is that the careers 'coordinator' is rarely, if at all, in a position of power or authority to actually coordinate – many are not in a senior management post or of senior teacher status or directly involved in whole-school planning (Cleaton, 1993; OFSTED, 1995c). A constant feature of careers teachers' work has been that they have had 'lots of responsibility but no power' (Watkins, 1994, p. 146). This was a source of frustration to many of the careers teachers interviewed, particularly those who had taken up their position during the National Curriculum upheavals when timetable time and resources were being renegotiated:

> Yes, with anything, if you want to maintain its [CE] status and
> also enhance it and develop it, and argue for funds, you need to be
> in a strategic position to do that. (CT4)

Until careers teachers are in a position of authority then the new terminology of careers coordinator, which implies a key role for careers teachers, will continue to mean little in reality.

It is too early to say whether the higher profile signalled by OFSTED and SCAA in conjunction with the recent financial initiatives for careers education and guidance mentioned earlier (see p. 134), will redress the damage inflicted by the National Curriculum and secure the position and status of careers teachers once and for all. However, the struggle for recognition and status which careers teachers have faced throughout their history, suggests that a note of caution is required.

ACKNOWLEDGEMENT

The current research mentioned in this chapter was supported by a research award from the Standing Conference on Studies in Education.

NOTES

1 Over the following two decades there was a great deal of tension between the two parts of the system with no clear resolution to the problems over division of labour. See Harris, 1990; Lawrence, 1993.

2 Careers education is usually referred to under the broader heading of careers education and guidance (CEG) emphasizing the dual roles – the curricular element of 'careers

education' and the individual, impartial and independent provision of 'careers guidance'. The focus in this chapter is on the careers education dimension.

3 Throughout the chapter I use the term 'careers teacher', which refers to teachers who are recognized as primarily responsible for careers education in their school. I use it because in some schools the title used is 'head of careers', 'head of PSE', or a variety of other titles. Interestingly, no careers teacher interviewed referred to themselves as the 'careers coordinator', which is the term used in the National Curriculum.

4 In 1969 the National Association of Careers Teachers (NACT) was established to represent teachers with a responsibility for careers work and to promote the development of careers education and guidance for young people in secondary school and tertiary education. In 1973 the association was renamed the National Association of Careers and Guidance Teachers to reflect the development of the guidance movement. Originally membership was made up primarily of careers teachers but this has broadened to include counsellors, careers advisers and the Inspectorate. There is an elected Council and Executive Council whose members represent the NACGT at meetings with government ministers and bodies such as SCAA.

5 In-depth interviews were carried out with teachers responsible for careers education in twelve comprehensive schools in a Midlands town between 1986 and 1988, and again in 1995. However, by the time the follow-up study was begun two of the original twelve schools had closed, one school was temporarily without a careers teacher and one careers teacher was on long-term sick leave. Informal discussions were conducted with careers teachers, careers advisers and others involved in careers education and guidance from various parts of the country at NACGT annual conferences.

6 It is beyond the scope of this chapter to discuss these in any great detail. What can be said here is that while there is evidence in the research schools that the money has helped secure more and improved resources this has not, as yet, translated into enhanced status, particularly for teachers who have only recently become involved in careers work. The traditional subject and departmental hierarchies are still present and have been strengthened, in many ways, by the National Curriculum.

7 This scepticism was clear in the comments made by the careers teachers in the research but it was also evident in the articles and correspondence in the NACGT's quarterly journal, *Careers Education and Guidance*, during the introduction of the National Curriculum. The name of the journal changed in 1991. Prior to then it had been called the *Journal*.

8 In 1987 the NACGT carried out a survey of careers education in schools. A similar survey was carried out on behalf of NACGT and the Institute of Careers Guidance in 1993.

9 Whether cross-curricular themes are still on the agenda is debatable. The evidence from Whitty's work and others suggests that schools have tended to concentrate on those cross-curricular themes which were already on the curriculum whilst ignoring those which were historically weak or non-existent. Some of the leading figures in the guidance world feel that the cross-curricular themes are 'dead' and that the government has conveniently 'dropped' them. However, for some, the cross-curricular themes are still very much alive with support coming from the cross-curricular interest and lobby groups, as well as support for themes which did not appear on the NCC list such as media studies, political education and consumer education (Dufour, 1990).

REFERENCES

Bowe, R. and Ball, S. J. (1992) Doing what should come naturally: an exploration of LMS in one secondary school. In G. Wallace (ed.), *Local Management of Schools: Research and Experience*. BERA Dialogues No. 6. Clevedon: Multilingual Matters, pp. 36–52.

Buck, M. and Inman, S. (1993) Making values central: the role of cross curricular themes. *Careers Education and Guidance*, February: 10–14.

Cleaton, D. (1987) *Survey of Careers Work*. London: Newpoint Publishing.

Cleaton, D. (1993) *Careers Education and Guidance in British Schools*. Stourbridge: Institute of Careers Guidance.

DES (Department of Education and Science) (1986) *Working Together – Education and Training*. London: HMSO.

DES (1987) *The National Curriculum 5–16: A Consultative Document*. London: HMSO.

DES (1988) *Careers Education and Guidance 5–16*. Curriculum Matters 10. London: HMSO.

DES (1989) *The National Curriculum: From Policy to Practice*. London: HMSO.

DES/DE (Department of Education and Science/Department of Employment) (1987) *Working Together for a Better Future*. London: HMSO.

Dufour, B. (ed.) (1990) *The New Social Curriculum: The Political, Economic and Social Context for Educational Change*. Cambridge: Cambridge University Press.

Evans, K. and Law, B. (1984) *Careers Guidance Integration Project. Final Report*. Hertford: NICEC.

Goodson, I. (1983) *School Subjects and Curriculum Change*. London: Croom Helm.

Goodson, I. and Ball, S. J. (1984) *Defining the Curriculum*. Lewes: Falmer Press.

Harris, S. (1990) Careers teachers and their teaching careers. A study of careers teachers, their routes into careers education and positions within schools. PhD thesis, University of Nottingham.

Harris, S. (1992a) Careers teachers: who are they and what do they do? *Research Papers in Education*, **7**(3): 337–57.

Harris, S. (1992b) A career on the margins? The position of careers teachers in schools. *British Journal of Sociology of Education*, **13**(2): 163–76.

Harris, S. (1994) Entitled to what? Control and autonomy in school: a student perspective. *International Studies in Sociology of Education*, **4**(1): 57–76.

Harris, S., Rudduck, J. and Wallace, G. (1996) Political contexts and school careers. In M. Hughes (ed.), *Teaching and Learning in Changing Times*. Oxford: Basil Blackwell, pp. 32–50.

Lawrence, D. (1993) The rise and fall of the local government careers service. *Local Government Studies*, **19**(1): 92–107.

NACGT Journal (1987) President's view, October, 2.

NACGT Journal (1988) Presidential address, October, 2.

NACGT Journal (1989) President's comments, June, 2.

NCC (National Curriculum Council) (1989) *The National Curriculum and Whole Curriculum Planning: Preliminary Guidance*. Circular Number 6, York: NCC.

NCC (1990) *Curriculum Guidance 6: Careers Education and Guidance*. York: NCC.

OFSTED (1995a) *Framework for the Inspection of Schools*. London: HMSO.

OFSTED (1995b) *Guidance on the Inspection of Secondary Schools*. London: HMSO.

OFSTED (1995c) *A Survey of Careers Education and Guidance in Schools*. London: HMSO.

Roberts, K. (1971) *From School to Work*. Newton Abbot: David Charles.

Rowe, G., Aggleton, P. and Whitty, G. (1993) Cross-curricular work in secondary schools: the place of careers education and guidance. *Careers Education and Guidance*, June, 2–6.

Saunders, L., Hewitt, D. and MacDonald, A. (1995) *Education for Life. The Cross-curricular Themes in Primary and Secondary Schools*. Slough: NFER.

SCAA (School Curriculum and Assessment Authority) (1995) *Looking Forward. Careers Education and Guidance in the Curriculum*. London: HMSO.

Watkins, C. (1994) Whole-school guidance? *British Journal of Guidance and Counselling*, **22**(1): 143–50.

Watkins, C. (1995) Personal-social education and the whole curriculum. In R. Best, P. Lang, C. Lodge and C. Watkins (eds), *Pastoral Care and Personal-Social Education*. London: Cassell, pp. 118–40.

Whitty, G., Rowe, G. and Aggleton, P. (1994) Discourse in cross-curricular contexts: limits to empowerment. *International Studies in Sociology of Education*, 4(1): 25–42.

Whitty, G., Aggleton, P. and Rowe, G. (1996) Competing conceptions of quality in social education. Learning from the experience of the cross-curricular themes. In M. Hughes (ed.), *Teaching and Learning in Changing Times*. London: Basil Blackwell, pp. 51–69.

Chapter 10

Continuing Professional Development and the National Curriculum

Gill Helsby and Peter Knight

INTRODUCTION

> we have come to realise in recent years that the teacher is the
> ultimate key to educational change and school improvement. The
> restructuring of schools, the composition of national and provincial
> curricula, the development of bench-mark assessments – all these
> things are of little value if they do not take the teacher into
> account. Teachers don't merely deliver the curriculum. They
> develop it, refine it and reinterpret it, too. (Hargreaves, 1992, p. ix)

This quotation comes from the Foreword to a collection of writings about teacher development (or the lack of it) in the context of widespread educational 'reforms'. Although most of the contributors were from North America, the sentiments are highly relevant to England in the wake of the Education Reform Act of 1988, which not only introduced a system of local (financial) management of schools (LMS), but also required all state schools to work within a closely defined, assessment-driven National Curriculum. If Hargreaves's view is accepted, then the extent of these changes, and the importance invested in them by the government in terms of 'raising standards' and 'improving quality' in education (DFE/WO, 1992), point clearly towards the need for major investment in the continuing professional development of teachers.

Five characteristics of these curriculum reforms are particularly salient to this theme of teacher development:

- Curriculum content was prescribed in considerable detail for both primary and secondary schools: for some teachers this meant having to master new topics, while some others found themselves having to teach a new subject, such as integrated 'technology'.
- Attainment Targets (ATs) were developed and teachers obliged to measure pupils' learning against pre-specified criteria. In most cases, these ATs were new, as was the concept of gearing teaching to the advancement of nationally established, detailed criteria: the 1989 curriculum contained 296 statements of attainment for mathematics alone.

- The technical, rational and centralist approach to curriculum design promoted through the National Curriculum was frequently at odds with teachers' own deeply held convictions about developing their teaching in ways that met individual pupil needs: accordingly teachers, particularly although not exclusively those working in primary schools, were often faced with the challenge of reconciling within their own practice conflicting notions of pedagogy.
- The new curriculum was both extensive and demanding, allowing teachers little, if any, space in which to develop their own interests, while simultaneously requiring that they continually assessed and recorded learners' achievements. To this degree, teachers' autonomy was circumscribed, while the demands of the job were intensified.
- The curriculum was not static but subject to regular revisions, so that schemes of work planned in 1989 were, in mathematics and technology for example, obsolete within three years.

As has been shown in other chapters, these changes have had many ramifications. Three are noteworthy in the context of this discussion of professional development. First, there was an obvious and pressing need for new learning, to build or extend knowledge of subject matter; to develop pedagogical processes appropriate to the new requirements; and to foster mastery of teaching to, and assessing against, the AT statements.

Secondly, it was unclear whether the National Curriculum had so reduced teachers' autonomy that they had become little more than 'technicians' (Harland, 1988), who therefore needed instrumental instruction, or whether they remained 'professionals' who needed a broader programme of *professional* development that would allow them to deploy their knowledge through the exercise of judgement within the National Curriculum framework. While the priority was to ensure that teachers grasped the requirements of the new curriculum, the question was whether professional development would be overwhelmed by this instrumental priority. Was emphasis to be laid on controlling and managing teachers through a legally enforced system of centralized prescription, increased accountability, close monitoring and surveillance rather than on developing and empowering them? Alternatively, would teachers be encouraged to cultivate the higher level capacities associated with curriculum development?

Thirdly, there is no doubt that teachers' workloads increased dramatically in these years (Campbell and Neill, 1994a, b), which raises questions about how teachers were to find the time, energy and will for the substantial reskilling implied by the new curricula. This is significant since, although teachers were directed to engage in five days of formal in-service (INSET) activities each year, reskilling depends also upon a wide range of more informal activities, such as the development of new schemes of work, reading, discussion with colleagues, curriculum review, planning new lessons, developing new approaches, choosing new teaching materials, attendance at conferences organized by professional associations and, importantly, reflection.

In trying to understand the impact of the National Curriculum on teachers' learning, it is necessary to ask what formal provision was made, what teachers thought of it, what other forms of learning took place, how teachers felt about these new demands for new learning and whether this reskilling may best be characterized as 'professional' or 'technical' development.

THE NEED FOR PROFESSIONAL LEARNING

It has been claimed that government changes to the English educational system since 1988 have eroded teacher autonomy, with the result that teaching is becoming deprofessionalized and is changing into a technical job. If that were the case, it might be argued that there would be, by definition, no place for continuing professional learning. Instead teachers would periodically undergo training or instruction to enable them to deliver unproblematic requirements in an efficient manner.

However, secondary-school teachers interviewed in 1994 as part of a major research study into The Professional Culture of Teachers and the Secondary School Curriculum[1] described their work in terms that they saw as characteristic of a profession, pointing to the importance of higher education-based entry qualifications, to the need for specialist knowledge, to their exercise of non-routine judgement, to a service ethic and to a commitment to doing the job properly as opposed to working fixed hours. They also drew attention to deficiencies in their pay, in their status and in the respect accorded to their work, arguing that teaching is not a profession in the same way as law and medicine. Nevertheless, these teachers' descriptions of their work (see below) suggest an occupation that, in its complexity and emphasis on individual, informed, non-routine decision-making, requires professional learning and not simply technical training. The categorization of occupations as 'technical' and 'professional' is neither simple nor uncontentious. Moreover, the claim that teaching might be regarded as a profession because practitioners have to engage in individual, informed, non-routine decision-making is, of itself, worth amplification. However, these important conceptual issues can only be recognized here, not elaborated.

Many of the secondary teachers interviewed accepted that their autonomy and power to set the curriculum had been constrained by the National Curriculum framework. However, that does not lead to the simple conclusion that teachers' professional standing had thereby been eroded, since professionals do not necessarily have unbounded or even high levels of autonomy. In England, many professionals work within bureaucracies, acting as council lawyers, civil service advisers or architects within large commercial enterprises. In continental

Europe, professionals frequently work within state bureaucracies (Burrage and Torstendahl, 1990; Torstendahl and Burrage, 1990). Autonomy, it might be said, is divisible. Although the National Curriculum did limit teacher control of the curriculum in terms of defining the content and the learning goals, it did not obliterate it. The loss of the power to define the curriculum framework was not missed by the majority of mathematics teachers, for example, who argued that there had long been a *de facto* mathematics curriculum for secondary schools. For all subject departments there remained the tasks of interpreting the curriculum requirements and of casting them into the forms of school policies and schemes of work, activities that require the exercise of autonomous judgement.

Moreover, as many of these secondary teachers made clear, they retained a high degree of choice over pedagogy. Indeed, many valued this bounded autonomy in the classroom, which included choice of classroom management strategies, control over the pace and focus of lessons, freedom to match teaching to the different needs of the learners and their unscripted, frequently improvised interactions with children, both individually and in groups, and with colleagues. Although some teachers felt that their pedagogy was constrained by curriculum overload, many believed that classroom management had remained largely untouched by the changes since 1989. Interestingly, Alexander (1992), writing of primary classrooms, argued that a major weakness of the National Curriculum was its indifference to matters of pedagogy, leaving the teachers with substantial autonomy in what he saw as the key aspect of learning, while regulating the less important area of curriculum content and learning goals. It can be argued that, if autonomy is a defining characteristic of a profession, then teachers continue to exercise substantial, albeit bounded, autonomy. In this respect, they do not compare unfavourably with many other professionals, although legal and medical professionals in the Anglo-Saxon world do generally have greater autonomy than teachers.

It follows that, while technical knowledge of curriculum content and of the ATs is clearly necessary, it is not sufficient. Teachers also need to be skilled in the deployment of insightful judgement in a framework of bounded autonomy. On this reading, the National Curriculum made greater professional demands on teachers, requiring that they refine their understandings of their subjects; collaborate with colleagues to plan schemes of work, to monitor progress and to refine the schemes; teach with ATs in mind; diagnose and remedy learning problems; and reflect upon their pedagogy with a view to continuous quality improvement.

Two points are worthy of note. First, much professional learning will be informal, in the sense of not being directly associated with attendance at INSET courses. Secondly, as Schön (1983, 1987) has argued with respect to professional learning, and as writers on organizational management such as Peters (1992), Drucker (1993) and Handy (1994) have argued, this learning needs to be seen as a life-long business, and not as a one-shot exercise. Within the fast-changing and turbulent environment within which they must operate, organizations and their members need to develop the capacity to renew themselves rapidly and effectively, and this requires transformative, as well as assimilative, learning.

The empirical question is, then, how far teachers' experiences of professional development since the introduction of the National Curriculum square with this view of the nature of professional learning. In the rest of this chapter we will examine the recent changes which have been made at national level to the formal structures for teacher development and support, before turning to secondary school teachers' experiences and perceptions of continuing professional development in the early and later years of National Curriculum implementation.

CHANGES TO IN-SERVICE EDUCATION AND SUPPORT STRUCTURES

The changes to the formal structures of in-service education and support for teachers (INSET) which have accompanied the educational 'reforms' of recent years, have seriously restricted the opportunities for personal, professional development (see, for example, Evans and Penney, 1994; Gilroy and Day, 1993). It is possible to trace a movement away from a system of INSET which, in the 1960s and 1970s, was locally controlled and relatively generously funded, towards one which is now heavily managed from the centre within tight budgetary constraints (Helsby, 1993). In Scotland, Hartley (1989) has identified a sharp owing in professional development policy away from a collaborative and human relations management approach which emphasized teacher autonomy and 'extended professionalism' (Hoyle, 1974) and towards a hierarchical model based upon Taylorist philosophy, which tends to deskill teachers by prescribing their development needs in terms of technical competences which are to be inspected and assessed.

In England and Wales there has been a similar trend, which has culminated in the current funding system that ties the entire national INSET budget to government-defined priorities, especially to those connected with management training and with National Curriculum implementation. Although the new legal requirement for teachers to undertake five days of school-based in-service training each year appears to leave scope for local initiative, in practice these training days have tended to be dominated by school management concerns and by the pressing need to address practical questions of National Curriculum implementation: the 'how' rather than the 'why' questions of teaching (Day, 1993; Hartley, 1989). At the same time, control by schools of their own INSET budgets has led to an understandable shift of focus away from longer-term individual development, which is hard to quantify, and towards what has been described, in the context of further education colleges, as 'demonstrably improved performance in the workplace' (Blackmore, 1992, p. 31).

Significantly, responsibility for the current national review of continuing professional development provision for teachers has been given to the Teacher

Training Agency, a body that has already exerted strong central control over initial teacher *education*. Moreover, the loss of responsibility for schools that opted for grant-maintained status and the increasing delegation of budgets for local education authority (LEA) services to schools through the Local Management of Schools has seriously reduced the capacity of LEAs to continue to offer advisory support to teachers. This capacity has been further eroded by the responsibilities placed upon LEA staff to monitor National Curriculum implementation, and later exacerbated by an emphasis on 'improvement through inspection' (OFSTED, 1993) and the clear separation of inspection and advice.

Consequently, opportunities have decreased for teachers to attend LEA-based meetings or training sessions at which they can exchange views and experiences with colleagues from other institutions. This factor, coupled with the increasing pressures to compete rather than collaborate with other institutions, has meant that development activities have become increasingly school-based, with all the associated dangers of insularity and parochialism. Drawing upon their experiences in North America, Bullough and Gitlin (1994) have argued that confining continuing professional development activities to individual school contexts in this way can inhibit critical thinking by discouraging the scrutiny of institutionally accepted roles and relationships.

TEACHERS' PERCEPTIONS OF CONTINUING PROFESSIONAL DEVELOPMENT AND THE EARLY NATIONAL CURRICULUM

Our evidence of teachers' views of their own professional development, and of the formal INSET and support which they have received in the years following the introduction of the National Curriculum, comes from two sources. Firstly, a large-scale programme of teacher surveys and interviews undertaken between 1991 and 1993 as part of the Lancaster TVEI Evaluation Programme,[2] included specific questions on professional support and development. Secondly, the on-going ESRC-funded study mentioned above (see note 1) produced both questionnaire and interview data on teachers' perceptions in this area

The TVEI data are based upon one-to-one interviews conducted between autumn 1991 and spring 1993 with some 200 secondary teachers in two LEAs, and also upon a survey targeted at all secondary teachers in three LEAs in 1992 and early 1993, which elicited over 2000 completed questionnaires. This research was undertaken in the early years of National Curriculum implementation, when teachers were still coming to grips with both its original and its fast-changing requirements and when it might, therefore, have been expected that formal opportunities for professional support and development would have been plentiful. Campbell and Neill (1994b) found that secondary-school teachers spent an average of 2.1 hours a week on INSET activities but our evidence suggests that a majority of respondents were nevertheless dissatisfied with the provision. Only about a quarter felt that they had received adequate professional development in their own curriculum area, whilst over a half positively disagreed with this statement. At the same time, more than three out of five agreed that they were having difficulties keeping up with current professional demands. Some of the open-ended comments from the survey pointed towards a reduction, rather than an expansion, of support:

> At a time of greatest demand on staff because of changes there is less time and support available to cope with it.

A lack both of resources and of training for National Curriculum implementation was identified:

> Vast changes through an ill-thought out National Curriculum and no training or funding to implement.

The major concerns over the changes in recent years are:

> (1) the frequency and uncertainty of actual changes;
> (2) the overall absence of extra funding and training necessary to introduce and support such changes.

Moreover, teachers felt that insufficient time was allowed for them to assimilate and plan for the changing requirements:

> Too many changes in too many areas pushed through too quickly with too little support and not enough time given off timetable to come to terms with them.

> Most institutions are not giving teachers time to properly initiate and develop the many and varied prescribed practices, therefore they are *always* underdeveloped and unsatisfactory.

Fewer than one in three respondents believed that the system of professional development had improved in the last two to three years or that the organization of INSET within the institution was working well. The proportion of teachers disagreeing with these statements was just over and just under a half respectively. A notable criticism concerned the lack of development opportunities in more generic, as opposed to subject-focused, areas because of national INSET priorities:

> It's been difficult recently because INSET requirements have been so oriented towards the National Curriculum. I would have preferred more on teaching and learning.

> We are beginning a period of little or no support in areas that matter to teachers.

Restricted access to external courses was a concern:

> Total disillusionment about staff development. Any work placements, course funds, etc. handed out as perks to 'favourites'.

> INSET provision is useless – one might as well not bother asking
> because one knows the answer will be negative.

> It is getting more difficult because of LMS to get out on courses.

Some also commented on the poor quality of compulsory school-based training days:

> There's a general feeling that if you have to have them they should
> have some clearly defined purpose – sometimes they're a bit
> woolly, they need more structure and they need to be related to
> what we need.

However, a minority of teachers expressed contradictory views both on the amount of support:

> I've never known so much INSET – it's almost a cause for concern,
> since so many staff are out.

and on the quality of school-based training:

> There has been a lot of school-based INSET: we can afford it and
> can often deliver it better ourselves.

One possible explanation of such discrepancies may lie in the marked differences in response between senior managers, middle managers and main professional grade (MPG) teachers. In particular, senior managers were more than twice as likely as MPG teachers to say that the system of professional support and development had improved in recent years and that institutional INSET worked well. At the same time, the evidence suggested that senior managers enjoyed vastly greater access than other teachers to LEA support, to meetings with colleagues from other institutions and to personal professional development, a point echoed in one of the comments:

> Professional support etc. limited for MPG teachers.

Overall, half of the survey group believed that there were important gaps in their professional expertise, although in this case MPG teachers felt themselves only slightly worse off than either middle or senior managers. Some felt a keen sense of isolation because of the lack of remedial support:

> Very little in the way of staff development or advisory help is
> offered – it is sink or swim – ALONE.

Where there were opportunities for MPG teachers to work with others, these were predominantly in-house. Thus well over three out of five engaged in internal planning meetings with colleagues, but only about two in five had the opportunity to meet teachers from other schools or to receive LEA support.

> The collaboration created by TVEI between schools has been
> eroded by LMS – instead of cooperative consortia developing

initiatives we have separate institutions guarding their 'market edge'.

More need for LEA support and guidance in my area – we feel on our own.

CONTINUING PROFESSIONAL DEVELOPMENT AND THE LATER NATIONAL CURRICULUM

Interview data from the Professional Culture of Teachers (PCT) study tell a similar story. Approximately one in three of the teachers interviewed in late 1994 and early 1995 *spontaneously* made some reference to the need for continuing professional development, particularly in the context of the increased demands of the National Curriculum. One teacher did feel that there had been a major expansion in INSET since the 1980s:

> It's an ever-more essential part of teaching nowadays because of
> the changes that are taking place. When I started ... we weren't
> told anything about in-service training ... we thought that once
> you were trained as a teacher, bang, that was it and you were off
> teaching and you learnt on-the-job basically and gained
> experience. And in-service came through in bits in those early 80s,
> for me anyway, and it's just an ever-present thing everyday now
> ... there is too much INSET, but there is a definite need for
> INSET to keep pace with the rate of change.

However, this was an exceptional point of view. Far more frequent were the complaints of a lack of opportunity for in-service education at a time when it was particularly needed:

> So much change and so little INSET.

According to some of the teachers interviewed, access to INSET courses appeared to be governed by the availability of funding, school priorities and by teachers' relative position in the hierarchy:

> there's been not that much money available for in-service training,
> most staff ... are self-taught on computers ... most people work at
> home so that they can keep ahead of what they're doing at school.

> I think in all my four years, I've only been on one, one-day course,
> and that was on my day off ... people at the bottom, like me, don't
> get very much support at all in the way of courses.

Often access to courses was restricted to heads of department:

> many of the courses I would have liked to have gone on, my head
> of department has gone on ... I'd like to have done a lot more just

> to keep up to date with things, and as well to find out what
> teachers in other schools are doing, because I don't seem to have
> much contact with them, which I think I would if there were more
> opportunity to do some INSET.

Alternatively it was dominated by management training for senior staff:

> a fantastic amount of investment has gone into the professional
> development of the senior team, an increasing amount, and what
> they're getting is management input, not necessarily specifically
> educational management theory and practice ... but at the same
> time the middle managers are not being given the same
> opportunities because the urgency about developing them is not
> necessarily perceived in the same way.

Several references were made to the important support role played by colleagues:

> One of my weaker areas at the moment is IT ... but I'm developing
> that with their [departmental colleagues'] support. I can go to
> them [with a problem] and they will troubleshoot, so it means that
> you can actually then develop, I suppose in terms of my own
> abilities, by using the professional expertise of other members of
> staff in department

However, the evidence also suggested that the general 'intensification' of
working life (Apple, 1986) and pressures of time were beginning to erode such
opportunities:

> I felt [in the 1970s] there was a little bit more breathing space, you
> could talk to colleagues more ... I think you'll find, because of the
> pressures of your subject area, you find you really don't get a
> chance to talk to other colleagues outside, say, the maths area and
> I think everyone's the worse for that.

> [Of NC] The forums for debating this [are] being eroded ... local
> groups of teachers find it very difficult to get together ... meetings
> are few and far between.

Lack of time because of increased workloads was also affecting teachers' abilities
to think and plan:

> We've had so many things imposed externally now that I feel there
> has been no time for reflection, because we're always having to do
> the new development. And I find now that the amount of time I
> have to spend on administration and developments is ...
> encroaching on what I think are very fundamental ... what the job
> is all about ... I think there was a time when I could have the
> amount of development time that I wanted, I could be involved in

new developments ... but now I just find I'm overwhelmed by all
the things I've now got to deal with, and we don't have time to mix
as a staff.

This contrasted sharply with the opportunities provided by past involvement in
an MA course:

it provided the opportunity to stand back, to see from a distance
what I was doing or trying to do as a teacher ... I found it
provided a very useful insight, an opportunity to focus in on things
which, when you're involved in them, you don't see.

Moreover, there were concerns about the focus of INSET activities, which
were sometimes characterized as instrumental rather than professional, bureaucratic rather than developmental:

The INSET sessions which are given over to departments ... are
too few and far between to make any significant impact on what
we need to do, and unfortunately what we tend to have to do is use
INSET time for standardization meetings at exam time ... so a
good six to nine hours of work which could be used for curriculum
development is used up on GCSE ... moderation and
standardization.

Reductions in LEA support were highlighted by several teachers; for example:

the LEAs have disappeared ... a lot of teachers now are going
through a sort of bereavement because they don't actually now
have anybody out there they can turn to ... that whole layer of
consultancy has disappeared, so put that together with the fact
that there isn't the funding now to send people on the sort of
courses you would like to, you've got an enormous great chasm
that's appeared.

There were also suggestions of a growing feeling of isolation amongst some
teachers:

we all seem to be in our own little boxes doing our own little things
... advisers now don't advise, they inspect. When I started as head
of maths, we used to meet regularly in various teams of heads of
maths from around the county, prepare courses, discuss teaching
methods, all that sort of thing, and with the onset of LMS, it's all
gone ... the backup for it, to feed good practice to the chalk face, is
virtually non-existent.

it's difficult to see other staff ... there's no forum for ideas or
concerns to be expressed, and that contributes to this feeling of not
being professional: you're just an isolated body in a classroom.

However, there were some who had found that the National Curriculum provided a prompt for professional development, especially through working with colleagues:

> In the initial stages you pick up the document ... and think 'how are we going to do this?' and it's actually brought us closer together ... we were driven by the fact that National Curriculum was coming in ... we were willing to develop ideas and courses for young people, we were willing to look at what we were doing and adapt it, modify and change it ... we knew we had to work together, we knew the only way forward was to come together as a group ... we've learnt how to relate to each other, because we didn't have to do that before, you could sit in your own little empire, but we've actually broken down the barriers.

EXPERIENCES OF PROFESSIONAL DEVELOPMENT

In the PCT study, 121 of the teachers returned post-interview questionnaires asking about their experiences of INSET and their beliefs about the best forms of professional development. They were asked to indicate any of 13 forms of INSET in which they had participated in the previous twelve months. This gives a picture of their engagement with different forms, although it does not tell us anything about the frequency of that engagement. As such it complements the observations volunteered in the interviews and, to some extent, it contradicts those data and the data from the TVEI study.

The main experience of INSET for survey respondents was school-based, accounting for 43 per cent of their INSET activities. Interestingly, these activities were split more or less evenly between work on a teaching subject and work on more general, cross-curricular themes. The next most common category of activity (26 per cent of all those named) comprised one-off meetings with colleagues from other schools. This relatively high incidence may be accounted for by the number of heads of department in the sample, who had greater access to out-of-school meetings than their junior colleagues. Here the subject focus predominated, with subject-centred activities outweighing cross-curricular ones in the ratio of four to one. A similar proportion of non-award-bearing activities were also subject centred. No data were collected about the foci of the award-bearing courses. Overall, but excluding award-bearing courses, activities focused more on subject teaching than on general and cross-curricular themes, the ratio being close to two to one. This is consistent with the data reported above.

Teachers were overwhelmingly positive about the professional value of all thirteen forms of INSET activity, with 79 per cent rated as of professional value and only 8 per cent reckoned to be of no value. There did not appear to be any systematic tendency to rate any form of INSET as more or less valuable than any other form. Moreover, there was no relationship between satisfaction and whether the teachers felt that they had some say in the content of an activity. These findings were not expected, since some discontent with INSET activities was noted above. However, the questionnaire invited evaluations of specific forms of INSET, whereas the interviews saw people talking about their general experiences of INSET. This is a useful reminder that different research approaches will often lead to different understandings of the same phenomenon.

It was also anticipated that INSET activities which involved thinking about general issues, reflecting upon one's own practices, and considering the wider implications of policy decisions and activities that distanced teachers from immediate practical concerns, would be regarded as more 'professional' than narrowly focused activities that centred on receiving information, completing specific tasks, acquiring specific skills and examining classroom materials. Teachers believed that 51 per cent of the INSET activities in which they had been engaged were characterized by this narrow focus, with 27 per cent mixing the narrow and the wider concerns and 22 per cent concentrating on the broader issues. There was no association between teachers' ratings of the professional value of activities and their categorization of the activity as broad, narrow or mixed. This is consistent with the feelings described above that the National Curriculum had led to a more instrumental approach to INSET. Given that teachers needed instrumental support, it is not surprising that they saw value in it, nor that they also valued more 'professional' INSET.

The returns were analysed to see if there were any differences in the experiences of new and more experienced teachers. The number of responses in some categories was low and no consistent pattern emerged. Where differences were identified, for example showing that teachers with 21–25 years of service had more say about what happened in school-based, subject-specific INSET activities, it seemed plausible to attribute this to the older teachers' status, since they were often heads of department, rather than to their length of service alone.

Teachers' preferred forms of professional development

In the PCT study, 105 teachers answered a question that asked them what they saw as the best form of professional development. Here, the focus moves from INSET to professional learning in a broader sense. Interestingly, the main response drew attention to the more informal aspects of professional development. Fifty teachers mentioned working with colleagues, whether in their own school or with teachers from other schools. The flavour of these responses is shown by such comments as: 'Meeting other teachers, especially within my subject, discussing developments, ideas, etc. Cross-fertilization of ideas'; 'Conversing with colleagues over current practices and issues, so sense and degree of isolation is reduced'; and 'Being given the time and opportunity to talk to other teachers – learn their strategies for dealing with situations.'

The second most important feature of desirable professional development could be described as work that embodied 'the practicality ethic' (Doyle and Ponder, 1977). This category includes curriculum development, workshops, acquiring skills, and action planning; in the words of some of the respondents:

> Practically based courses where there is (a) practical exercises to produce classroom materials, (b) awareness-raising workshops to develop the individual teachers, (c) practical exercises to develop leadership and managerial skills, (d) exchange of ideas and programmes of study with practical applications from other professionals in other schools.

> Relevant, hands on, applicable to classroom, supported, allowing time for implementation before a further dose. It doesn't matter whether it is in or out of school.

> PSE (personal and social education): training courses on teaching techniques, resources available, counselling. Subject-related courses: examining new teaching/assessment techniques, reviewing new resources – new teaching materials – IT development.

However, there was also a recognition that there were things to be learned from speakers, through externally mounted courses and through higher education: 'Visiting speakers are useful in a subject-specific category'; 'SMP [School Mathematics Project] courses are the best ones I've been on for years'; 'In school or out of school subject specific with outside help from specialist'; and '[I got a] higher degree'.

Other, less common observations drew attention to: (1) the importance of professional development based on the identification of individual needs (fourteen teachers):

> Using a person's interests, develop them in a useful way for the benefit of the institution and reward them in some way (not necessarily financially) so that they feel in control of their own professional life;

(2) the importance of reflection upon one's own work (seven teachers) – 'INSET gives an opportunity to reflect on wider issues as well as one's own role within one's place of work'; (3) the financial restrictions that limit the scope for professional development (eight teachers) – 'Training [should be] properly funded so that [there are] no worries that colleagues have to do extra to cover for [your] absence'; and (4) the problems of having enough time to do it (twelve teachers) – 'Provision of more *time*, more support with cash/resources'. A variant of this was where four teachers said how valuable it would be if periods of study leave, or sabbaticals, were available: 'secondment for quality time to get quality results,

preferably leading to a qualification (good motivator)'; *'secondment* – one year at least after twenty years' teaching ought to be available'.

The questionnaire given to teachers before the interviews asked about influences on their professional development. The most common response, coming from 86 of the 147 returning this questionnaire, was that teachers' own experience was an important influence, closely followed by colleagues in the same department (77 cases) and their own beliefs and convictions (74 cases). When asked which was the most important influence upon their professional development, the 124 who replied put experience at the head of the list (40 cases), followed by either colleagues in the same department or their own beliefs (23 cases each). Initial teacher education (ITE) was fourth in terms both of frequency of citations as an influence (39 out of 147) and of identification as the most important influence (cited by 12 of the 124). Perhaps not surprisingly, teachers of 1–5 years' experience placed far greater emphasis on ITE than did other teachers, although they still gave priority to experience and they valued just as highly the influence of their own beliefs and that of colleagues in the same department.

Formal INSET activities were cited as important influences by 17 of the 147 who completed that questionnaire, placing it eighth in the rank order. Only four of the 124 nominated INSET as the most important form of professional development for them.

A conclusion that might be drawn from these data is that professional development is a complex, often informal process. While INSET provision may be necessary, and while it may be that our questions invite an underestimate of its significance through not probing for the *indirect* influence of INSET, it can be said that focusing on INSET as if it were the heart of professional development flies in the face of these teachers' reflections on their own learning. It would follow that a government wishing to prepare teachers for the changes wrought by the National Curriculum would do well to conceptualize professional development as something much greater and much more complicated than INSET provision alone.

CONCLUSIONS

There is little gainsaying that the National Curriculum has demanded considerable professional learning by teachers. Not only have many teachers had to master new content and new learning goals, but some have also had to learn new subjects, while all have had to develop new schemes of work, to choose new learning materials, to learn how to assess pupils against prescribed criteria, and to consider appropriate pedagogies for effective National Curriculum learning. In many cases, these changes have been accompanied by greater collaboration between teachers, itself requiring new skills and a degree of change in working practices for some teachers. INSET provision to support this has tended to be instrumental and has not been on the scale that teachers would have wished. However, much informal professional development has taken place in what have been trying times for teachers. There is also a suggestion that access to INSET has been easier for teachers with managerial responsibility, a finding also reported by Campbell and Neill (1994b). This aligns with other indications in the PCT data that changes since 1988 may be producing a more hierarchical occupation, opening up a gap between managers and workers. This needs further investigation. There are also hints in the data that younger teachers, who have been trained to teach the National Curriculum, were less critical of it than the older teachers. However, the study was not designed to establish whether this was so, although it is a topic for further research that could give an interesting perspective on future development needs in the profession.

The National Curriculum has, in practice, given rise to INSET provision which has been predominantly instrumental and formal and to which access has been limited for some teachers. Professional development, as identified in the opening sections of this chapter, has largely been an outcome of teachers' conscientious and informal engagement with the ramifications of the new curriculum. Teachers, coping with change, seem to have been the main agents of their own professional development. While that may reflect well on the commitment of the profession, it has placed considerable pressure upon teachers, and left many feeling beleaguered and unsupported. It might also be asked whether this *ad hoc* and 'do-it-yourself' model of professional development is appropriate to a national system that is geared towards a wholesale improvement in children's learning.

Perhaps the more interesting conclusions relate to our conceptualization of professional development, particularly in the context of the current concern with the quality and the reform of educational provision. First, we need to make a distinction between two approaches to quality in education. The one sees quality as something to be achieved through a system of bureaucratic accountability, signs of which may be seen in the data we have presented here. The other, which we believe to be more powerful and more appropriate to educational settings, is centred on the idea of trust and empowerment, and focuses on continuous quality improvement rather than on quality control. The empowerment that lies at the heart of this second idea implies that teachers are seen as professionals, exercising judgement and creativity, rather than as technicians, following directions. Moreover, this approach, by definition, implies continuous learning, continuous professional development. INSET is one means by which that development may take place but it is clearly not the only way. Eraut (1994) has described the importance of experience in professional development and the well-established notion of action research centres upon the idea of informed and systematic reflection on experience as a way of bringing about professional development and continuous quality improvement. Sockett (1993) has also argued that professional development in teaching is closely allied with personal development, since teaching is a moral activity that demands certain personal qualities.

This perspective leads us to two conclusions. The first is that professional development must be understood as something far more extensive than participation in INSET, which implies that research into this area, which is quite scanty, needs to investigate informal professional development as well as formal provision. The latter is the tip of the iceberg: visible but a small portion of the whole. The second point is that such research needs to be phenomenographic, to explore professional development as seen by individuals with their own biographies, values, identities and desires. This research needs, therefore, to be located within a life histories approach and to look at the process of development through longitudinal studies: cross-sectional studies cannot do justice to the shifting, subjective realities of the linked processes of personal change and professional development. The data we have reported here begin to capture something of the process but they also make us aware of its complexity.

The National Curriculum has undoubtedly stimulated professional development and, in a sense, has forced teachers to rethink their work. At the same time, it has created problems of overload and excessive change, resulting in an intensification of working life which has left little time for reflection and learning. If continuous quality improvement is to be the goal, we need to conceptualize professional development better, to research it more imaginatively and to put it at the heart of that commitment. The modernist idea that rationally planned INSET provision takes care of professional development is appropriate neither for the multiple realities of post-structuralist thinking, nor for the complexities of continuous quality improvement.

NOTES

1   The ESRC-funded study exploring The Professional Culture of Teachers and the Secondary School Curriculum ran from January 1994 until June 1996. The researchers involved are Gill Helsby, Peter Knight, Gary McCulloch, Murray Saunders and Terry Warburton.

2   The Lancaster TVEI Evaluation Programme was based upon the local evaluation of TVEI in a consortium of fifteen LEAs. Directed by Gill Helsby and Murray Saunders, it ran from 1984 until 1994.

REFERENCES

Alexander, R. (1992) *Policy and Practice in Primary Education*. London: Routledge.

Apple, M. W. (1986) *Teachers and Texts: A Political Economy of Class and Gender Relations in Education*. New York: Routledge.

Blackmore, P. (1992) The professional development and vocational training divide in further education staff development. *Journal of Further and Higher Education*, **16**(3): 30–8.

Bullough, R. V. and Gitlin, A. D. (1994) Challenging teacher education as training: four propositions. *Journal of Education for Teaching*, **20**(1): 67–81.

Burrage, M. and Torstendahl, R. (eds) (1990) *Professions in Theory and History*. London: Sage.

Campbell, R. J. and Neill, S. R. St J. (1994a) *Primary Teachers at Work*. London: Routledge.

Campbell, R. J. and Neill, S. R. St J. (1994b) *Secondary Teachers at Work*. London: Routledge.

Day, C. (1993) Reflection: a necessary but not sufficient condition for professional development. *British Educational Research Journal*, **19**(1): 83–93.

DFE/WO (Department for Education/Welsh Office) (1992) *Choice and Diversity: A New Framework for Schools*. London: HMSO.

Doyle, W. and Ponder, G. (1977) The practicality ethic in teacher decision-making. *Interchange*, **8**(3): 1–12.

Drucker, P. F. (1993) *Post-Capitalist Society*. Oxford: Butterworth-Heinemann.

Evans, J. and Penney, D. (1994) Whatever happened to good advice? Service and inspection after the Education Reform Act. *British Educational Research Journal*, **20**(5): 519–33.

Eraut, M. (1994) *Developing Professional Knowledge and Competence*. London: Falmer Press.

Gilroy, D. P. and Day, C. (1993) The erosion of INSET in England and Wales: analysis and proposals for a redefinition. *Journal of Education for Teaching*, **19**(2): 141–57.

Handy, C. (1994) *The Empty Raincoat: Making Sense of the Future*. London: Hutchinson.

Hargreaves, A. (1992) Foreword. In A. Hargreaves and M. Fullan (eds), *Understanding Teacher Development*. London: Cassell.

Harland, J. (1988) Running up the down escalator. In D. Lawton and C. Chitty (eds), *The National Curriculum*. London: Institute of Education, pp. 87–98.

Hartley, D. (1989) Beyond collaboration: the management of professional development policy in Scotland, 1979–89. *Journal of Education for Teaching*, **15**(3): 211–23.

Helsby, G. (1993) Creating the autonomous professional or the trained technician? Current directions in in-service teacher support. *Evaluation and Research in Education*, **7**(2): 65–82.

Hoyle, E. (1974) Professionality, professionalism and control in teaching. *London Educational Review*, **3**: 13–19.

OFSTED (1993) *Corporate Plan*. London: Office for Standards in Education.

Peters, T. (1992) *Liberation Management: Necessary Disorganisation for the Nanosecond Nineties*. London: BCA.

Schön, D. A. (1983) *The Reflective Practitoner*. London: Temple Smith.

Schön, D. A. (1987) *Educating the Reflective Practitoner*. San Francisco: Jossey Bass.

Sockett, H. (1993) *The Moral Base for Teacher Professionalism*. New York: Teachers' College Press.

Torstendahl, R. and Burrage, M. (eds) (1990) *The Formation of Professions*. London: Sage.

Name Index

Subject Index